George Howell

Trade Unionism - new and old

George Howell

Trade Unionism - new and old

ISBN/EAN: 9783742898593

Manufactured in Europe, USA, Canada, Australia, Japa

Cover: Foto ©ninafisch / pixelio.de

Manufactured and distributed by brebook publishing software
(www.brebook.com)

George Howell

Trade Unionism - new and old

SOCIAL QUESTIONS OF TO-DAY

EDITED BY H. DE B. GIBBINS, M.A.

TRADE UNIONISM
NEW AND OLD

SOCIAL QUESTIONS OF TO-DAY.

Edited by H. de B. GIBBINS, M.A.

Crown 8vo, 2s. 6d.

MESSRS. METHUEN announce the publication of a series of volumes upon those topics of social, economic and industrial interest that are at the present moment foremost in the public mind. Each volume of the series will be written by an author who is an acknowledged authority upon the subject with which he deals, and who will treat his question in a thoroughly sympathetic but impartial manner, with special reference to the historic aspect of the subject, and from the point of view of the Historical School of economics and social science.

The following form the earlier Volumes of the Series:—

1. **TRADE UNIONISM—NEW AND OLD.** G. HOWELL, M.P., Author of *The Conflicts of Capital and Labour.*   [*Ready.*

2. **POVERTY AND PAUPERISM.** Rev. L. R. PHELPS, M.A., Fellow of Oriel College, Oxford.   •   [*Nearly Ready.*

3. **THE CO-OPERATIVE MOVEMENT OF TO-DAY.** G. J. HOLYOAKE, Author of *The History of Co-operation.*   [*Nearly Ready.*

4. **MUTUAL THRIFT.** Rev. J. FROME WILKINSON, M.A., Author of *The Friendly Society Movement.*

5. **ENGLISH SOCIALISM OF TO-DAY.** HUBERT BLAND, one of the Authors of *Fabian Essays.*

6. **THE COMMERCE OF NATIONS.** C. F. BASTABLE, M.A., Professor of Economics at Trinity College, Dublin, and Author of *International Commerce.*

7. **ENGLISH LAND AND ENGLISH MEN.** Rev. C. W. STUBBS, M.A., Author of *The Labourers and the Land.*

8. **MODERN LABOUR AND OLD ECONOMIES.** H. DE B. GIBBINS, M.A. (Editor), Author of *The Industrial History of England.*

9. **CHRISTIAN SOCIALISM IN ENGLAND.** Rev. J. CARTER, M.A., of Pusey House, Oxford, Editor of *The Economic Review.*

10. **LAND NATIONALIZATION.** HAROLD COX, M.A.

11. **THE EDUCATION OF THE PEOPLE.** J. R. DIGGLE, M.A., Chairman of the London School Board.

12. **CONTINENTAL LABOUR.** ALICE OLDHAM, M.A.

BY

GEORGE HOWELL, M.P.

Fellow of the Royal Statistical Society ;
Author of " The Conflicts of Capital and Labour," "Handy-Book of the
Labour Laws," &c. &c.

𝔐𝔢𝔱𝔥𝔲𝔢𝔫 & 𝔠𝔬.

18, BURY STREET, LONDON, W.C.

1891

PREFACE.

DURING the last couple of years there has been what may be termed a revival amongst the Trade Unions of the country, and consequently there has been a demand for Trade Union literature. One result of that demand was the republication of my work, *The Conflicts of Capital and Labour*, brought down to date. I may perhaps be permitted to refer the reader to that work for an exhaustive treatment of the more historical phases of the Labour Movement, and also the more debatable questions connected with its economic aspects. The present is in no sense a reproduction of that work, nor is it an epitome of its contents. It is written in view of the later developments of Trade Unionism, with especial reference to what may be termed the new departure in the organization of labour.

GEORGE HOWELL.

HAMPDEN HOUSE, ELLINGHAM ROAD,
SHEPHERD'S BUSH, LONDON, W.
February 1891.

CONTENTS.

CHAPTER I.

ORGANIZATION OF LABOUR.—Part I.

EARLY PERIOD.—THE GUILD SYSTEM.

CHAPTER II.

ORGANIZATION OF LABOUR.—Part II.

SECOND PERIOD.—UNDER STATE REGULATION.

CHAPTER III.

RISE AND PROGRESS OF COMBINATIONS OF WORKMEN.

CHAPTER IV.

TRADE UNIONISM : ITS ORIGIN, DEVELOPMENT, AND PROGRESS.

CHAPTER V.

THE "OLD TRADE UNIONISM."—Part I.

CONSTITUTION AND GOVERNMENT.

CHAPTER VI.

THE "OLD TRADE UNIONISM."—Part II.

PROVIDENT BENEFITS, AND STRIKE PAY.

CHAPTER VII.

THE "NEW TRADE UNIONISM."—Part I.

CHIEF CHARACTERISTICS OF THE NEW TRADE UNIONS.

CHAPTER VIII.

THE "NEW TRADE UNIONISM."—Part II.

STATE AID, STATE REGULATION, AND STATE CONTROL.

CHAPTER IX.

CHAPTER X.

TRADE UNIONISM:
NEW AND OLD.

CHAPTER I.

ORGANIZATION OF LABOUR.—Part I.

EARLY PERIOD.—THE GUILD SYSTEM.

Frith Guilds—Town Guilds—Merchant Guilds—Craft Guilds—Contests for Supremacy—Guilds instituted Free Association—Sought to regulate Industry and Labour—To limit and regulate Apprentice-ships—Laid the Foundations for Local Government—Contained the Germs of Modern Trade Unionism.

TRADE UNIONISM is an outgrowth of, if not exactly an offshoot from, the old Guild system of the Middle Ages. This fact is clearly shown in the admirable preliminary essay by Dr. Brentano, in *English Gilds*, edited by the late Mr. Toulmin Smith, and published by the Early English Text Society in 1870. That essay formed the basis of the two first chapters in the *Conflicts of Capital and Labour*, by the present writer, the information contained in the essay being condensed, and in some respects amplified by reference to other sources, and to the Guild statutes and ordinances then and subsequently available. Trade Unionism not only owes its origin to the Old English Guilds, but the earlier Trade Unions were in reality the legitimate successors of

B

the Craft Guilds, which flourished in this country down to the time of the suppression of the monasteries and other fraternities by Henry VIII., in the thirty-seventh year of his reign. It is therefore important that all who write or speak upon the Trade Unionism of to-day should know something of the history, constitution, objects, and work of the old guilds. Without the knowledge derived from a study of the Guild system, the organization, rules, and operations of Trade Unions cannot be properly understood. The materials for that study are so fully collected, arranged, and dealt with in the works above alluded to, that there is no need for any elaborate treatment of the subject in this volume. A brief recapitulation of the chief characteristics of the guilds only will be attempted, sufficiently to indicate the points of contact, and to explain the underlying and controlling influences which have been continuously at work.

1. **The Frith Guild.**—This, the oldest form of guild-life, was a fraternal alliance for mutual protection against usurped authority, political and industrial. The Frith Guild was partly religious, partly social, and partly industrial. The distinctively Religious Guild, and the Social Guild, respectively, appear to have developed out of the earlier form of Frith Guild ; but in each the members seem to have met for fraternal purposes, the objects being religious observances and exercises, the distribution of alms, or Christian charity amongst the members, the furtherance of education, as far as it then existed, the celebration of feasts, representation of religious plays, the performance of secular plays, the enjoyment of pastimes, or recreation, and mutual assistance in cases of need by contributions, benefits, and insurance, in a primitive kind of way. At the meetings held, festivities

were indulged in on the occasion of marriage, anniversary festivals, rejoicings at births, mutual condolence and religious exercises at death, and social feasts on occasions of public or private events, deemed suitable for such gatherings, and in some way affecting the members, or some of them. The guild was to a great extent responsible to the authorities for the conduct of its members, and in return exacted obedience to its ordinances and statutes, as they were called. This early form of the guild was at first mainly an extension of the family circle, but it soon widened so as to embrace not only blood-relations, but neighbours. In the early history of communities, the guild played an important part, protecting the rights of its members, avenging their wrongs, extending their privileges, fostering their interests, and otherwise exercising a beneficial and restraining influence when brute force was in the ascendant, and law and public institutions were in their infancy in this country. Some of the very earliest forms common to those guilds have come down to us, not exactly perhaps in their original shape, but in their essence; certainly they were to be found in the earlier Trade Unions, especially in the modes of initiation of members, in providing assistance in cases of need, in the burial of the dead, and sometimes in church parades —latterly revived somewhat.

2. **The Town Guild.**—As the earlier village communities expanded into townships, the social and industrial conditions changed. Neither the Frith Guild of the enlarged family, nor the Social Guild of the more or less blood-related coterie, any longer satisfied all the requirements of the people, the circumstances of the case, or the times, socially, or even industrially. Consequently there was instituted the Town Guild, consisting of the freemen, mostly landed proprietors

and others, having a stake in the country.   In some places
this was termed the Burghers' Guild, the government of the
town, or township, being practically in the hands of the
guild.   That the supreme authority was to all intents and
purposes centred in the Burghers' Guild is evident from
a variety of circumstances, not the least interesting being
the fact that the Town Guild of Sleswig closed the gates of
the town against the king, the citizens mustered at the
sound of the guild-bell, seized the king and slew him, and
those who tried to defend him, because his son had slain
Duke Canute, the Alderman of the Guild.   In the earlier
period, no doubt, the Town Guild more or less represented
the inhabitants of the township, exercised judicial as well
as local authority, and preserved law and order generally
within its jurisdiction.   It also prevented the incursions of
marauders, and restrained the barons from undue exactions,
at a time when the king and the court were nearly powerless
to enforce the laws and charters in force.   In London they
seem to have attained a high state of development in Anglo-
Saxon times.   In the reign of Athelstan (901 to 925) it
appears that the Frith Guilds united to form one guild for
the better government of the town, its ordinances being
binding even upon non-members.   In this guild was vested
the power of regulating the trades and occupations carried
on within its boundaries, and even beyond, in some cases.
The foundation was thus laid for the incorporation of towns
by Royal Charter, and of the Municipal Institutions of
later times.   In a rude kind of way, the Town Guild was
representative, the aldermen and wardens being chosen on
the elective principle.[1]

[1] See *Conflicts of Capital and Labour*, chap. i. §§ 6 and 11, pp.
18, 19.   Also Dr. Brentano, *English Gilds*, pp. 97, 98.

3. **The Merchant Guild.**—With the development of industrial life, as contradistinguished from agricultural pursuits, there came a time when the traders in the townships claimed equal rights and privileges with the possessors of landed property within the township. At first, doubtless, the owners of land, and those who carried on trade, were identical. Leaseholds had not then been invented, all occupiers being in fact the owners of the dwellings in which they resided, and carried on their business. But the pursuits of agriculture, and occupation in some special trade within the township, could not for long be prosecuted together. Traders and dealers developed into separate classes, and these soon found it to be of advantage to constitute a guild, the only form of association then known, for mutual protection and advancement. Possibly the terms of exchange were made too exacting by the property owners, who, to some extent, held the key to the position, by reason of the fact that they made the ordinances which controlled prices, and held in their hands the power to withhold food supplies, partially at least, if the citizens became obstreperous. That contentions arose at a very early date is certain. It is equally certain that the possession of land gave priority in matters of government and control. At Canterbury the Guild of the Thanes had precedence over the other two guilds in the city, the aldermen being selected from the Guild of the Thanes, the members of which were owners of estates within its jurisdiction. At Berwick all the existing guilds were, by a decision of the townsmen, united into one guild, all the separate possessions being consolidated. But this was at a later date. The distinction between the earlier form of guild, and the offshoot termed the Merchant Guild, arose out of the circumstances of the particular town, and

does not distinguish a distinctive period in guild-life. In some places the Merchant Guild arose at a very early date, indicating that in these places some of the citizens had devoted themselves to trade and manufactures as a separate and distinct class from those who were engaged in agriculture. Some were traders in the produce of the field and farm, supplying the inhabitants with food; others in the materials of manufacture, while others were handicraftsmen —builders, clothiers, shoemakers, &c.

The growth of a separate trading class, many of whom were craftsmen, no doubt early led to some jealousy in the management of the affairs of the township. Some of them became opulent citizens, comparatively speaking, at that date. Many had as high claims to social distinction as the landed proprietors; and they soon claimed equal rights in the administration of the guild, and of the township. The possession of property in land was common to all; it was merely a question of extent or degree. All were freemen of the township, and all were masters in their particular handicrafts. Hired handicraftsmen were not then known; each had learned his trade, under the regulations of the guild ordinances, and worked at it, not only without feeling shame, but with a manly pride, as a pursuit worthy of all praise. The idea that trade was humiliating, if not dishonourable, originated with the patricians. The establishment of the Merchants' Guild was at once a protest against this snobbish idea, and a declaration in favour of equal rights, as citizens, not only to be allowed to pursue their own avocations in peace, but to take part in administrative duties. The contest for equal rights was long, and sometimes bitter. The patricians sought to exclude the traders and merchants from some of the guilds. Those whom they tried to exclude found sympathizers in the ranks of those who had been members of the Frith Guilds, or their descendants, but who were not eligible for membership to the Town Guild. For the old Frith Guild was expansive, not exclusive. The struggle had a two-fold object: (1) The right to an equal share in the government of the township in which they resided; and (2) the right of regulating their own industry. Landowners had already begun to tax traders. The traders and merchants sought to make land pay its full share of local and other burdens. Besides which, the members of the Town Guild sought to exclude the mere merchant and trader from participation in the corporate property and revenues, much of which had arisen and accumulated out of the increased values resulting from trade. In the end the Merchant Guilds were victorious; they wrested the power from the hands of the then exclusive class, and shared in all the privileges which membership of an opulent guild could confer. They regulated their own industry, and assessed the taxes leviable upon property.

4. **Craft Guilds.**—In the earlier years of the institution of Merchant Guilds, and during the more severe periods of their struggle, the craftsmen were allowed to be members of such guilds. There was no distinction between the man who traded in cloth, and the man who made it, or worked it up into garments. But no sooner had the merchants and traders succeeded in achieving their victory, than they also sought to perpetuate their privileges and monopolies by exclusiveness. For example, Article 25 of the Statutes of the Berwick Guild make it a condition of membership that the craftsman "must forswear his trade for a year and a day." If a butcher dealt in wool or hides, he must forswear his axe; if the corn-merchant baked bread, he was

not eligible as a member of the guild. As the township grew, and population increased, men devoted themselves more and more to a particular branch of industry as a distinctive calling or occupation. Hence arose a class of handicraftsmen, trained to the trade. The merchant traded in the materials, or in the products of manufacture or other merchandise ; and he sought to deprive the craftsmen of their share in the regulation of their own trade. As these were fast growing into a distinctive class, they were by no means content to be hustled out of the guild, or be denied admission thereto. Most of them were small masters, who made their own wares, and disposed of them by sale, barter, or exchange, in money or in kind, as the case might be. All had been regular apprentices to the craft, for there was no other portal through which they could pass into the status of the handicraftsman class, except by marriage, and then only if the woman was a widow, or daughter of a freeman of the guild. Thus, the earlier craftsmen, who established the Craft Guild, were small masters and their apprentices, for the journeymen handicraftsmen had scarcely come into existence at that date. The latter, however, were being created by the force of circumstances, and the expansion of trade, and we find that they also asserted their independence, and claimed participation in the advantages conferred by the guild. As these guilds regulated everything pertaining to trade, it is obvious that sheer necessity compelled those outside to combine in some similar fashion.

Then arose a contest more prolonged and more bitter than that between the Town Guild and the Merchant Guild. The number of Craft Guilds extended more rapidly, and covered a wider range, than the two previously-named classes of guilds. In the weaving trades, building trades, and those engaged in the manufacture of clothing, boots and shoes, and the like, we find distinctive traces of guilds of the free-handicraft class at early date ; and also, following close thereupon, of a separate class of "operatives," hired men, who formed the journeymen section of a somewhat later date. The most powerful of the earlier craft-guilds, if not actually the first in point of time, were the Weavers' Guilds, the members of which, in some form or another, continued to fight labour's battles all through the guild period, and down the closing years of the eighteenth century. The next in importance were the Masons' Guilds, the members of which were perhaps the earliest genuine journeymen—men who travelled from place to place, to work at the cathedrals and other ecclesiastical structures, at the palaces of the princely, and at the baronial castles of the Middle Ages. In many instances actual conflicts with the Merchants, or Town Guilds were only averted either by the inclusion of the craftsmen in those guilds, or by the masters joining the Craft Guild. In those cases the more restricted and less hostile battles were fought out by contentions as to the internal government and administration of the guild. The craftsmen fought for a voice in the selection of the master and wardens; sometimes they waived all right as to the appointment of master, but insisted upon electing the wardens. In other cases the battle for ascendancy was hot and prolonged, so much so that the supreme authority in the township, and even the authority of the Crown, had to be called in to put an end to the strife. When this was done, the dispute ended in favour of the masters. But the general outcome of the long and severe industrial and political conflict was favourable to the Craft Guilds. They either triumphed over and subdued the opposing guilds, or attained such share in the management, and in the regulation of trade, as satisfied their aspirations, procured for them the control of their own affairs, and secured to them their privileges.

The period covered in the preceding brief sketch of the guild system, and industrial life in England extends from very early, probably before Anglo-Saxon times, down to the reign of Henry VIII., and the suppression of the monasteries. It is perhaps sufficient first to indicate their origin, development, and, growth, and the chief departures in policy and government, during some seven or eight centuries in English history. We are not here concerned with the political aspects of the earlier or later struggles of the guilds, to obtain control in the government of the township, or the contentions of different guilds, or kinds of guilds, for supremacy and ascendancy one over the other, except in so far as those struggles and contentions pertained to social and industrial life, the regulation of trade, and the pursuits of labour. We look, however, into their internal economy and government as the prototype of the modern Trade Union, in order to discover the germs of that associative principle which has influenced to so great an extent the industrial condition of England, and moulded the life of her great army of workers, in nearly every department of manufacture and trade. To-day that principle is operating with intensified force. Indeed, it would seem that the fruit of ages of incessant labour had ripened prematurely, or else that it has been gathered while yet too green, judging by the history and experience of the last two years. The chief points of interest in the constitution and working of the guilds, illustrative of their history, as the predecessors of Trade Unions are :—

(*a.*) The guilds, in all ages, and of all kinds, instituted, preserved, and handed down from generation to generation the right of free association, to discuss grievances and provide remedies, to assist each other in case of need, to sustain each other in resisting wrong, to mutually advance each other's interest, and generally to promote the welfare of the members of the particular guilds. Originally the Frith Guilds sought to extend the government of the family to blood-relations, outside the family circle; then to widen the fraternity to neighbours, and others having something in common; and latterly, in another form, to associate together those engaged in particular avocations, or seeking the attainment of a common object, or end.

(*b.*) The guilds endeavoured to regulate the conditions of the trade in which the members were engaged. In the earlier guilds this simply meant mutual restraint, for the mutual good of all, inasmuch as the Frith Guilds represented the whole village community, or the township, as the case might be. When diversified interests arose, in consequence of the altered conditions of industry and trade, each branch of industry sought to regulate the number who should follow the particular handicraft, by a restrictive system of apprenticeships, the mode in which the trade should be carried on, the prices and quality of articles; and, later on, the hours during which labour was to be performed, both in summer and winter. The regulations in many instances became so minute, and eventually so oppressive, that frequent revolts occurred, and often new guilds were instituted. Generally the disputes were settled by the master and wardens, at other times by the commonalty in the Town Guild, sometimes by statute, decree, ordinance or charter by the Executive Government of the country.

(*c.*) The initiation of members, the binding of apprentices, and their reception into the guild at the end of their term, the modes of payment, and the benefits provided in the regulations or ordinances of the guild, in cases of sickness, death, lack of employment, or dire distress, resembled, in very many particulars, the practices in vogue, and the rules in force in the Trade Unions of modern times. The solemnity of " initiation " is to a great extent preserved, but for its full significance we must look to some of the Affiliated Orders of Benefit Societies, such as the Foresters, the Odd-fellows, the Druids, the Old Friends, &c. With respect to modes of payment, or contributions, there is more regularity in the modern Trade Union ; and in some of the older and better unions the provident benefits have been extended, and are carried out in consonance with commercial prin-ciples, on a sound financial basis. The burial of the dead guild-brother was common to all the earlier guilds; and often also the saying of masses for the repose of his soul. Relief in sickness, and assistance in distress, were generally volun-tary, either out of the guild funds, or by collections, as each case arose and came before the members.

(*d.*) The Guild system laid the foundations both of local government, and of free association, and introduced a kind of social discipline which was necessary to secure the proper discharge of the duties of, and the functions in connection with, the communal life of the Middle Ages, in all its varying forms. And it expanded as time went on, from the coterie, within the village community, to the whole body of persons having common rights and privileges, or common interests, in the city, township, or district, comprising the whole body of the people. Limited at first to the freemen property owners, they subsequently took in the free handicraftsmen, and then the freed-men who had been villeins on country manors, under feudal, ecclesiastical, or other service, until they embraced all sections of the people. In process of time they again became restrictive, in the sense of including only either a section, or a single profession or occupation.

Under whatever form they were instituted or constituted, and in every form, the English Guilds, during their prolonged existence and activity, certainly from the end of the eighth to the middle of the sixteenth century, are found to have in them the germs of what, in later times, developed into Trade Unions, distinctively representative of the respective branches of industry with which they were and are associated. Those old guilds, in a sense, created the conditions under which trade developed, and industry was carried on. Each and every trade was regulated by the statutes or ordinances of the several guilds. The master and wardens had the supreme control, subject to the approval of the members. The quality and size of the materials, the mode in which they were to be made or worked up, the places at which, and the manner in which they were to be sold, and even the prices of the materials and goods, and subsequently the wages and hours of labour, were all determined by the guild. Their decisions had, to all intents and purposes, the same authoritative effect as positive law. When the guilds were suppressed, the laws abrogated, or the ordinances had no longer binding legal effect, the whole system of guild-life, as applied to industry, became crystallized into trade customs, which had the force of law. These continued to operate for centuries, and still operate indirectly in modern industrial life.

CHAPTER II.

ORGANIZATION OF LABOUR.—Part II.

SECOND PERIOD.—UNDER STATE REGULATION.

Guild System virtually ended with the reign of the Tudors—Effects of the system upon Trade, Manufacturing Industry, and Labour—Revolt against Guild System, by Handicraftsmen—Statutory Regulation—Statute of Labourers—Effects of Legislation—Increasing demands for Legislation—Restraint of Labour by Law, Ordinance, and Custom—Influence of the Protestant Reformation in England—Newer Conditions of Labour—Elizabethan Legislation—Wages, Hours of Labour, Apprentices, Hiring and Discharge of Workmen—Controlling the ever-varying Conditions of Industrial Life—Effects of Legislative Restriction upon Capital and Labour—Extension of Legislative Control—Its Character and Effects—Statutes in Restraint of Trade, in Reigns subsequent to that of Queen Elizabeth—Trades and industries interfered with by Regulation, and its general effects.

THE Guild system, as the dominant force in the social and industrial life of England, virtually ended with the reign of Henry VIII., certainly with the reign of Edward VI. Nevertheless, as corporate bodies and trading companies under charter, they continued not only to exist, but to exercise considerable authority in numerous places, even to the extent of "grinding the faces of the poor." This is evident from the recitals in the Statutes 2 and 3, Philip and Mary, cc. 11, 12 and 13, and especially in the first-named statute, concerning weavers. In some cities and towns, and in a limited number of industries, they tried to exert a commanding influence throughout all the subsequent reigns, from that date until towards the close of the eighteenth century, and indeed, in a few places, they maintain some remnant of exclusive power even to this day, in a few instances.

The widespread effects of that system upon the industrial and trading life of England, with its guild ordinances and regulations, may be seen by reference to the statutes of the realm, as early as about the middle of the fourteenth century, in which statutes the State seeks to modify some of the regulations in force, and to practically abrogate others. By proclamation, ordinance, and decree, efforts were made in the same direction, at an earlier date. As before seen, revolts and secessions occurred in the guilds themselves, at an early date, against the exclusiveness, exactions, and monopolies which were practised. But each new guild seems to have fallen into the same evil ways, when once it had been firmly established. If the guild-brothers found the ordinances and regulations to be oppressive, it is easy to perceive that the commonalty outside the guild would feel the oppression still more acutely; but, as a rule, the non-members would be powerless to protect themselves from the aggressions constantly made.

Institution of Statutory Regulation.—With the dawn of the fourteenth century the revolt of the people against the absolute government of the guilds becomes more distinctly apparent. But so interwoven were their ordinances with all that concerned social and industrial life, and even, to some extent, the then local and political life of England, that their all-powerful influence pervades the statute law for several centuries. The first Statute of Labourers bears the

impress of their wide-reaching mastery in all matters pertaining to labour.   At the same time the enactment marks
their decadence as the governing authority, inasmuch as they
could no longer enforce their regulations, without the aid of
statutory law.   It also shows that the action of the guilds,
and the demands of their members, had become such as to
involve a public danger, unless restrained by statute.   Had
the first Statute of Labourers been restricted to husbandry
—servants of the farm, labourers on estates, and workmen
generally employed upon manors—it might have been contended that it had no reference to the Guild system, that it
was entirely outside the purview of guild law.   But its provisions were not so restricted.   The Statute 25 Edw. III., st.
I. (1350-1) was, in reality, originally an Ordinance of the
King and Council, then a statute as quoted, namely 23 Edw.
III., 1349.   But by the Statute 2 of Rich. II., c. 8 (1378), it
was expressly enacted that this ordinance should be affirmed,
and held for a statute.   After reciting in the preamble the
reasons for its enactment; upon "the Petition of the Commonalty," because the servants, having no regard to the
ordinance, refused to serve "unless they have liveries and
wages to the double or treble of what they were wont to
take," the statute proceeds to enact clauses with respect to
yearly and daily wages, modes of hiring, &c., of all servants
in husbandry.   Then, in Chapter III., it deals with artificers
in the building trades—carpenters, masons, tylers, plasterers,
and their servers, or labourers; and, in Chapter IV., with
shoemakers, tailors, saddlers, tanners, curriers, goldsmiths,
and others, all of whom were associated with the respective
guilds of their several trades.   The reference to liveries, as
well as to wages, is conclusive that the statute dealt with
persons who were members of the various guilds.

The statute referred to (25 Edw. III., st. I.), and others subsequently enacted of the same class, or with similar objects, sought to wed statute law to the existing guild ordinances, to effect a fusion where possible of local regulation and general law. Public policy demanded that something should be done, and dissensions in the guilds rendered it practicable, at least to essay the attempt. The government of the country had become to some extent settled; each township was no longer a law unto itself. Forms of industry had sprung up which were to some extent outside the pale of the guilds, even of the later Craft Guilds, although the latter everywhere sought to regulate each new industry as it arose. Had Scotland been at that date united to England, and had one of her representatives to the British Parliament been that most prescient of all her gifted sons, the author of the *Wealth of Nations*, it is possible that posterity might have been spared the industrial difficulties of later times by the enactment of enabling laws, instead of embodying economic heresies in the statutes of the realm, to be wrangled over, extended, modified, aud subsequently repealed, centuries thereafter.

Extension of Statutory Regulation.—Having once resorted to legislation affecting labour, it was but natural that recourse should be had to it again and again, as new conditions or fresh complications arose. Like begets like, in legislation, as in the animate world. The Statute of Labourers became the progenitor, so to speak, of a family of laws, the progeny of which multiplied exceedingly, after their kind, generation after generation. Further regulation by statute, in the succeeding reign, was immediately followed by an ordinance, made by Richard II., requiring returns of the guilds, as to their constitution, aims, statutes, and means. A.

C

partial inquiry had been instituted in the reign of Edward
II., about the year 1321, in consequence of abuses said to
exist in connection with the Weavers' Guild of London.   In
1436-7 an Act was passed (15 Hen. VI., c. 6), "for the
Regulation of the Ordinances of Guilds, Fraternities, and
Companies," enacting that they should not be used against
the common profit of the people, and requiring that their
ordinances should be approved and enrolled before the
Justices of the Peace, and by them revoked, if not found
to be wholly loyal and reasonable.

During the succeeding reigns, covering a period of about
160 years, the organization of labour was subjected to the
operation and restraints of two distinct forces, for the most
part antagonistic to each other, both being more or less
detrimental to the freedom of labour.   The guilds ought to
enforce their ordinances and regulations wherever they had
the power so to do; while the statute law sought to restrain
them in the exercise of their authority, and also over industry
—the object of both.   The Justices of the Peace had full
power in the administration of the law, but in many cases
they were identified with the guild system.   In some places,
therefore, the guilds were not only left unmolested, but were
fostered and protected.   In certain places they maintained
their power and authority, by reason of the fact that the
local government of the town was so inwoven with the guild
system that the two elements could not be divorced.   If
disputes arose between the separate and respective guilds,
the danger of suppression was frequently averted by mutual
concession, and sometimes by a kind of amalgamation.
But, in whatever form authority was ultimately exercised,
this one fact is obvious, namely, that, either by guild
ordinance or regulation, or by statute, the customs, modes

of hiring, hours of labour, conditions of work, matters of wages, and even prices, were regulated on the lines which had been instituted by, or under, the English guilds, in one or·another of their multiform operations, as the sole arbiter in questions affecting industry. In the unequal struggle which was then going on, labour, properly so-called, was placed at a disadvantage. The dominant influence in the guild had been and was necessarily that of the master craftsmen, for journeymen handicraftsmen were the outgrowth of a later stage of development in manufacturing industry. The contentions, previously adverted to, were therefore between the small masters, who constituted the guild members, and mostly arose when the system of manufacture had so far advanced as, in their opinion, to necessitate, in some degree, a more restrictive system of trade, in the sense of confining its operations to distinctive branches, each in the hands of men who attended to a particular branch, to the exclusion of all others.

Effects of Protestant Reformation upon Labour.—The Protestant Reformation in England, and the suppression of the monasteries and other religious houses consequent thereupon, or in connection therewith, towards the end of the reign of Henry VIII., produced two results directly affecting the conditions of labour, and led to others, more remotely affecting industry, in later times. Up to that period the indigent poor were relieved and cared for by the ecclesiastical authorities in the various districts, and by the conventual, monastic, and other institutions connected with the Romish Church. The Reformation put an end to this system of beneficence and alms, and rendered necessary the institution of the Poor Law, or a system of parish relief. The poorer craftsmen, on the other hand, were supported by the respective guilds, out of the funds collected for that and other purposes, and by means of the property left as legacies by the brethren of the fraternity, or the voluntary gifts of the richer and more prosperous members during their lifetime. Bequests and gifts for those purposes were common in early times, not only to the "religious houses," but to the guilds of the craftsmen. Those modes of relief, in cases of distress, were either discontinued, or so considerably diminished, that other agencies had to be resorted to. In the second place, guild law and regulation lost so much of their force as to become practically of no effect in many industries, while in all it was weakened by the operation of Statute Law, and by the decline of their power and authority, as a consequence of the Reformation, as well as by internal dissensions. There had also, by this time, grown up a distinct handicraft class, operatives or journeymen, men who were no longer masters, but were employed by the day, the year, or some other term, as hired workmen. This change in the conditions of labour necessitated changes in the law. Even the Craft Guilds had degenerated into close corporations, for the most part, the hired handicraftsmen being accorded scant protection by the guilds, representing the respective industries in which the workmen were employed. Wealth was increasing, trade and commerce were expanding, and men were growing rich by manufacturing industry; but the toilers had missed their chance of obtaining their full share of the prosperity.

Substitution of State Regulation for Guild Law.—The reign of Elizabeth marks an altogether newer development in the history of labour. Guild law and authority were virtually superseded, and there was substituted therefor a code of legislative regulation, applicable to most of the

industries then existing in this country. The Statute, 5 Eliz.,
c. 4 (1562-3), was an endeavour, and on the whole a worthy
endeavour, all things considered, to codify existing law respecting the several matters therein dealt with, in such manner
as to protect alike the master, and his hired servant, or
apprentice.   The preamble recites that "there remain and
stand in force a great number of Acts and statutes concerning
the retaining, departing, wages, and orders of apprentices,
servants and labourers, as well in husbandry as in divers
other arts, mysteries, and occupations ; yet partly for the
imperfection and contrariety that is found, and doth appear
in sundry of the said laws, and for the variety and number
of them ; and chiefly for that the wages and allowances
limited and rated in many of the said statutes are in divers
places too small, and not answerable to this time, respecting
the advancement of prices of all things belonging to the
said servants and labourers ; the said laws cannot conveniently, without the great grief and burden of the poor
labourer and hired man, be put in good and true execution ;
and as the said several Acts and statutes were, at the time
of making them, thought to be very good and beneficial for
the commonwealth of this realm (as divers of them are), so
if the substance of as many of the said laws as are meet to
be continued, shall be digested and reduced into one sole
law and statute, and in the same an uniform order prescribed and limited concerning the wages and other orders
for apprentices, servants, and labourers, there is good hope
that it will come to pass, that the same law (being duly
executed) should banish idleness, advance husbandry, and
yield unto the hired person, both in time of scarcity and in
the time of plenty, a convenient proportion of wages."

Section 2 of the Statute then repeals the provisions of the

then existing eight special statutes, commencing with the 25
Edw. III., st. I. (1349), and ending with the 21 Hen. VIII.,
c. 16 (1529). That the statute was intended to deal justly
with the artificers and hired men included within its provisions, is evident from the fact that the Statute 2 and 3
Phil. and Mary, c. 11 (1555), "An Act touching Weavers,"
is not included in the statutes repealed by 5 Eliz., c. 4, which
Act is wholly in the interests of the handicraft weaving class.
Section 4 then enumerates the sciences, crafts, mysteries, and
arts affected by the statute, comprising all the distinctive
handicrafts of the time, and in subsequent sections those engaged in husbandry and other occupations similarly affected.
Those who framed the provisions of that important statute
attempted much more than a mere consolidation of existing
statutes, they endeavoured to solidify into a code existing
customs and guild ordinances as far as practicable, and where
they could not interfere with the latter, as in Norwich and
Godalming, saving clauses were introduced, preserving the
liberties of those places, and also the charters and liberties
of corporate towns. The Act prescribed the terms of service,
the hours of labour, the fixing of wages by the Justices of
the Peace, the period of apprenticeship, the proportion of
apprentices to journeymen, modes of discharge, conduct of
the master or mistress towards apprentices, and *vice versâ*,
and most other things touching employment and daily
labour. Taking into account the times and circumstances,
the previous action of the guilds, their ordinances and
regulations, the legislation that had been enacted, and the
general conditions of industry at that stage of our history, it
was an ideal code of labour law, protecting at once the hired
worker and apprentice, and the master by whom they were
employed. Its defects were natural and inherent. Law

had gone out of its province. It had sought to regulate and control the ever-varying conditions of industrial life ; and in so doing it left to future generations a legacy of wrong, the evils of which still cling to our industrial system. The Acts are now repealed, but some of their effects remain to shadow the wayfaring toiler in his pilgrimage through life.

The Act of Elizabeth was the inevitable outcome of the legislation initiated by the Statute of Labourers, in the reign of Edward III., and of the subsequent statutes by that Act repealed. The 5 Eliz., c. 4, became the parent of numerous other Acts, passed in later reigns, covering a period of over 250 years. The State having once entered upon the wild-goose chase of attempting to regulate labour, thereby re-straining the development of the individual in the pursuit of his own welfare, it found no halting-place. As new industries arose, the law had to be extended. Each fresh discovery and invention was more or less handicapped in its application to industry. Capital was fettered, employers were harassed and hampered, and manufacturers were impeded by such laws ; and, worse than all, they afforded but scant protection to the workmen. It so happened, however, that the latter sought to perpetuate them, because they feared that by repeal they would fare worse than under the law. The capitalists and employers, on the contrary, sought their repeal ; and for about two centuries the contest raged fiercer and fiercer, on the one side for the retention of the laws, and on the other for their repeal. One of the most mischievous things in connection with this struggle was that the law, in so far as it gave protection, or even fancied protection, to the workmen, was badly administered; it might even be said mal-administered, or the Acts were not put in force at all. Moreover, some of the later Acts were more adverse to labour than that of Elizabeth, or the earlier one of Philip and Mary, and the later one of James I. Look where we will, there is no bright spot in the history of labour struggles during this period. The workmen had been accustomed to regulation during long centuries, first under the Guild system, and then under statute law. And they were used to perpetuate regulation, when it served the purposes of employers, or a section of them, so to use them; and then they were deprived of the especial provisions which might have been to their advantage. They were taught a new lesson in geometry—that a part is greater than the whole; and for a season they appear to have swallowed the proposition, and believed in its soundness.

Further Legislation Relating to Labour.—Obviously, such a piece of far-reaching legislation required a good deal of bolstering up. A buttress had to be added here, an inverted arch there, and in some instances even, the foundations needed under-pinning. Then there had to be lateral extensions, if only for inclosure purposes. During a period of from 240 to 250 years, the most approved legislative architects were called in, experts were examined, and experimental remedies were applied to amend the defects, and to strengthen the legislative edifice. It seems not to have entered into the heads of any of those consulted, that the foundations were utterly bad, and that the structure itself was an absolute incongruity, altogether incapable of renovation, and valueless for any useful purpose. But the legislative builders, from the early part of Elizabeth's reign, proceeded with their work, under succeeding reigns, according to the designs furnished by legislative architects for the time being in power and authority. Sometimes one style was adopted, at other times another,

just as fashions change in Society, and with as little reason.
The Statute of Elizabeth bears some traces of symmetrical
design, of fitness, of being planned by a skilled draughtsman.
It was a kind of rude Gothic, perhaps, without much orna-
mentation ; but it was adapted to the purposes for which it
was intended.   It was certainly homogeneous in character;
there was a oneness and completeness about it in all its parts
which commands something like respect, even if we dispute
its value.   In subsequent reigns we find additions and altera-
tions by unskilful hands, by men with little knowledge of
structural details, or of the severe principles of architectural
style.   Classic, Norman, florid Gothic, bastard Gothic, Queen
Anne's style, all sorts of styles, and no style at all, were added,
or patched on to the existing pile, as it suited the taste of
the age, the change in fashion, or altered circumstances of the
times, until the whole had become a hideous structure in the
days of George III., of no use except to hinder and obstruct,
and dangerous to the public because of its dilapidations.

The Statute of Elizabeth applied to all the crafts and
trades of the time.   Its provisions were extended to other
crafts and trades as they arose or developed, and those
relating to existing trades were "strengthened," as new
conditions affected industry and modes of labour.   During
the reigns of the Stuarts, James I., Charles I., Charles II.,
and James II., new Acts were passed, exhibiting at least
activity, if not wisdom, in law-making.   William III. could
not escape the contagion ; in his reign also fresh laws were
enacted, or newer provisions were added to existing laws.
In the reign of Queen Anne further legislation took place,
nearly a score of statutes being passed affecting labour in
one way and another.   Already the pile of statute law
relating to labour was ponderous and huge, hampering it

under the guise of regulation. But there was no halting-place. *Finis* was nowhere written at the end of any chapter. There were always more blank pages to be filled up. In the reigns of the three Georges, increased activity was manifested to fill up the volume; and some astonishing specimens of the handicraft of statesmen, in respect of Labour Laws, distinguish those reigns. Some repeals had been effected; changes were introduced; and new laws and provisions were added. Industry groaned under the weight of regulation, restriction, and control. There was a revolt against it, first by one party, and then by the other, as it suited them, or as the nature of the industry demanded. It almost looked, at one period, as if the whole trade of the country would be crushed beneath the load of legislation; and it would have been had not other countries been similarly stupid as regards the same kind of legislation, or at least such legislation as compassed nearly the same ends. The employers of that period thought that the only way to avert ruin was by enacting repressive laws against labour. These were tried with cruel effects in the reign of George III., as the succeeding chapter will show. Freedom for industry, and liberty for labour, were not even dreamed of those days—regulation and repression were the only two agencies devised by the wisdom of our forefathers.

It has been already stated that the Statute of Elizabeth applied to all the handicrafts of the time, and that in subsequent reigns provisions were added for the regulation of new industries as they arose. It would be difficult to find a single trade, of any consequence, existing prior to the close of the last century, which was not subjected, in one way or another, to State regulation and control. Among those specially dealt with, in specific Acts, might be mentioned the textile industries, including the woollen trade, the silk trade, the cotton trade, the flax and linen trades, the hosiery trades, and hempen manufactures. The clothing trades of all kinds, in the manufacture of articles, and in the making up of materials by tailors. The boot and shoe trades, and all leather trades, in the manufacture and preparation of materials, the hides and skins, and all subsequent processes, and the manufacture and making up of all sorts of articles. The manufacture of hats and caps, gloves, articles of personal adornment, and utensils for home use. The building trades, in all branches, were subjected to legislative provisions of one kind and another, including the unskilled labour which served the artizans and mechanics. Bakers, butchers, grocers, and vendors of various wares and articles of merchandise, were under some kind of regulation; in addition to which many of them were under restraint by vexatious revenue laws, in the shape of customs and excise laws, licenses, or other restrictive provisions. A return to the policy of those times is now advocated, as a necessary part of a legislative limit of the hours of labour to eight per day. In the correspondence on this subject in the *Star* newspaper one of the writers urged the fixing of a minimum limit of eight hours, a minimum wage, and a maximum price of commodities. If a cure for this frenzy be possible, probably the best cure will be a careful perusal of the legislation prior to the commencement of the present century, and a careful study of its effects. It nearly killed our early trade, and nearly starved our people. It needs no prophet to foretell that the same results would follow if such laws were re-enacted.[1]

[1] See "Eight Hour Discussion" in the *Star* newspaper, November 22nd, 1890, and reply thereto in issue of November 25th, 1890.

CHAPTER III.

RISE AND PROGRESS OF COMBINATIONS OF WORKMEN.

Combination arose from Necessity, out of Changed Conditions—Hiring of Labour, Masters and Handicraftsmen—Combinations first arose in connection with Manufacturing Industry—Specific effects of the Statute of Labourers upon Labour—Increase of Hired Handicraftsmen, consequent upon Expansion of Trade, and Accumulation of Wealth—Difficulties of Labour necessitated Combination—Consequences of State Regulation of Labour—Associative effort hindered— Legislation to put down Combinations—In Restraint of Trade— Nature and Extent of Prohibitory Law—Efforts to Repeal Statutory Law—Dawn of the Nineteenth Century—State of the Nation— Growth of Combination, a Result—Mostly non-political—Political Agitation resorted to—Effects upon Labour—Results, Repeal of the Combination Laws.

COMBINATIONS among workmen arose out of sheer necessity. They were an outcome of circumstances, some of which were the outgrowth of industrial development, expanding trade, and the progress of civilization; while others were the result of abnormal conditions resulting from the Guild system and statute law. When the craftsman was his own master, with perhaps one or two apprentices to assist in the productions of his craft, the guild to which he belonged exercised a restraining influence in regard to competition, by preventing his fellows from gaining any considerable advantage over him, and at his expense. Of course this was done at some personal sacrifice, and loss in other respects, because rightful emulation was to a great extent stifled. This very fact was indeed one of the chief causes which led to splits in the guilds, and to the formation of new ones, representing other interests. But each in its turn followed the old lines, and became exclusive in its character. Monopoly was the object, and each body fought for its own special privileges.

When the expansion of industry required more sub-division in labour, for the purpose of increasing production, and the wealth of some of the masters had so increased as to enable them to hire labour, when hired labour was to be had, the hired workmen found that they needed some kind of associative machinery to act as a buffer between them and the masters, the latter having the law and the ordinances of the guild at their back. The earlier attempts in the way of combination were, of course, of the most elementary kind; they were indeed little more than mere temporary expedients, resorted to as occasions arose, and abandoned, for the most part, when the crisis was over. But most workmen in those early times must have had some idea of the value of associative effort, for they saw samples of its efficacy in the Guild system. As imitation is natural in all ages, nothing is more probable than that the earlier handicraftsmen sought mutual protection against the guild-masters, by combinations of their own, whenever a sufficient number were to be found, engaged in the same trade or industry, willing to combine, or at least to make the attempt. Besides which many of the free-handicraftsmen were members of existing guilds, although they were gradually losing their power and influence in the management of affairs, and in directing the policy to be pursued. The instincts of self-protection, and the desire to safeguard the interests of the new handicraft class, gave birth to combination, as those instincts and desires had previously given birth to the Craft Guilds.

Origin and Object of Combination.—Combinations first arose in those trades which took the lead in instituting manufacturing industry, on a sufficiently large scale to bring together and employ a number of hired handicraftsmen. They were intended for the mutual protection of this class of workmen against encroachments upon the customs and privileges of the trade, as the outcome of guild law, and exactions in one form or another, whether as regards the hours of labour, the amount and quality of the work to be done, reductions in the prices, or wages paid for such work, or other conditions of employment. The first combination of which we have any authentic record appears to have been instituted in the woollen trade, the handicraftsmen in which established their own guild. Perhaps the masons were also among the earlier trades to found a real workmen's guild. It is also pretty certain that shoemakers, tailors, tanners, curriers, farriers, carpenters, tylers, saddlers, and goldsmiths, acted in concert, either in Craft Guilds, or in some other form of association for mutual protection and support. These and other trades are mentioned in the *Statutum de Servientibus*, or Statute of Labourers, 25 Edw. III., st. I. (1349). No doubt those earlier combinations, in whatever rude form they were constituted, were instituted and founded as a protection against, and sometimes as a menace to, the existing guilds, many of which had degenerated into mere coteries for the benefit of the privileged classes of that date. It is probable indeed that the Statute of Labourers was instigated and prompted by the guilds, or some of them, with the view of restraining the independent action of the free-handicraftsmen of the towns. It was at once a declaration of war, and a proclamation of disability as regards one of the contending parties.

There are two very curious circumstances in connection with the enactment and proclamation of the Statute of Labourers, both of which, if they have not escaped observation hitherto, have been overlooked or disregarded : (1) It is generally thought that the statute was passed in consequence of the high wages demanded during and after the plague. Had this been the case, the tenets of modern political economy could be pleaded in justification of the workmen. Scarcity means dearness, plenty cheapness ; and when two or more employers compete for one workman, labour becomes necessarily dear, and *vice versâ*, cheap, when labour seeks in vain for employment. But the fact is that, *before the plague*, wealth had so increased, and the demand for goods and luxuries of all kinds had been so largely augmented and amplified, that employment was plentiful, and remuneration, in the shape of wages and prices, had advanced with steady strides. In fact, some superstitious people regarded the plague as a punishment by heaven for the luxuriousness, gaiety, and wealth-seeking propensities of the people. (2) The other circumstance was the alteration and reduction made in the English coin about this time, namely, that although it was lacking in weight, yet it was made to pass at its former value. Other coins were also caused to be made, of equal value with the sterling money, which had the effect of raising the prices of provisions and commodities, which usually rise or fall according to the plenty or scarcity of money, and which led servants in husbandry, artificers and labourers to demand an increase in wages. The Statute of Labourers reduced those wages to the same rates as given before the plague.[1] The plague doubtless led to a scarcity of labour, and to further demands for higher wages ; but it also caused a scarcity of provisions and commodities, and consequently raised prices. From an economical point of view this was inevitable. But the statute was aimed chiefly at labour, though the sellers of victuals by retail, innkeepers and herbergers (*i. e.* harbourers, or those who lodged people) were included in its provisions. Had the statute been a mere temporary expedient, to prevent undue exactions at a time of great peril or distress, applicable to manufacturers, provision merchants, traders of all sorts, and to handicrafts-men of all kinds, it might have been justifiable. But it was the first blow by legislative action to the then growing desire to combine on the part of the workmen. The old guilds being worsted in the conflict, they resorted to statutory enactment ; the law ended the matter by becoming inimical both to guild and combination.

The exact position of the handicraft-class at that time was this : Those who were hired workmen were increasing enormously in proportion to the number who were free craftsmen, members of the Craft Guilds, from which they were either excluded altogether, or were so numerically weak, that although they were in the guild, they were out of it, in the sense of guiding its policy, or managing its affairs. "The prodigious extension of commerce," and "the incredible influx of riches," the spoils of successful wars gave an impetus to manufacturing industry and home trade, such as it had never before experienced, and for the most part it

[1] See *Parliamentary History*, vol. i. p. 292 ; also *Kennet*, p. 224. For the state of the kingdom, see *New and Impartial History of England*, by Spencer, Barnard, and others, p. 185.

was as extended as it was sudden.   The workmen naturally sought to participate in the increasing wealth and prosperity ; the guilds, representing the master craftsmen, resisted ; then statute law was called in to enforce obedience to ordinances and regulations, which events had rendered obsolete or unjust.   The handicraftsmen had thereafter to contend against two, almost all-powerful forces—the existing guilds, and statutory enactment.   The former were, at that period, declining in power and influence, and were doomed to extinction at no distant date; while the latter contained within it the seeds of enormous growth and extension, and was destined to produce evils incalculable, during ages and generations yet to come.   Even during the reign of Edward III. a plentiful crop of statutes grew up, consequent upon the provisions of the *Statutum de Servientibus*. For example, in the thirty-seventh year of his reign, the prices of poultry of all kinds were fixed by statute ; merchants were " not to ingross merchandises to enhance the prices of them, and shall use only one sort ; " " handicraftsmen, (artificers of various kinds) shall use but one mystery, but workwomen may work as they did ; " for the regulation of the art and workmanship of goldsmiths ; " of the diet and apparel of servants ; " and of all other people also in several separate Acts ; and for regulating the size, make, and prices of cloth.   Numerous other statutes were passed bearing upon labour, production, commerce, and trade, during this reign ; " the Statute and Ordinance concerning Labourers " being confirmed by 42 Edw. III., c. 6 (1368), when it was enacted that "commissions shall be made to Justices of the Peace, to hear and determine matters concerning the same."   A return to Parliament of the whole of the Acts, ordinances, and proclamations respecting labour, including

D

the regulation of wages, prices, hours of work, conditions of employment, modes of manufacture, and sale of goods, would cure many of the craze for legislative enactment so common just now.

The foregoing partial catalogue of statutes affecting labour, and manufacturing trade generally, indicates to some extent the nature of the struggle of the earlier handicraftsmen, and the difficulties against which they had to contend, over and above those connected with the guild system, which was also used to their detriment in most cases. The workmen sought by combination to minimize the evil effects of legislation, and to obtain justice at the hands of those who administered its provisions. Sometimes they were found to be supporting the statute law, as against the action of the guilds; at other times they supported the guilds as against the law. Often the influence of the handicraftsmen was sought and used by the defenders of each in turn, as it suited their purposes. Curious, indeed, are some of the records of that long and bitter struggle. They convey lessons of admonition, and of circumspection also, if read aright. But now comes the most deplorable part of the story.

Effects of State Regulation.—The effects of the regulation and control of industry, whether by the guilds or by the statute law, singly, in their respective domains, or jointly, as the one or the other operated in a particular district, or trade, were found by the workmen to be antagonistic to their interests, and disastrous in their results. But the fight against them was unequal. In the former contest, it was one form of free association pitted against the other; and in the end the victory remained with the Craft Guilds, as against their wealthier opponents, in the Merchant or Town Guilds of that

date.   Now it was against "constitutional authority," in so
far as that term can be used to describe a Parliament which
was far from being representative. The laws had been
passed; they must be administered, at least, until they had
been repealed.   Their administration was partial, bad,
often iniquitous, always mischievous, but there was no
remedy. The handicraftsmen had but one resource open
to them—combination.   But a combination to upset the
provisions of the statute law soon became a conspiracy,
subsequently sedition, then treason.   There was the law ; it
must be maintained ; the remedy was an appeal to the
Justices, or appeal against their decisions, if deemed to be
unjust.   The law itself was adverse to the interests of
labour ; its administration was in the hands of men opposed to labour ; and new conditions were arising which
separated classes more widely than they had hitherto been.

It would almost appear that the forces then opposed to
combination were crushing ; certainly they were formidable.
The earlier attempts could not have in the least succeeded
had not the existing conditions of labour rendered some
form of association indispensable.   And brave men were
found who were prepared to risk their all, even their liberty,
and in some cases even their lives, in maintaining the right
of free association, for mutual protection and support.
Wages having been arbitrarily fixed by law, it was also, and
subsequently, enacted that no man should take more than
the statutory amount, or the amount fixed by the justices,
even when tendered ; and that no employer should pay, or
tender, more than the State regulated wages in the particular industry.   The simple enforcement of such laws was
not only a barrier to combination, but it also led to it, and
promoted it.

Statutes in Restraint of Labour and Trade.—Then followed a series of statutes directed specifically against combinations of workmen. Others were also enacted which operated with a like effect, such as those dealing with "idle persons, rogues, and vagabonds." The first statute specifically directed against combination, as such, appears to have been 34 Edw. III., c. 9 (1360-1), an Act in which "The Statute of Labourers is confirmed, altered, and enforced." After mitigating the penalty as to labourers, the Act proceeds to abolish and render null and void all alliances and covines of masons and carpenters, and to order that each such artificer shall be compelled to serve his master, and do every work that to him pertaineth. Chapter X., of the same year and reign (1360-1), goes further, as regards labourers and artificers, and empowers the sheriff to pursue and seize those that absent themselves out of their services, in another town or country, and to outlaw those not found. If found after outlawry, he was to suffer imprisonments till he agreed to do as required by law, and had made satisfaction to the party, and for the falsity to be branded with an iron, formed to the manner of the letter **F**, burnt in the forehead, signifying *Falsity*. But this latter cruelty was not to be perpetrated except with the advice and consent of the Justices, after a respite for a given period. This statute also declared that there should be paid no wages for festival days; thus further reducing wages, for festival days in that period of our history were more numerous than in after times, or than now even with Bank Holidays.

The remaining years of the reign of Edward III. were fruitful in legislation in restraint of trade, the liberty of workmen, and the freedom of labour. The succeeding reigns were scarcely less so, down to the accession of Queen

Elizabeth.[1] In the latter reign matters in this respect changed somewhat, but it was merely a new departure upon the old lines. Regulation increased, and was extended as new industries arose. Statutory regulation required statutory enforcement, hence we find repression to prevent complaints, and of combinations to obtain redress of grievances, and suppression, by law and proclamation, when the workmen dared to combine and risk all the penalties. The predicament in which workmen found themselves was this : Labour—*i. e.* wages, hours, conditions of employment, modes of working, and even the occupations men should follow— was regulated by statute, and by the laws and customs of the Guild system, when the whole circumstances surrounding and conditions affecting labour had changed; and, moreover,

---

[1] The statutes in restraint of labour and of trade are too numerous to be set forth in detail, but the following list gives some of them, all of which interfered with the freedom of the workmen, some also with that of the employers, all with industry.

a. 25 Edw. III., st. I.
　34 Edw. III., c. 10.
　37 Edw. III., cc. 5, 6, 7, 8, 9, 10, 11, 12, 13, 14, and 15.
　38 Edw. III., c. 2.
　42 Edw. III., c. 6.
　50 & 51 Edw. III., cc. 6 and 7.
　12 Rich. II., c. 3, 4, 5, 6, 7, 8, 9, 10, and 14.
　13 Rich. II., st. I., cc. 8, 10, 11, and 12.
　14 Rich. II., cc. 4, 5, and 14.
　17 Rich. II., c. 8.
　21 Rich. II., confirming 13 Rich. II., c. 12.
　4 Hen. IV., cc. 14, 35.
　7 Hen. IV., c. 17.

a. 2 Hen. V., c. 4.
　2 Hen. VI., c. 7.
　6 Hen. VI., c. 3.
　8 Hen. VI., c. 8.
　11 Hen. VII., c. 22.
　12 Hen. VII., cc. 1, 3, and 4.
　14 & 15 Hen. VIII., c. 2.
　21 Hen. VIII., c. 16.
　33 Hen. VIII., st. I., c. 9.
　2 & 3 Edw. VI., c. 15.
　1 Mary, st. II., cc. 11 and 12.
　1 Mary, st. III., cc. 7 and 8.
　1 & 2 Phil. & Mary, cc. 7, 14.
　2 & 3 Phil. & Mary, cc. 11, 12, 13, and 16.
　4 & 5 Phil. & Mary, c. 5.

the workmen were prevented from taking such action as they thought best to ameliorate their condition, advance their wages, or alter the hard and fast lines of statutory hiring and of service. The only chance of escape was by mutual association, for mutual protection, and this was denied to them. But, in spite of law and of other difficulties, they would and did combine, with the result that the criminal law was strengthened and extended, with the view of stifling discontent and resisting every effort to obtain a relaxation of the law where oppressive, and of amending it where it was thought to offer any advantage to labour. Besides which the laws against labour were rigidly enforced ; those in its favour were laxly administered.

Laws Prohibiting Combination.—The scope and nature of the laws specifically directed against combination, and known subsequently under the name of "Combination Laws," may be inferred from the following brief description : First of all, the Statute 33 Edw. I., st. I. (1305), was brought to bear in order to stamp with conspiracy "all who do confeder or bind themselves by oath, covenant, or other alliance, as relates or extends to combinations or conspiracies of workmen, or other persons, to obtain an advance of, or fix the rate of wages, or to lessen or alter the hours or duration of the time of working, or to decrease the quantity of work, or to regulate or control the mode of carrying on any manufacture, trade, or business, or the management thereof; or to combinations or conspiracies of masters, manufacturers, or other persons, to lower or fix the rate of wages, or to increase or alter the hours or duration of the time of working, or to increase the quantity of work, or to regulate or control the mode of carrying on any manufacture, trade, or business, or the management thereof, or to oblige workmen to enter into work." The statute, 3 Hen. VI., c. 1 (1425), applied to "the annual congregations and confederacies made by masons, in their general chapters assembled;" the 33 Hen. VIII., st. I., c. 9 (1541-2), "An Act for servants' wages," applied to Ireland; 2 and 3 Edw. VI., c. 15 (1548), dealt with "victuallers and handicrafts-men"; 5 James I. (1411) dealt with "the fees of craftsmen, and the price of their work," in Scotland; in another Act, with "the fees of workmen," also in Scotland; and in yet another Act, with masons and others. The price of silk-workmanship was dealt with in the Act 7 James I., Scotland (1413). The 5th of Mary—Scotland (1547)—dealt with "the price of craftsmen's work, and of meat and drink in taverns." The size and prices of stuffs were dealt with by 7 James VI. (1574), Scotland, and silk-throwing was regulated by 13 and 14 Chas. II., c. 15 (1662). Later on tailors were regulated under 7 Geo. I., c. 13 (1720-1). In 1725, "An Act to prevent unlawful combinations of workmen employed in the woollen manufactures, and for the better payment of their wages," was passed, 12 Geo. I., c. 34 (1725-6). This was followed by 3 Geo. II., c. 14 (1730), "an Act to prevent unlawful combinations of workmen in all trades," in Ireland; by 22 Geo. II., c. 27 (1748-9), extending 12 Geo. I., c. 34, which was again extended by 29 Geo. II., c. 33 (1755-6). In the reign of George III. some fifteen or sixteen other Acts were enacted prior to the year 1800, when a new law "to prevent unlawful combinations of workmen" was passed, 39 and 40 Geo. III., c. 106 (1799—1800). The enactment of those named and other statutes conclusively show that combinations were prevalent, and that the law was practically powerless to stamp them out, or put them down. Fines, disablement, and imprisonment did not relieve distress, or remove the causes of discontent.

Revolt against the Combination Laws.—Towards the close of the last, and in the early years of the present century, very determined and resolute efforts were made to institute associations of some kind for the protection of workmen, and the advancement of labour. Some men dared openly to combine ; others did so secretly. In many trades the attempts to do so were persistent, in some cases continuous, often, however, only spasmodic ; but such, nevertheless, that the criminal law was frequently set in motion to circumvent or thwart the men's designs, crush the incipient organization, or to punish the daring innovators, who sought to associate, for disregarding the law. Tumults, riots, even bloodshed, sometimes resulted from these attempts ; but they were persisted in. It is said that "perfect love casteth out fear ; " in this case it was dire distress and misery, caused by low wages, the dearness of provisions, and the scarcity of employment, which banished fear. When they could not openly combine, the workmen resorted to violence, outrage, rick-burning, destruction of machinery, attacks upon the dwellings of the masters or employers, or upon the places where the manufacture was carried on. Prosecutions were instituted, when the offenders were apprehended, and condign punishment followed upon conviction ; but in many instances the perpetrators of overt acts were not discovered, and none would betray the wrongdoers, simply because of the injustice which had led to the wrong-doing. Discontent, and industrial revolt, were common, if not general ; and then there was a scare. But the only result of the scare was further repression ; as the "Combination Laws" had failed in their effect, or were ineffective for the objects intended, other laws were brought into requisition, namely, those enacted for purely political purposes, such as the Sedition Acts, the Corresponding Societies Acts, and even the Acts relating to treason. There was very little excuse for thus stretching the law in order to reach workmen, as such, for their meetings, as a rule, were not political, certainly not in the earlier stages, although they became so when redress was denied to them.

Condition of England at dawn of the Nineteenth Century.—It is said that, in the natural world, the darkest period is the hour before the dawn; it is even so in the history of nations, and of progress. The closing year of the eighteenth century opened most gloomily for the people.[1] The Bakers' Company of London, in appearing before the Lord Mayor to set the assize of bread, reported that the average price of wheat was 96s. 1¾d. per quarter, and of flour 88s. 10d. per sack; whereupon the Lord Mayor "gave the bakers a whole assize," which advanced the price of the quartern loaf to 1s. 3d., commencing from January 1st, 1800. The Select Committee of the House of Commons, in reporting upon the supply and price of corn, bread, &c., urged "that the bakers should be prohibited from selling bread until twenty-four hours after it is baked." A Bill for that purpose was immediately passed, forbidding "any baker or other person within the Metropolitan area after the 26th day of February, 1800, and any baker or person residing in any other part of Great Britain, after the 4th day of March, 1800, to sell, or offer, or expose for sale, any bread until the same shall have been baked twenty-four hours at the least." On February 20th, 1800, resolutions were moved

[1] Compare Gibbin's *Industrial History of England*, pp. 173 and 186—197.

in the House of Peers, by his Grace the Archbishop of
Canterbury, respecting the scarcity of grain, and an agreement was signed by the great majority of that House, that
not more than one quartern loaf per week, for each individual in their respective families, should be permitted to
be consumed; in which agreement the House of Commons
most readily concurred." Even the use of pastry was to be
discontinued until the 10th day of October, 1800. The use
of potatoes, rice, and other ingredients was suggested to be
mixed with flour, to lessen the price of bread. But the
scarcity continued, and the next assize of bread fixed the
price of the quartern loaf at 1s. 5¼d. When the Royal Family
prohibited the use of pastry in the Royal household, the
price was subsequently raised to 1s. 6d.; the price of coal in
London was £4 the chaldron. Other commodities, as well
as provisions, were proportionately high, and the laws
against forestallers and ingraters were rigidly put in force,
in all parts of the country. To make matters worse, there
was great scarcity of employment, and the wages of those in
work were exceedingly low. The natural result followed;
there were riots and tumults, bakers and provision merchants'
houses were attacked, and the military dispersed the mobs
"without quarter." Then, it was alleged by the Court of
Common Council, that there would have been a fall in the
price of corn and flour, had not the access to the corn-
market been impeded.

As a companion picture to the foregoing, here is an
extract from the newspapers of the year 1800: "Conspiracies have been set on foot by journeymen of various
trades, to enforce an augmentation of wages, which have
been very properly resisted by the masters, and repressed
by the magistrates. . . . Some of them are to be tried at

Quarter Sessions. In general we do not conceive the high price of provisions to fall with that degree of severity upon any of those classes of men which can authorize even complaint in their mouths. They do not certainly bear more than their share of the general pressure, and if every man who feels the burthens of these times is to revolt from his employment, and to discontinue his industry, society is disorganized at once." At that time, when the people were in a state of semi-starvation, it was computed that "the number of coach and post-horses in the kingdom consumed as much corn as would keep about 1,000,000 persons, at a quartern loaf, each person, per week. On November 9th, 1800, a proclamation was issued, forbidding a public meeting of journeymen, artizans, mechanics, and tradesmen, which had been proposed to be held, to petition the King and the Parliament, with reference to the high price of provisions. This was followed by a further proclamation urging the utmost possible frugality in the use of every species of grain." The riots and tumults of that year were mostly bread riots, politics having had very little part or lot in them. Three men were committed to Coldbath Fields prison, by Sir William Addington, for hissing at his Majesty on his way to the House of Peers. Two of the three were shoemakers. At Twickenham, a basket-maker was committed to Tothill Fields Bridewell, for using disrespectful expressions against his Majesty, and the Government of this country. But it was not in London alone that discontent existed. In all parts of the country there was dire distress, and social revolt. The period is thus described by a writer who had examined over 1000 newspapers issued in 1800—"The laws were harsh, commerce restricted, the slave-trade flourished, the press-gang was in active operation, the pillory was in frequent use, footpads and mounted highwaymen were numerous, duelling and drunkenness were fashionable." [1]

Labour Agitations and Political Movements.—Up to the end of the last century labour agitations and industrial combinations were nearly always separate and distinct from political movements ; only occasionally did the two forces unite or coalesce. The fact is, the journeymen were non-voters, as a rule, and therefore were, politically, of no account. In certain cities and towns the freemen had votes, and these were courted at election times, to be despised, if not spurned, when the event was over. It could not be otherwise, for their votes were bought at so much apiece, and those who bought them, sold them again at a profit, only in another way. The voteless journeymen saw this, and resented it.[2] By degrees the workmen, seeing no chance of escape from their industrial thraldom in any other way, joined forces with the political malcontents, and demanded a reform of Parliament, the abolition of abuses, and the repeal of the Combination Laws. It is not very clear to what extent the political factions agreed in the demands of the workmen for social amelioration, but the latter foresaw that something would be gained by the alliance. During the first quarter of the present century we find that the political and social elements co-operated in many public movements, with the result that both sections gradually begun to reap partial advantages. Some legislation took place as regards Friendly Societies, ere the eighteenth century closed ; this was followed by the first Factory Act, in 1801—1802. The workmen became bolder also in the

[1] See *The Year* 1800, by F. Perigal, 3rd edition, 1861.
[2] See Gibbin's *Industrial History*, p. 189.

matter of combination, the weavers, shipwrights, shoemakers, tailors, compositors, and some others, taking the lead. Strikes also were prevalent, as the reports of investigations into the nature and extent of combination abundantly show. There were also numerous prosecutions, resulting in fines and imprisonment, all of which tended rather to increase the discontent than to allay it. It was pretended that the law was equal for employers and employed, but there is no instance of a successful prosecution against employers for combining, although it was just as illegal to combine to keep down wages as to increase them.

Repeal of the Combination Laws.—But the dawn of a more humane period was casting its lighter shadows across the dark background of the picture. The tips of the loftier hills were beginning to be tinged with slanting streaks of a roseate hue. Humane men had heard the cries of the oppressed workmen. They had touched a chord of infinite fibre, which subsequently vibrated throughout the land. Some, perhaps, only regarded the unenfranchised workmen as a fulcrum by which to sustain the lever which was being brought to bear to raise the merchant princes, who had grown up in various parts of the country, to some level of authority and power with the governing classes, representing the landed interest, then the privileged orders of society. Whatever the motive, the result was the same. The inquiries instituted in 1817, 1818, and down to 1824, and the outrages which occurred during those years, drew attention to the subject, and ended in a repeal of the Combination Laws, in 1824, to be again the subject of Parliamentary inquiry in 1825, when the Act of the previous year was repealed, and another enacted, as a substitute, in its place.

Labour was not completely unfettered by the 5 Geo. IV., c. 95 (1824), or its substitute 6 Geo. IV., c. 129 (1825). It was not intended to be a full charter of rights for the workmen. Mr. Wallace, in introducing the Bill, stated that its " principle was to make all associations illegal, excepting those for the purpose of setting such amount of wages as would be a fair remuneration for the workmen." Whatever its object, or the reservations in the minds of those who framed the measure, the Act gave freer scope to the workmen, and enabled them to associate together to promote their own welfare, in their own way, so long as they did not use violence, threats, intimidation, or force, to achieve their objects. They were empowered by law, for the first time certainly during more than five centuries, to fight for their own freedom, at least to a limited extent. The laws of master and servant still remained,[1] and, in principle, they were in conflict with the 6 Geo. IV., c. 129 ; but in effect the repeal of the Combination Laws enabled workmen to institute lawful associations for mutual protection and advancement, and they were not slow to utilize the power which that statute gave to them in those respects.

[1] The old Laws of Master and Servant were temporarily repealed in 1867, but they were only finally repealed in 1875.

CHAPTER IV.

TRADE UNIONISM : ITS ORIGIN, DEVELOPMENT, AND PROGRESS.

Trade Unions, successors to the Old English Guilds—Traces of their descent visible in Forms, Ceremonies, Methods, and Policy—Earlier difficulties, Law and Custom favoured Capital at the expense of Labour—Rise of an " Operative Class " of Hired Handicraftsmen—Examples of early Trade Unionism—Growth of associative effort—Benefit Clubs and Societies—Imitations of the Guild System—Apprentices—Labour Organizations towards the close of the Eighteenth and early years of the Nineteenth Century—Repeal of the Combination Laws in 1824, immediate effects thereof upon Labour—Extended associations—Federations of Labour—Institution of newer and better type of Trade Unions—Amalgamated Society of Engineers—Model upon which later Unions have been mostly founded—Progress of Trade Unions, 1851 to 1860—Progress continued, 1861 to 1870—Further Progress, 1871 to 1880—Changed Conditions of Labour—Legal recognition of Trade Unions—Protection of their Funds—Severe strain upon the Unions, from 1875 to 1880—Depression in Trade—Test of fitness and of ability to cope with a great Industrial Crisis—Further progress of Trade Unions, 1881 to 1890—Revival of Trade Unionism—Growth in Numbers, and in Funds—Federations—The Dockers' Union and Strikes—Trades Union Congresses—Institution, Progress, and Labours of Trade Congresses—The Dundee and Liverpool Congresses—Trade Unions becoming more Political—The present position, power, and influence of Trade Unions.

IT is now universally admitted that Trade Unions are the legitimate successors to the old English Guilds. The parents had deteriorated and degenerated ere the birth of this younger born of their progeny; and it is to be feared that the offspring retains traces of the degenerate times which gave it birth. Ailments are more often hereditary than healthful vigour; certainly the former develop more speedily, or at least they obtrude themselves sooner upon the eye of the observer. In this instance, the little stranger was not welcomed; and it had the misfortune to have a bad accoucheur and a worse nurse. Nevertheless the Trade Union, in all its earlier developments especially, carries the stamp of its lineage in nearly all its features. In many ways indications of the fact that Trade Unions owe their origin to the old English Guilds, are to be found in their forms and ceremonies, their observances and methods, and in their general policy. In some cases the Unions have discarded that which was bad in the old system, and retained the good; in other instances, it is to be feared that they acted contrariwise, by clinging to the bad, and forsaking the good; such is the perversity of poor human nature. There is this excuse for them by way of palliation. There was a conspiracy against them, to strangle them at their birth. The guilds denied their paternity, and sought to destroy them; the law not only refused protection, but virtually declared them outlaws; and then statutes were passed specifically adverse to them, with the view of permanently stamping them out of existence. They were nursed in secret, and fed by discontent. No wonder that they grew up very Ishmaels of the desert, their hands being against every man, and every man's hand against them. This hard usage of the past may have had a bad effect upon their character, and tainted their action. First impressions seldom are effaced, either from individuals or systems. Sometimes they become hereditary.

In previous chapters the organization of labour has been traced through the periods of guild-life and statute law, and we have seen how the workmen endeavoured to protect themselves by combination.   The incipient germ of the Trade Union is discernible at an early date in some of the combinations, confederacies, or alliances then formed.   But, in most of them, the essence of the old guild prevailed. The workmen had not emerged from tutelage ; they relied upon the old forms, and sought refuge behind the old ramparts.   They were cramped in their action, and could not strike out into a new path.   Law and custom en- compassed them on every side ; and they had been taught to believe in both.   When they lost faith in existing agencies, the law prevented them from establishing new ones, which, if established, might have averted centuries of suffering and of wrong.   Had the journeymen, who were fast becoming a distinct class, in the later years of the existence of the Craft Guilds, and who soon grew to be numerous enough to institute independent associations of their own, in certain specific industries, been permitted to combine, in a lawful and peaceable manner, British industry would have become organized centuries ago.   It was most wanted, and needed, when the new industrial system was first instituted,[1] and the hiring of workpeople necessarily constituted a part of the manufacturing extension, which was everywhere elbowing out the cruder form of the domestic workshop.   Wages, prices, the hours of labour, conditions of employment, and other essential matters might then have been arranged in such a way that the laws of economic science would have had fair play.   As it was, the whole tenor of law and custom were in favour of capital,

---

[1] See Gibbin's *Industrial History of England*, pp. 175—186.

as against labour; the former asserted its rights, with little heed to its duties and responsibilities; while the latter was compelled to perform all its duties and responsibilities, almost without the recognition of its rightful dues, certainly without their attainment or enforcement.

Institution of Trade Unions.—The difficulties in the way of instituting Trade Unions, which should be to the handi-craftsmen what the old guilds had become to the masters, were enormous. Even without the intervention of law they were great, for systematic hiring, in the sense in which we now understand the term, was only very partial down even to a rather late period in the eighteenth century. Wages were often only part-payment; board, and even lodging, frequently formed part of the remuneration of labour; and the workman himself did not always wholly depend upon the mere wages of service,[1] for husbandry of some kind was common even among the craftsmen, particularly in the smaller towns, and in nearly all the villages. The produce of the garden, the allotment, or the field, helped to feed the workpeople so largely engaged in domestic industry, which could be put aside as occasion required, especially in summer. This state of things applied to skilled craftsmen, such as masons, carpenters, smiths, and others, whose employment was general throughout the country. In a less degree, even weavers, shoemakers, and tailors, possibly hatters also, took their turn in the garden and the field. It was only when numbers of hired handicraftsmen employed in the same trade, or branch of trade, were congregated together in one place, or within a circumscribed or tolerably definite area, that any real union of the workers could be successfully carried out. Combination for some specific purpose could

---

[1] *Industrial History of England*, p. 154.

be, and was, resorted to, as we have seen. But there is also abundant evidence of the fact that these combinations were disbanded when the object was attained. Indeed, very frequently they were abandoned on the mere promise that the reforms demanded would be conceded. Only in very few instances had they the essential elements of permanency in them. The law was partially responsible for this state of things; but custom, and the influence of an old system, which survived in many places, had something to do with the hesitancy of the workmen to embark on a new sea of troubles, not knowing whither they might be taken or driven.

Some of the earlier combinations very nearly approximated to a regular trade society in organization, though too much after the type of the later Craft Guild. For example, we find evidence of the existence of some form of continuous labour combination among the framework knitters, from 1710 to 1725, and of active political work in 1778 and onwards. The compositors, and others connected with printing, show signs of activity in 1775, 1785, and 1792. In 1798 five members were prosecuted for conspiracy for "unlawfully meeting together to restrain and injure the master-printers." The hatters were active in labour questions as early as 1772. The shipwrights of the port of Liverpool were a political force, by means of their organization, in 1790, but their association was a guild composed of freemen, having and exercising the Parliamentary franchise. Sheffield boasted of its trade organizations before the close of the last century, for we find some rather warm contentions in various trades, the masters on the one side, and the workmen on the other, combining for specific purposes. Foremost among workmen were the cutlers, in 1790; the scissor-grinders, in 1791; and the scissor-smiths, in 1792. In the

cotton industry we hear of the combination of the calico-
printers, in the year 1802. But perhaps the nearest approach
to a *bonâ-fide* Trade Union, something akin to those of
later times, was the " Institution," established at Halifax in
1796, and one at Leeds, about the same time, by the cloth-
workers of Yorkshire. Even those " Institutions " were,
however, modelled upon the old Craft Guild, for masters
as well as journeymen were members. It is evident
from various contemporary references that weavers were
among the first to institute associations of the kind, for an
Act expressly prohibiting their combinations was passed in
1775, 12 Geo. I., c. 34. The contributions to the Halifax
Institution was threepence per week, to the Leeds Institution only one penny per week, the workers in the villages
contributing as well as those working in the towns.

Probably the reason why we hear more of combinations
of workmen towards the close of the eighteenth, and the
beginning of the present century, was that modes of self-
help were being promoted and legalized.[1] The Friendly
Society Club was recognized as a useful institution, and an
Act was passed for their " encouragement and relief " in
1793 ; this Act was amended and extended in 1795. The
workmen in some trades took advantage of this legislation,
and combined under the cloak of Friendly Societies. The
" Good Intent " Society of Silk Weavers, instituted in 1806,
is an example of this form of association. Still, the efforts
of workmen to advance their interests, and to undo the
mischiefs of past legislation, were cramped in every direction. Free association being denied to them, some secret
societies were doubtless formed, but the reasons for their

---

[1] This subject is more fully dealt with in the volume on *Mutual
Thrift*, in this series.

secrecy were not criminal; they were not founded with a criminal intent, except in so far as seeking to mitigate the evils of legislation, by combined action, could be construed as being criminal. It was an offence against the law to combine; and seeking to evade the provisions of unjust and disabling laws was punishable, while resistance to them brought the offenders within the penal clauses of statutes specifically directed against sedition, treason, and conspiracy. A legitimate trade society could not be lawfully established prior to 1824. Up to that date they were unlawful associations in restraint of trade, or under the ban of some other fiction of law. But their growth and vitality is undeniable, even before the passing of the Act, 5 Geo. IV., c. 95. Many of those who had primarily demanded the repeal of that Act came to the conclusion that, in consequence of the enormous development of combinations as soon as it had passed, they had been called into existence by it. No such thing. They had been created and nursed in secret; the latitude allowed by the Act brought them into daylight and prominence. The workmen were freed from danger, but they were confronted with responsibility, and the attempt to retrace the step signally failed. The law was re-enacted in 1825, after an inquiry into its operation and working.

Character of the Earlier Unions.—All labour associations up to that date were founded more or less upon the later forms of the old English Guild system, that is to say, upon the Ordinances and Regulations of the Craft Guilds. They had no other model upon which to frame their rules or constitution. They often differed from each other as to objects, and in the means for attaining them; but they had the one common ground of protecting the interests of the workmen, however they might differ as to the methods. Many desired the revival of the Guild system. Those were frequently supported by the smaller masters, and by the fraternities of freemen in corporate towns. Others sought the maintenance of law and custom, believing, in their innocence, that restrictive law was the bulwark of liberty. Some thought that both objects were good, in so far as they went, but that circumstances warranted a revision of the law, and an amendment of the Guild system. A few were far-seeing enough to perceive that freedom was better than either, and that combinations, or associative effort, would best enable them to work out their own redemption. All seemed to be agreed that the limitation of apprentices was good, and all sought to perpetuate the system, as being the embodiment of law and long custom. Here the workmen and the employers split ; and the apprentice system was thereafter practically abolished, in so far as restrictive law was concerned. Some regarded the fixing of wages and the hours of labour as beneficial, and supported it, believing that their troubles arose from administrative neglect of statutory provisions. Legal enactment in some form they could not get away from, the idea was ingrained in their very nature. They had been used to it. In the matter of association, their methods were crude and transitory. With few exceptions, the contributions consisted of temporary levies, for temporary purposes. They assisted each other in labour contests to some extent, and gave temporary relief in cases of sickness or distress. The only real "benefit," which was well-nigh universal, was "funeral benefit," to ensure decent burial. In cases of prosecution the members were defended in the courts of law, and sometimes the wives and families of those convicted and imprisoned were provided for.

Modern Trade Unions.—For all practical purposes, the modern Trade Union started on its pilgrimage in 1824. Prior to that date nearly all was incubation and infancy. A few Unions established in the earlier period have survived to this day; but these have mostly been reorganized. The Consolidated Society of Bookbinders was founded in 1792; the compositors in 1801; the iron-founders in 1809; some branches of the engineering trades in 1823 and 1824; the shipwrights in 1825; the glass-bottle makers in 1827; have all survived to this day. From the final repeal of the Combination Laws, in 1825, the real work of organization commenced. During the next twenty-five years there was great industrial activity, in many ways and forms. There was great political activity also, and the energies of the pioneer Unions were applied to such movements as that for Parliamentary reform, and for other objects. This was especially the case up to the passing of the Reform Act, 1832. Then commenced, in real earnest, the organization of the Labour Unions, upon a more permanent basis. In 1833 and 1834 we find them a distinct political power, backed by numbers and funds. Politicians courted them and assisted them. They numbered among their friends Dr. Wade, Mr. Francis Place, Rev. Mr. Bull, Joseph Hume, M.P., Thomas Attwood, M.P., and other then well-known public men. Those two years present the nearest parallel to 1889 and 1890, as regards labour movements, of any years upon record. Judging by the reports in the *Pioneer* newspaper, an organ of the Unions, nearly every trade in the country had its Union, and strikes were rife, not only among workmen, but among women. Of the latter we find washerwomen, female straw-workers, bonnet-makers, female operatives in the textile trades, and many others. London shopmen also combined, and attorneys' clerks threatened to do so. Prominent among the men's Unions were masons, carpenters, bricklayers, plasterers, cabinet-makers, smiths, shoemakers, tailors, printers and compositors, chair-makers, potters, japanners, locksmiths, engineers, textile operatives, coopers, gas-workers, sawyers, saddle and harness-makers, stove-makers, Sheffield workmen, nail-makers, agricultural labourers, and others.

The parallel is nearly complete in other particulars. There were those fascinating conceptions of a "Grand National Consolidated Trades' Union," also of "The Grand National Guild of Builders," and further, a "National Labour Exchange," for London. Strikes were prevalent in most industries, and help was generally rendered by those in work to those on strike. The prosecution of the six Dorchester labourers was the signal for such concerted action, and evoked such unbounded enthusiasm as had never before been witnessed or exhibited in labour agitations. But the elements of permanency had not even then been sufficiently developed to be adequately embodied in the constitutions and rules of the Unions. After a period of unwonted activity and vigorous effort, the majority of the Unions subsided; while those that weathered the storm and remained, had all their work to do to consolidate their organization, and place it upon a permanent basis. The cause of Unionism progressed, however, and they had attained such prominence again, by the year 1838, that a further inquiry was instituted into their objects and organization. But nothing came of the inquiry, not even a report, the evidence only being published. In 1846-47 there was another revival of Unionism; many strikes occurred, some prosecutions were instituted, and federation was again the chief topic of the day. The workmen were gradually feeling their way towards a solid basis upon which to establish an institution which was destined to exert an enormous influence in all matters relating to capital and labour, both in the then near and also distant future.   As yet the Unions were little more than fighting machines, erected upon insufficient foundations. Sometimes the foundations gave way, or the machines themselves would not work ; often the havoc which took place in the conflict resulted more from the misuse of labour's weapons than from the heavy artillery of capital's guns.   The leaders of the Unions, for the most part, were 'prentice hands; they had not learned to handle masses of men, nor to direct a steady fire upon the outworks of the enemy.

Provident Benefits and Trade Unions.—In the year 1850 an event occurred which has left and will leave its mark upon the Trade Union movement for all time.   Up to this time the different branches of the engineering trades had each their own Union of some kind.   But they found " that they were in too isolated a state, and therefore not able to command what they were really entitled to."   After some conferences, a delegate meeting was held in Birmingham, in September 1850, when it was resolved to amalgamate all the separate societies into one Union, under the name of " The Amalgamated Society of Engineers, Machinists, Millwrights, Smiths, and Pattern Makers."   At that delegate meeting the questions of over-time and piece-work were discussed, with the result that steps were subsequently taken to abolish these practices in all shops, except that overtime, when absolutely required by the exigencies of the case, was to be paid for at double rates.   Extra rates had been generally paid since 1836, but the practice was not universal, and many strikes took place in consequence of the lack of uniformity in practice, especially in Lancashire. From the initial action thus taken in 1850, resulted the great engineers' strike. This phase of the question need not, however, be further pursued. The event of supreme importance was the basis upon which the amalgamation was constituted, and the benefits which were provided in the society's rules, for all members of the Union. This practically is what is now denominated the "Old Trade Unionism," a system instituted only forty years ago. It is quite true that some of these benefits are to be found in two or three of the older Unions. The Iron-founders' Society, for example, began with some of them thirty years previously ; the Steam-Engine Makers' Society, twenty-five years previously ; other Unions may have had one or two of the objects in their rules, even at an earlier date. But in 1850 the provident benefits were systematized, and were made an integral part of the constitution, and internal economy of the Union. The contributions were made to cover all benefits and all purposes, except that extra levies might be added by the votes of the whole of the members for specific purposes, or on occasions of great emergency.

The constitution and rules of the Amalgamated Society of Engineers have become the models of many of the later Unions. Some of those established long prior to 1850 have since that date been re-organized on the same basis as the Engineers. Many of them have not been able to incorporate all the benefits in their rules ; a few have kept the provident and trade benefits separate and apart, but the tendency has been to approximate to the Engineers' Society as far as practicable. Among those most nearly approaching to the ideal of a trade society in these respects are the boiler-makers and iron-shipbuilders, the iron-founders, the steam-engine makers, the moulders of Scotland, the carpenters and joiners, the operative bricklayers, the compositors, the tailors, the railway servants, and some others.

Progress of Trade Unions.—Trade Unionism made rapid strides between 1850 and 1860, but no new features were developed. The records, so far as available, seem to show that quiet organization was going on in various trades. The period was also remarkable for some great strikes, notably the great Preston strike in 1853 ; the great miners' strike in Yorkshire in 1858; the boot and shoemakers' strikes in 1857, 1858, and 1859; the strike and lock-out in the building trades in 1859-60 ; in the flint-glass trades in 1859-60 ; and the chain-makers in 1859-60. Those disputes, and the circumstances connected with, or arising out of them, directed public attention to the subject of labour organizations and of trade disputes generally. Efforts were from time to time made to institute Boards of Conciliation and Arbitration to deal with such questions, but they never achieved any marked success. Employers usually resented any " outside interference," and the workmen seemed to have very little faith in the impartiality of any umpire. The efforts of Mr. Mackinnon and of Lord St. Leonards in this direction were almost futile; but the legislation they inaugurated remains on the Statute Book, to testify to their zeal, to this day.

The next decade, 1871-80, saw further developments in labour organization, and also an extension of Trade Unionism. During four or five years Great Britain enjoyed an expansion of trade and increased prosperity to an extent never before realized or approached. Prices of commodities and goods went up enormously, vast profits being netted in nearly every industry in the kingdom. Naturally the work-

men sought to share in the benefits and advantages of the
flush in trade.　The result was that labour organizations
also expanded, new societies sprang into existence, a
revival took place in those already formed, and national
federations were attempted on a large scale.　Strikes were
prevalent in all trades; in some the wages went up to a
higher level than had ever before been attained; and all
workmen seemed to have made a forward step towards
better remuneration for labour, and better conditions of
employment.　During that period, although labour disputes
were common, almost universal, one fact stands out pro-
minently to the credit of all concerned—workmen and
employers alike—namely, that much of the old bitterness
had passed away.　The battles were fought with vigour,
persistency, even with stubbornness, but right royally for
the most part.　Generally there was an absence of riotous
proceedings on the one side, and of an appeal to the forces
of the Crown on the other.　Formerly it had been the
common, almost usual, practice to call out the military in
the event of a great strike, especially in the iron and coal
districts; but this was no longer thought to be necessary.
The press was usually pretty severe in its comments upon
the action of the Unions and the exactions of the men.
The colliers were rated soundly for their supposed love of
champagne, and for pianos, and all were treated with the
usual homilies about driving trade from the country by their
demands for high wages, shorter hours of labour, and other
claims, and also for their alleged neglect of work, and of
laziness in the performance of their duty.

Further Progress: Changes in the Law.—Undoubtedly some of changes in the attitude of capital and
labour towards each other were due to the action of the

Legislature in passing the Trade Union Act, 1871. Up to that date Trade Unions were under the ban of the law. The repeal of the Combination Laws gave to workmen freedom to combine; but combinations in restraint of trade were unlawful associations still. The trade society, which represented such combinations, was unrecognized as a lawful association, and, consequently, their funds were unprotected. An officer of the Union, having access to the funds, could embezzle them with impunity. Happily few did so, or even attempted to do so; but in the cases tried in the courts, those who had done so were acquitted, and were practically told that they could rob the society without fear of legal consequences. The Unions were thus denied that security for their property which was accorded to all other bodies. The Trade Union Act remedied that state of things. It also gave other advantages to these labour organizations; they were recognized as lawful corporate bodies, capable of holding property in land, and they had the right of legal remedy by the simple process of registration. In some other respects the Legislature was timid. A part of the original Bill was even reactionary; this was eventually carried as a separate measure, under the title of the Criminal Law Amendment Act. An agitation was then commenced for the repeal of this obnoxious measure, and in 1875, after a brief inquiry as to the effect of that law, and other labour statutes, the whole were repealed by the " Labour Laws, 1875." This was followed in 1876 by an amendment of the Trade Union Act, a measure which conceded all the demands of the Trade Unionists up to that time. Legislation was now tolerably complete. Labour was freed from restrictive law. The Trade Unions, representing labour, were placed on an equality with all other associations; they could pursue their policy and carry out their objects without fear. Thenceforward liberty was accorded to all alike, and also such protection as was needed to prevent that liberty from being infringed.

The second half of the decade was not so propitious. Trade declined, prices fell, and wages were lowered. The Unions endeavoured as far as possible to resist the downward tendency. Great strikes followed in several industries, in many instances resulting in disaster, distress, and almost ruin to some of the older organizations. But nothing could prevent reductions in wages—down they went, in some instances as low as before the great accession in trade, in the five years previously. But this was not the case in all industries, for many of them retained some of the advantages which had accrued to them in those five years. Fortunately the concessions as to working-hours were to a great extent maintained, partially in some trades, in others wholly. The strain upon the Unions was immense; those built upon a solid foundation were shaken to their very centre, others fell to pieces like a house of cards. The great Federation of Miners, called the "National Association," fell to pieces, never to be revived on the same basis up to this hour. By the close of 1879, the drain on the resources of the largest and most successful Unions was such that many could not have withstood it much longer. Those were years of severe trial; they tested the principles upon which the institution was established, and they indicated the form of association which could weather the storm and tempest of depression in trade, the dangers of which were intensified by its long duration. It needs but a very superficial acquaintance with the history of those years, and of the annals of labour organizations during the same period, to be able to decide as to relative value of the different kinds of trade societies, and their capacity to live through intense industrial difficulties, and survive the ordeal. Those founded upon the model of the Amalgamated Engineers were shaken and strained, but they rode into harbour unimpaired. The Masons' Society, which was a near approach to that of the Engineers, fared not so well; many others fared badly; some have never recovered; several have since been remodelled with a view to their being able to meet similar difficulties, should they ever unfortunately recur. This aspect of the question must be studied by all who desire to understand the comparative value of "the old" and "the new" Trade Unionism.

The decade now closing, 1881-90, has witnessed many changes, not so much in the organization and work of the Unions, as in men's conception regarding them. For the most part, the entire decade has been one of progress. Trade Unionism has lived down the aversion formerly entertained towards it. Gradually the public have learned that they are an important social and industrial force; and politicians have recognized in them a great political power. They have won recognition where formerly they were abused and tabooed. If imitation be the sincerest form of flattery, as is alleged, then Trade Unions have been flattered to their hearts' content. They may even claim to be fashionable. Has not His Royal Highness the Prince of Wales received and fêted their representatives at Sandringham? Have they not been complimented by Royal Commissions, upon which have sat some of their most respected representatives? Have they not been recommended by a Committee of the Peers of the Realm, as a cure for certain social evils? Has not Royalty, in the person of the German Emperor, met representatives of the Trade Unions of England at a Royal Conference at Berlin? Are not several of their representative leaders respected members of the British House of Commons? Are not others Justices of the Peace in some of the chief centres of industry? Are not many of them members of Town Councils, County Councils, School Boards, and other representative local bodies? Almost better than all, from a purely industrial point of view, and perhaps in consequence of the foregoing public recognitions, are not the representatives of the Unions officially recognized by leading employers and great capitalists, as worthy of sitting at the same Board, on terms of perfect equality, to discuss and settle labour questions without recourse to fierce industrial war? All this, and much more, had been accomplished ere the dawn of 1889, though some seem not to be aware of the fact, while others appear to take a pride in hiding or obscuring the facts. But history, although it might be distorted, cannot be obliterated, and truth will triumph, in spite of falsehood, misrepresentation, and suppression.

Revivals and New Departures.—During the last two years there has been a singular, almost an unprecedented revival of Trade Unionism. It began with the shipbuilding trades early in 1889, in consequence of a great revival of trade in all branches connected with that important industry. Other branches of the iron trade were similarly affected, and industrial movements for higher wages became general. Then followed the miners, mostly the coal miners, by whom considerable advances in wages were speedily won. In some districts the Miners' Unions developed enormously in numbers, and later on, another gigantic National Federation was instituted, similar, though not on quite the same lines, to that of 1873, 1878, and 1879. Those movements, and others, prepared the way for the institution of the Docker's Union, started in 1887, and registered in 1888. At first, and for a long time, its success was not great. Its members are stated to have risen to 2,500 at one time, they then fell to 300 ; at the date of the great strike the total membership is said to have been about 800 paying members. In the beginning, the Union did not make such rapid strides as the Agricultural Labourers' Unions in 1872, which are said to have reached a total membership of about 73,300 members in the three great Unions at that time established. The Dockers' Strike, however, at once gave an impulse to the Union, and members were made with unusual facility. No strike that ever took place evoked so much sympathy. The public mind had been prepared for it, and was pre-disposed in its favour, by the publication of the *Bitter Cry*, and numerous other publications and reports in the press. Of sympathy there was no lack, and help soon followed in abundance. The general public contributed direct, by letter and otherwise, £13,730 2s. 4d., including amounts sent through various newspapers ; trade societies contributed £4,473 11s. 2d. ; the Colonies, £30,423 15s. 0d., most of which came from Australia ; and foreign countries £108 14s. 7d. In nearly every labour contest previously, the workmen had to depend upon Trade Union funds alone ; they were denied public sympathy, and received no outside support. Even poor relief, in cases of dire distress, was often refused to the families of those on strike, so bitterly opposed⁻ were the employing class and all local officialism to labour disputes. The change was remarkable, and the circum-stances were novel in the extreme. The attitude of the public betokened a more favourable tone towards the poorest workmen.

F

Trades Congresses.—The last twenty years have also witnessed the growth of an institution in connection with Trade Unionism, of it but not inside it—namely, the Trades' Union Congress. Started in 1868, it nearly came to an untimely end in 1870, in which year no Congress was held. Since 1870, however, the Congress has met yearly, the last, in September 1890, being the largest ever held. This institution is supported wholly by *bonâ-fide* Trade Unions, outside help not only being resolutely refused, but absolutely prohibited. The Parliamentary Committee, which is the governing body elected by the Congress, is charged with the duty of carrying out the resolutions passed at the annual gathering, mostly as regards legislative action and measures proposed for legislation. During its existence all measures affecting the interests of labour, and the welfare of workmen, have been watched with sedulous care, and many have been introduced and carried at the instigation of Congress, several by its own initiation. As a rule, the Congress, and its representative committee, have avoided purely political questions having a party complexion ; but not wholly so. Even questions upon which there is great diversity of opinion are generally either eschewed, or are treated tenderly. This policy has helped to keep the Congress together. For legislative purposes there must be a consensus of opinion. It is not necessary that there shall be absolute unanimity, but the opinions of even a strong minority have to be considered. By pursuing this course the Congress has been able to carry successfully numerous important measures, and to impress the seal of its approval upon many others, governmental and otherwise.[1]   Perhaps

[1] For a detailed review of the history and work of successive Congresses, see *Conflicts of Capital and Labour*, chap. x.

the wise prudence which has characterized the proceedings and legislative efforts of the Congress, and its elected representative body, the Parliamentary Committee, has helped to disarm opposition to the Trade Union movement in later years. The qualities of statesmanship have been shown in a high degree, both by the selection of subjects for legislative treatment, and by the manner in which they have been handled and prepared for Parliamentary debate. This is shown by the fact that nearly all the measures proposed have been embodied in law, if not always exactly on the precise lines contemplated.

The two last Congresses have deviated from that course. That of September 1890 carried some resolutions, and attempted to carry others, which have had the effect of producing schism, and even of some secessions, the results of which cannot as yet be foreseen. The more important of these resolutions will be discussed in another chapter, suffice it here to say that there was anything but unanimity in the discussions, or in the resolves of the Congress. The very size of the gathering, instead of adding to its strength, brought only weakness and diversity. The discussions were centred upon one subject mainly, and that one the chief cause of the dissensions which followed. It was made the stalking-horse upon which the election of secretary and of candidates for the committee turned. But even on the most crucial occasions over one-fourth of the delegates abstained from voting. The rift in the lute might have been comparatively slight, but its tones are altered. Instead of harmony, there is discord; there is a jarring sound which grates upon the ears, both of the performers and of the listeners, who look on.

Trade Unions and Politics.—A change is also perceptible

in many Trade Unions. They are tending more and more to mere political activity, as industrial bodies. If Trade Unionists as such took a more active part in political movements, the country would be the gainer in the long run ; but to turn the Unions into party political machines will at once destroy their significance and usefulness as industrial associations, and render nugatory their influence in contested elections. Courted and cajoled at first, they will be bribed afterwards, with the view of "holding the balance of parties;" and when their influence is reduced by corruption, or internal divisions, then they will be kicked aside as of no further account. The tares are being sown most industriously, and they have a propensity for growing much faster than wheat. Only the true husband-man can discriminate between the two; if the former are allowed full scope to mature, they will choke the latter, and utterly destroy the crop. The warning is needed before the mischief is done; later, it will be but cruel mockery, adding insult to injury, at the harvesting-time.

The Trade Unions of this country have passed through many trying vicissitudes, have endured much obloquy, have encountered numberless difficulties, have surmounted many obstacles, but they have made enormous progress, notwith-standing all the troubles with which they have had to contend. They are now, at the close of this year of grace 1890, in the plenitude of their power, strong in numbers, wealthy in funds and resources, powerful in the province of party political warfare, commanding in social influence in so far as the masses are concerned, and a dominant force in the industrial world. All this has been accomplished in the teeth of difficulties which at times appeared to be insur-mountable, in spite of opposition the most formidable, and of legislative enactments which were thought to be absolutely crushing by their multiplicity, and their overwhelming compulsion and restraint.   But the Unionist leaders in the past were far-seeing men ; they were plucky withal ; they sought for a freedom which was broadening down from precedent to precedent, taking their stand upon the principles of liberty for which Sidney died on the scaffold, and Hampden bled on the field of battle.   The objects for which the earlier Unions fought were mainly the right to combine, to associate together for the mutual protection and advancement of the interests of their members, and to obtain for them their rightful dues in the competitive industrial struggle which is their lot in life.   That victory they have practically won. Whether or not the Unions will retain the influence they have attained will depend upon the policy which they pursue, and the means they take to carry that policy out. Having triumphed over persecution, will they show the capacity to endure, as a dominant force, and to direct the destinies of labour ?

CHAPTER V.

THE "OLD TRADE UNIONISM."—Part I.

CONSTITUTION AND GOVERNMENT.

The Term a Misnomer—The Modern Union practically Instituted in
1850—Origin of Provident Benefits—Essential Characteristics of
Trade Unions—(I.) Voluntary Associations—Compulsion Incon-
sistent with their Constitution and Aims—(II.) Objects of Trade
Unions : Protection of Trade Privileges—To Secure and Maintain
High Rate of Wages—Shorter Hours of Labour—Abolition or
Restriction of Overtime—Regulation of Piece-work—Sub-contracting
—The Butty System—Apprentices—Refusal to Work with Non-
Union Workmen—Other and varied Objects, Local and General—
Means for their Accomplishment—Their Policy not to be Judged by
isolated acts, but by General Conduct and Results—(III.) Constitu-
tion and Government of Trade Unions—Democratic in Character—
Doctrine of " Restraint of Trade "—Rules and Bye-Laws—Equality
as regards Voting upon all Matters of Policy and Government—
Management, by Popular Representation and by Direct Vote—
Officials and their Salaries — Delegations — Central Executive
Authority—Office Work—Official Reports—Annual Reports and
Balance Sheets—Trade Unions Constitutional Bodies, Representative
in Character and Modes of Government.

THE term, "Old Trade Unionism," is a misnomer. There
is also something akin to impertinence in its use. What is
now called "the Old Trade Unionism" is about forty years
old, the policy which the expression is supposed to describe
having been adopted, as a system, about the middle of the
present century. The elements of that policy are to be

found in some of the Unions of an earlier date, and a few had actually introduced the Provident principle, in a crude kind of form, towards the close of the last century. From 1824 to 1834 the principle was extended, but it was made an integral part of the constitution of only a very few Unions. Among those who had formulated a scheme of friendly or provident benefits, in connection with the purely "trade benefits," may be mentioned the steam-engine makers, the iron founders, and a few others. The records of those attempts survive to this day. But the benefits were very restricted, being confined to one or two objects. Of course the germs of this policy are to be found in the English guild system, dating from the earliest period. The decent burial of deceased members was one of the duties of the guilds, from their first inception, down to their extinction, as corporate industrial bodies; and nearly all the earlier combinations of labour, if at all of a permanent character, continued and maintained the practice. Relief in cases of sickness and distress was also a part of their internal economy, but, as a rule, this was effected by voluntary collections, as occasion required. Assistance in cases of dispute with employers came into existence at a later date, when journeymen handicraftsmen became a distinct class. But even this was, for a long period, merely a temporary expedient, resorted to for the time being during the dispute. The system of regular contributions, for definite purposes, only dates back about one hundred years. During one half of that period the objects were confined to trade purposes only, such as strikes, defence in cases of prosecutions, and to "funeral benefit." Other benefits were added subsequently, as Trade Unionism progressed and developed, and as they recognized the importance of consolidating their power and conserving their energy for the great industrial conflicts which they had to face.

It is probable that several reasons, individual and combined, may have influenced the earlier unions towards adopting a system of friendly benefits, as part of, or in connection with, the organization of the trade society. In the first place friendly societies were legalized and encouraged in the last decade of the last century, thus affording a kind of shelter under which to combine. Secondly, mutual assistance being the essence of a Trade Union, nothing was more natural than that some provision should be made for the common casualities of life among workmen, such as sickness and privation. Thirdly, the earlier Unions found great difficulty in keeping their members together; the bond was weak and insufficient. The members dropped away when the emergency which called the union into existence had passed over. This was the experience of most Unions, is indeed the experience now in many industrial occupations. Fourthly, the funds of the Unions were unprotected, while those of the Friendly Society were protected by law. This last consideration operated strongly fifty or sixty years ago, and thenceforward until the year 1867 and onward to 1870. Other causes and circumstances may have influenced, doubtless did influence, the pioneers in the Trade Union movement in this respect. The original founders of the Amalgamated Society of Engineers, William Newton and William Allan, were capable and far-seeing men. Their vision was not bounded by the narrow horizon of *the present;* they looked into the far future, and they saw that they were creating an institution which would bear the test of time, would flourish and expand when they had passed away; and that it would become the stronghold of industrial freedom, and a citadel of protection to the members, so long as the present industrial system lasts. For forty years this Union has stood the test; its experience and records have stimulated others to emulation; and its constitution and management have helped, in a hundred ways, to dispel prejudice, to disarm opposition, and quell fears, whenever Trade Unionism has been attacked. The country generally, and Trade Unionists particularly, owe a debt of gratitude to the founders of this society, and also to the society itself, for its marvellous work during the last forty years.

In proceeding to describe the essential nature, characteristics, objects, constitution, and work of Trade Unions, that which is ephemeral, accidental, or merely incidental, will be excluded, except in so far as any feature or phase may be necessary for attaining a correct view of their organization and work. Candour and truth will resent any omission which may bear the impress of partiality, or any endeavour to hide disagreeable facts. An institution which cannot face the light of day is unworthy of the pen of an historian, unless it be for the purpose of laying bare its deformities, and its mischievous effects.

I. **Voluntary Associations.**—Trade Unions are, in their very nature, voluntary associations for mutual protection and assistance. Nominally, the old guilds were voluntary, but in each successive development they became more and more restrictive in their actions and arbitrary in their methods. The later guilds were distinguished by their exclusiveness, not by inclusiveness, and their degeneration into mere coteries was the forerunner of their decline and fall. The earlier Trade Unions were compelled to be voluntary, by reason of the stringency of the Combination

Laws. In all the movements, agitations, and demands of the earlier Unionists, the one claim only was advanced, namely, for the right to combine—to freely associate together for mutual protection and support. In the enrolment of members this principle is fully recognized. The candidate for admission, upon being initiated a member, stands before the lodge, or branch; he is then asked sundry questions, the chief being whether he is *willing* to become a member; and then whether he is willing to be bound by the rules of the union—a copy of which is placed in his hands. But, lest there should be any mistake about the matter, certain rules are read to him "in open lodge," and he is asked if he consents to be bound by those rules. This appears to be the universal practice in all Unions, without exception. The Unions could not exist upon any other principle. Compulsion is tyranny, cover it over by any high-sounding phrase you may. This fact is recognized everywhere by men of sense and experience.

All the earlier battles of the "labour party" were directed against compulsion, under the guilds, under statute law, and by employers. The compulsion then exercised was adverse to labour, and destructive of industrial freedom. Workmen fought for the liberty to combine; law forbade combination. Employers, taking advantage of the law, endeavoured to crush every effort at combination. Society generally, or public opinion, as it was then termed, supported the prohibitory laws, and also the action of capitalist classes, manufacturers, merchants, and traders, in the attempts made to put down all associative effort, called into existence in the interests of the workmen. Even since the repeal of the Combination Laws, aye, and down even to the present moment, employers have sought to compel men *not* to belong to a Trade Union. Many of the most costly and stubbornly-fought battles in which labour has been engaged have been waged in support of the right of association. The public, in its corporate capacity, as the State, instituted and maintained compulsion, and enforced it by coercion and punishment. The Trade Unionists, on the other hand, fought for liberty, but not for the liberty to compel. The man, (and the men) who seeks for the power to compel, violates the charter of Trade Unionism. Some people apparently cannot distinguish between right and freedom, compulsion and coercion. The employers who deny the right to combine, and the men who deny the right of not combining, are equally wrong. They seem to desire freedom for themselves, with power to coerce others. The two are inconsistent and incompatible. No such duality can co-exist in a free State. Fortunately, now, the law has pretty evenly settled the question. The right of free association is conceded; while the limits of social pressure are defined. On the whole, the equity of the law is indisputable; in its interpretation and administration there might have been a miscarriage of justice in a few instances, but not of a serious character, during the last ten years. Any such case would soon find a voice in the Commons House of Parliament, and any real grievance would have redress. Workmen and employers would be well advised to carry out the spirit and intention of the law, and not to seek to stretch it on the one hand, or relax it on the other.

II. **Objects of Trade Unions.**—The primary objects undeniably of a trade society are the maintenance and advancement of the industrial interests of its members. Trade Unions were established for those purposes. The exact form in which those advantages are sought to be secured depends entirely upon the nature of the trade in which the members are engaged, and upon the surrounding circumstances and conditions.

(1) All Unions are agreed upon one point, namely, securing and maintaining the highest rate of wages which the industry is supposed to be able to bear. In seeking to obtain that highest rate, it is seldom that the members trouble themselves to inquire into the rates of pay in other trades ; they find differences existing, fanciful and outrageous differences sometimes, but neither they nor their employers are exactly responsible for them. An advance is sought on the basis of pay, whatever that basis might be ; or a reduction is resisted in like manner. Nor is uniformity insisted upon, although there is a tendency to uniformity, in given districts, for the same kind of work, co-equal in quantity and quality. In branches of trade belonging to what might be called the same department of industry, the men in the several branches look for something at least approaching to relative uniformity. For example, in the engineering trade the mechanics of various classes approximate to the same rates, called the minimum rate, but which is virtually the standard rate ; but the rates of wages in different towns vary. London usually stands at the head of the list, for the highest wage ; whilst towns like Liverpool, Manchester, Leeds, and Birmingham may differ from each other in the amount paid to men of equal skill, doing precisely the same kind and quality of work. In the building trades there is an approximation to uniformity, in the wages paid in particular districts ; but it does not follow that masons, bricklayers, carpenters, plasterers, and painters get exactly the same amount per hour, which is now the

usual mode of payment. The Society in each case acts by
and for itself, in the interest of the members. Occasionally
there is co-operation in cognate branches of trade, because
an increase or a reduction would react upon the others.
Almost invariably, however, each Union acts independently
for its own trade and members.

(2) With regard to the hours of labour, there is more
uniformity than in matters of wages. What is termed the
normal working-day almost necessarily becomes the fixed
working-day for all engaged in the particular trade;
although it does not always follow that the hours will be
the same in all places. Still, there is a natural tendency in
that direction. For example, the ten hours' day was once
general in all branches of the building trade; the hours
are now 52½ per week; this also is pretty general. The
labourers work the same hours as the artizans. Where nine
hours are established as a working-day, in any trade, the
tendency is for that system to become general. But here
again a town or a district has its own minimum or maximum.
The hours of labour are not uniform in all places, even in
the best organized trades; but in the engineering trades
54 hours per week is nearly universal, this being regarded
as equivalent to a nine hours' day. Recently a further
reduction of one hour on Saturdays has taken place in the
North. Perhaps the chief reason why a reduction of
working-hours has been more stubbornly resisted by
employers than advances in wages is, because of the
natural tendency to uniformity in the hours of a normal
working-day. Wages may go up; they may subsequently
be pressed down; but a reduction in working-hours is not
so easily upset. The four o'clock on Saturdays, once
conceded, was never seriously tampered with afterwards; the

"Saturday half-holiday," once given, has remained intact.
The "Nine hours" has been attacked, but it has virtually
triumphed. There used to be a kind of fetish faith in a
ten hours' day, as though nature had ordained that all
"wage-earners" must work that length of time. There is
no particular efficacy in ten, nine, or even eight hours. The
requirements of trade, the necessities of the community, the
health and comforts of the workers, the wages of labour,
all these, and other considerations must and will determine
eventually the length of the working-day. Prejudice and
habit help to determine the hours of labour now; and the
Unions seek to enlist public sympathy where they can, and
to educate their own members as they may in favour of
shorter hours. By the efforts of the Unions from eight to
ten hours per week have been taken off, in most of the
skilled trades, within the last forty years. The yearning for
a further reduction of hours is unmistakable, and is
commendable.

(3) The question of overtime does not appear to be
quite so ripe for solution. In most cases the officers and
the leaders of thought in the Unions are in advance of the
desires of the members. There has long existed a kind of
undefined sentiment in favour of the abolition of overtime;
and it was thought that the demand for extra pay for all
time worked beyond the nominal day would in time put a
stop to it. Instead of which it has, in numerous instances,
rather stimulated the men engaged in various trades to
desire it. It is perfectly certain that the Unions have not
been able to put the practice down, although in the Boiler-
Makers and Iron-Shipbuilders' Society, steps in that direction
were recently taken with some effect. The Unions wisely
restrict their action to what is known as "systematic over-

time," as contradistinguished from occasional overtime in cases of emergency. The blame for the continuance of overtime must be borne pretty equally by employers and employed. If it be not a curse to both, it is certainly very little to their advantage. All labour done after the usual working hours is costly, above and beyond the extra pay. It is natural that it should be so; without charging the workers with any intentional loitering over their work, the quantity and quality will not, as a rule, bear comparison with that done in the usual hours of the working-day. And the workers are not materially benefited in the long run by the extra pay. Of course there are exceptions, but most workmen agree that workers of overtime, systematically pursued, reap no permanent advantage therefrom. It might not be possible to abolish the system altogether, at once and for ever, but its curtailment, within the narrowest limits, would be of advantage all round. Every nine or ten men, who work only one extra hour per day, keep one other man idle. By mutual restraint and mutual action, in concert with employers, the change might easily be affected, with injury to none, with benefit to all, as one not unimportant contribution to the solution of the great labour problem.

(4) Piece-work has long been a subject of warm debate both inside and outside the Unions. There is a kind of popular delusion current with respect to this question. It is thought, or at least the impression seems to be abroad, that Trade Unions are absolutely opposed to the piece-work system. Such is not the fact. In many trades day-work is practically unknown, the entire manufacture being carried on by piece-work. In other trades day-work is the rule, piece-work being almost unknown. The relative number

of those working on the two systems respectively is not
accurately known, but it is estimated that a majority of
those in Union work on the piece principle in some form.
Speaking generally, the piece-workers would resent any interference with their mode of working, while the day-workers
deprecate the introduction of piece-work into their trades.
Both systems have their own peculiar advantages. Each
industry must decide for itself as to which is most suitable
and most advantageous. There ought to be some kind of
mutual arrangement as to modes of working, so as to avoid
unnecessary friction. In the case of day-workers, the wages
are fixed at so much per hour, or so much per week, usually
consisting of a definite number of hours. The regulation
of wages in those trades is comparatively an easy matter.
But in the case of piece-work there are many difficulties in
some trades, in consequence of the great variations in style,
quality, and the nature of the materials. In some trades
there are very elaborate "statement lists," of a highly
technical character, for the regulation of prices. These are
often open to dispute. A slight change in fashion, in the
use of materials, or in methods of work, may make a considerable difference in the labour to be performed by the
worker—more being required in some cases, involving a
claim for an advance in the price; less in others, involving
the question of a reduction in the price. Every trade working under this system ought to have a Board of Conciliation,
to which could be referred the numberless small disputes
that constantly arise. Happily this is the case in many
industries; in others they are either being formed, or initial
measures are being taken to establish them.

(5) The gang, or butty system, is of a different character.
Trade Unions, as a rule, are strongly opposed to such a

method of working. In some few cases work has, it seems, to be performed on this system, but it is not so general as it was formerly. It is indeed open to question whether the system can be worked, to any large extent, without positive injustice. If one man in a gang from any cause absents himself from work, the others perforce suffer. There may be cases, and it appears that there are cases, in which some such system works better than any other. But the evils attendant on the practice have greatly restricted the field of its operations in recent years. Besides its natural disadvantages as a mode of working, the individual men in the gang are, in cases of dispute, denied the easy remedy at law given to day-workers for the recovery of wages. In the latter case the nearest magistrate can decide the question at once, and order payment; in the former case, the man has his remedy only in the County Court, or by other civil process. Indeed, this applies also to piece-work. The workman in the workshop, under the piece-work system, is raised to the dignified position of a contractor. If a dispute takes place over twopence or threepence, he has his remedy " at law ; " while his more fortunate fellow-workman, perhaps in the same shop, can go to the nearest magistrate to enforce payment for as many shillings or pounds.

(6) The task system is greatly modified now compared with what it was twenty-five or thirty years ago, chiefly owing to the action of Trade Unions. Formerly it was the common practice to give one or two " leading hands " sixpence or more per day extra, to "run" the other workmen engaged in the same kind of work. Of course, the strongest and quickest were selected for that purpose. The others, without the additional pay, had to "keep up," or their

G

places were speedily filled by other men. The "task," or "stint," as it is sometimes called, is still the practice in some shops. The mere fact of its existence in any shape shows that there is something wrong in the industrial system. It indicates either too much greed on the part of the employer, or moral laxity on the part of the employed, or that both have sunk to the low level of seeking a mean advantage over the other.

(7) The apprenticeship system used to be a constant bone of contention in many trades. At present the disputes are not numerous, but they occur sometimes. This was a legacy bequeathed to the Trade Unions by law and custom. Originated by the earlier guilds, it ran through the whole system, and survives in a few corporate towns to this day. The custom was early embodied in law; it formed one of the chief provisions in the Statute of Elizabeth, and centuries elapsed ere the stringency of the law was relaxed, and many more years before its provisions were wholly repealed. The Unions generally sought to perpetuate the law and custom of apprenticeships, believing, firstly, that the system ensured capable craftsmen; and, secondly, that this system regulated the supply of labour into trades. The first object was, and is, good. Everybody will admit the value of any provision or regulation which will help to secure competent workmen and good workmanship. Upon the second there is great diversity of opinion, the tendency being, in all branches of industry, to extend freedom, not to limit it. The Unions can, however, plead both custom and law in their favour; the severe strictures passed upon them are not therefore altogether just, even as regards the purely restrictive policy pursued. One great aim of the Unions is to keep up a standard of efficiency. The candidate for admission must

be able to earn the current wages of the district, or the prices ruling in the trade. Wages have a constant tendency towards a lower level. That tendency is always accelerated by a large influx of less skilled labour into any branch of trade; it is also accelerated by further minute sub-divisions of labour, requiring either only partial skill, or such skill as can be acquired in a short time. It is natural, therefore, that Trade Unions, representing the highest skill in their respective branches of industry, should seek to enforce apprenticeships with the view of keeping up the standard of workmanship, and with it the standard rate of wages. Excellence in work will rule the world; slop-work and scamping will ruin any industry. The nation that can and does produce the best goods will prosper; those who manufacture inferior goods will decay. Shoddy can only flourish for a season, like a green bay-tree.

(8) The practice of refusing to work with non-Union workmen is also a remnant of the olden times—it was guild law, and as such it survived as a custom after the guild system had ceased to exist, as a controlling force in industrial matters. The law gave no express sanction to this custom, and indeed all the Combination Laws were, by their very nature, prohibitive of any such practice. The legal aspect of this question has been touched upon in an earlier part of this chapter; it will be reverted to in a subsequent chapter later on. Looked at from its purely social aspects, much can be urged in favour of the utmost pressure being applied to induce workmen to belong to the Union. Those who persistently remain outside, neglect an obvious duty—the duty of manfully doing their part to keep up the current rates of wages, and maintain a maximum working-day. Non-Unionists are always ready to take

advantage of the fruits of others' labours ; they ought to partake of some share in sowing the seed, tilling the ground, and promoting the growth and maturity of the harvest, as well as reaping it and gathering it in. But this is not all that can be laid to their charge ; they hang on the outskirts of the Union as a drag, and, in times of dispute, they go in to take the places of men who are fighting, not for themselves only, but for the whole trade. Under military law a deserter is severely punished ; the man who fled into the enemy's camp to fight against his own comrades would be shot without mercy. This, and much more, can be urged in palliation of the bitterness displayed by Unionists against those whom they term "blacklegs." Nevertheless, apart from the legal side of the question, the policy of " retributive justice " is a doubtful one, to say the least. Efficient organization is the proper cure. If Union men so comport themselves that employers will seek them in preference to other workmen, the question will be solved. Besides which the Union should be made so attractive, by reason of its benefits and advantages, that even the men who habitually shirk duty and responsibility will seek its protection and obey its mandates, from necessity, if not from choice.

The foregoing comprise the chief objects of the Unions, in so far as their industrial purposes are concerned. Of course many and varied matters crop up from time to time, relating to modes of hiring and discharge, methods of payment, conditions of employment, local trade customs, and other things incidental to our vast and ever-varying industries, which the Unions take cognizance of, and deal with, as they arise. Their action must be judged, not by isolated acts, or strikes, but as a whole, just as we are in the habit of judging all other institutions. Perhaps the Church, as an institution, has been more severe in its attitude towards Trade Unions than any other—except the State itself.   But if the Church were judged by the same standard it would fare badly—and would not come out of the ordeal unscathed.   Imperfection is the lot of humanity, in the individual, and in the concrete ; it would have been marvellous indeed if Trade Unions had risen to a higher ideal than other institutions.   Even the State, the perfection of human wisdom, has not at all times attained and maintained the quality of perfection.   The "Anarchists" have tried it in the balances, and they declare that they have found it wanting.   They cry "Away with it ! Away with it !" "Cut it down, why cumbereth it the ground?"   Some who incline to view favourably the main objects of Trade Unions object to the means which they use to attain the objects. Here again something can be urged in their favour.   The means were improvised as circumstances arose.   They could not always choose the best means.   Every obstacle was thrown in their way.   But as the years have rolled on, and as legal and other obstacles have been removed, the Unions have improved their methods, are still improving them in many instances.   It is a case of evolution from the lower to the higher forms of concrete life.   As they grow in intelligence, and expand under the influences of freedom and legal recognition, they will divest themselves of the appendages which hampered their progress and retarded their earlier growth.   They have emerged from barbarism—retrogression on a large scale is not possible.

III. **Constitution and Government of Trade Unions.**—In their constitution and form of government, Trade Unions are essentially democratic. When "initiated" into the society, the members are supplied with a copy of the rules by which they are bound. After that, they are placed on a footing of equality with other members in all matters of government, revision of rules, voting upon all questions, and deciding upon all issues submitted to the body in its corporate capacity. (1) Formerly it was a prevalent notion that the published rules of a Trade Union were intended as a cloak to cover the real designs and objects of the society. It was thought, and generally alleged, that the real government of the Union was centred in a committee, partaking more or less of the nature of a secret conclave, and that the members were under a system of bye-laws of such a character that the Union dared not make them public. There was never any foundation for the statement so persistently made and reiterated. The only possible colouring for the allegation is to be found in the fact that the engineers so framed their rules that no expression in them directly implied that they were "in restraint of trade." This was done in order to obtain protection for their funds, by depositing the rules with the Registrar of Friendly Societies. The draft-rules for this purpose were submitted to Mr. Cockburn, afterwards Lord Chief Justice Cockburn, as counsel, to advise. But the real object of the Union was everywhere publicly known. If the word "strike," or the term "dispute" was not expressed in the rules, the payment was simply made under another name—well-known to the Registrar, to the Justices of the Peace, to the Government, by whom the permit of depositing the rules was allowed, and by the general public. There was no secrecy about the matter. The device was resorted to by reason of the unwise, foolish, most unjust laws which denied to such societies that legal protection to property which was accorded to all other corporate bodies and associations.

(2) Bye-laws were found to be necessary as soon as the Union expanded beyond a mere local society.   Just as we see in the United States, with its Federal Constitution and Laws, and the Constitution and Laws for the government of the several States, composing the Union.   But the bye-laws were in no case inconsistent with the rules any more than the Constitution for Massachusetts is at variance with the Federal Constitution.   In the earlier stages of federation, if the term can be so implied in this connection, the local Unions had more individual freedom than they now have under amalgamation.   But in every case the local members had an equal voice and vote.   Usually the bye-laws were simply lodge regulations, for the proper conduct of business —nothing less, nothing more.   In a few instances the local branches, or lodges, maintained what was termed a "schedule" of local customs relating to wages, hours of labour, walking-time, and in one or two cases what was called "watering-time," that is, a brief respite for tea in the afternoon, or some other kind of refreshment.   Bye-laws still exist in most of the Unions (for example, every compositors' "chapel" has its own rules, even in cases where non-Unionists are employed).   But it would be difficult for any man, however antagonistic to Trade Unionism, to find one which would or could justify the calumnies which were hurled against the Union up to the date of the publication of *The Conflicts of Capital and Labour*, in which work most of these allegations were refuted.   A very large number of the Unions are now registered under the Trade Union Acts 1871 and 1876, so that the rules have to be carefully revised in order that none of them shall be contrary to public law. But lest it might be thought that all the objectionable features have not been removed or modified during the last

five and twenty years, it might be pointed out that the search-
ing inquiry into the organization and rules of Trade Unions,
by the Royal Commission in 1867, found nothing in them
of a compromising character contrary to public policy, except
in so far as they were alleged to be in violation of an economic
theory, that is, " being in restraint of trade."

(3) In the matter of government all questions were
formerly, they are still usually, decided by show of hands
in "open lodge"; all present being free to take part in the
discussion, and eligible to vote. In recent years voting
papers have been frequently used; and for all general
purposes, where a vote of the members is taken throughout
the whole of the branches of a large society, ballot papers
are issued to all members. Even the question of a strike
has now to be submitted to the whole of the members in
most Unions. In certain cases, where the recognized rules
of the society, or the current rate of wages, or the normal
working-day, are interfered with by an employer, or firm,
the branch has the right to resist; but even this action is
subject to the approval of the Executive, or Council. In all
well-regulated Unions the power and authority are vested in
the members ; the governing body cannot act without their
sanction, either as expressed in the certified rules, or as
determined by a specific vote. In a properly constituted
Trade Union there is no such thing as anarchy. It is
doubtful whether the Benchers of Lincoln's Inn, or the
governing body of the "Temple," the successors of the
"Knights Templars" of old, conduct their business with
more regard to constitutional law, precedent, and accredited
usage than the modern Trade Union, now dubbed the
"Old Trade Unionism." The Unions recognize the fact
that order is the law of progress, and they act upon the

principle with conservative tenacity, in all they do.   The "anarchists," as a few wild dreamers delight in calling themselves, will have to reckon with the labour organizations of Great Britain ere they can do mischief with the British Constitution.   British statesmen, and the nation at large, are beginning to realize the fact that there is an enormous steadying force in the Trade Unions of the country.   If there be any danger at all, the danger is lest they may become too conservative, and thereby land us, politically and industrially, in the quagmire of reaction, by reverting back to dangerous precedents in legislation, fiscal policy, and industrial trammels in matters of trade.

(4) The management of the Unions is vested in officers, and in a governing body, elected by the whole of the members.   It is a representative institution more perfect in its character, and in the operation of its elective principle, than any form of government in the world.   The chief officer, in nearly all cases, is the secretary, sometimes called "general secretary," or "corresponding secretary," in the Amalgamated Unions, or societies composed of branches, or divided into districts.   He is elected annually by the members, by whom also his salary is fixed and voted. Gigantic as some of these Unions are, only in very few instances does the secretary's salary exceed £200 per annum.   Many draw less than that sum ; a few reach £208, one is as high as £250.   Only in two or three instances are there salaried presidents or treasurers.   The Council, or Executive Committee, are similarly elected, their remuneration being fixed by rule, usually at so much per night for each attendance.   It was customary up to within a few years ago to describe the officials and delegates of Trade Unions as "bloated officials," the insinuation being that

they were over-paid, over-fed, and under-worked; but this description was exposed in 1878 as a foul calumny, and has since been generally abandoned. It remained for one of the most prominent and blatant of the leaders of the " New Trade Unionism " to revive the calumny, and to speak of his colleagues, at the recent Trades Union Congress, as aldermanic in appearance, and to sneer at them for wearing " tall hats." Henceforward, presumably, a tall hat will be regarded as inconsistent with Trade Union principles, anti-democratic in politics, and as a badge of shame to the man who dares to appear at a Trades Union Congress, Trades Council, meeting of Unionists, or of politicians in the head-gear now nearly universal in this country. The public and the employers have advanced in this respect. They have abandoned the old vulgar prejudices and calumnies. The officers of Trade Unions are received and treated with the respect due to their representative capacity, and the foundations have been laid for healthier and better conditions between capital on the one hand, and representatives of labour on the other.

(5) The Executive Committee, or Council, of a Trade Union constitute the real governing body. They interpret the rules, " where silent," just as a Court of Law interprets an Act of Parliament. The interpretation is usually open to appeal, either to what is termed a general council, a delegate meeting, or the whole body of the members. They conduct the business, direct the secretary, deal with all matters of finance, and see that the rules are properly carried out. The administrative functions of this body are multifarious, and often very extensive. In Unions like the Amalgamated Engineers, Amalgamated Carpenters and Joiners, and similar bodies, their authority extends not only

over the whole of the United Kingdom, but to the United States, our colonies, and to foreign countries. The work is vast, often complicated, always onerous, generally laborious, but it is done with a regularity, an efficiency, and a promptitude which would astonish the Foreign Office, the Colonial Office, the Local Government Board, or the Board of Trade. It would put to shame the War Office and the Admiralty, with their red-tape and circumlocution. The work is usually performed by working members, in the evening, after their day's work is done.

(6) In addition to the ordinary duties connected with an elaborate system of book-keeping, of a large mass of correspondence, of disputes the most delicate, relating as well to internal affairs as to matters of wages, hours of labour, and other matters with employers, many of the Unions issue monthly reports, some fortnightly returns, which partake of the character of a monthly magazine. In these publications the state of trade is registered, disputes are commented upon, the income and expenditure are presented in abtract form ; anniversary meetings are reported, deaths and admissions are recorded, the voting of the members on specific subjects is tabulated, and the general progress of the society is indicated. Each member, by the payment of a very trifling sum, is entitled to a copy of these reports, in which they can see what is being done, and learn something as to the prospects of the near future.

(7) The annual reports of many of the Unions are perfect marvels in size, in the extent of the information given, in arrangement, and in the fullness of their details. So complete are some of them that any member can almost test the accuracy of the financial statements for himself, without the aid of the auditor. In these annual reports the branch

accounts are given with commendable fullness, as regards details, while the Executive, or Council's accounts are often most minute. The summaries, or tables showing the progress and work of the Unions, either from their establishment, or for a long series of years, are most complete, many of them would do credit even to the Royal Statistical Society. It is to be regretted that all the Unions do not publish an annual report and statement of accounts in the same way as the Engineers, Ironfounders, Carpenters and Joiners, Boiler Makers and Iron Shipbuilders, Steam-Engine Makers, and similar Unions. Some of them think that publicity would be prejudicial; that this is not the case is shown by the progress of those Unions which issue their reports without reserve, and thereby challenge the opinion of the world. It does not, however, follow that balance-sheets, or annual statements, are not issued in all other cases to the members, or at least to the lodges, or by the local Union to the members, if there are no branches. On the contrary, all registered Unions must send in a yearly statement to the Registrar of Friendly Societies; but for the most part the *Annual Reports* of that department of the Government are very meagre, and they are issued so long after date as to become practically useless, except as a mere historical record. The figures given in the next chapter will be found to be in advance of the Registrar's Report in all instances, so laggard and behind-hand is that office in its work. Even the Report of the Labour Correspondent to the Board of Trade for 1889 is not yet issued (January 31st, 1891), although it is usually far in advance of the Reports of the Registrar. A full and complete record of the work of Trade Unions is becoming more and more necessary year by year, and that record should be published at the earliest possible date, even at the cost of some slight addition to the expenses of the departments charged with the compilation of those records.

It will be seen from the foregoing pages that Trade Unions are essentially representative institutions, in their constitution and methods of work; and that the chief of these Unions do not shrink from publicity. If they were not always equally constitutional in their organization and operations, the fault lies at the door of the State, which denied to them a rightful place among the lawful institutions of the land. If men are compelled to do in secret what they ought to have a perfect right to do in the open, it is adding insult to injury to call their societies secret. Yet this was the position of Trade Unions up to and during the first quarter of the present century. For sixty-five years they have had partial freedom; but only since 1875—fifteen short years in British history—have they had that full liberty which they possess and exercise to-day. The period, since their emancipation from the trammels of law, is scarcely sufficient for the mass of British workmen to realize that they are free, that the law is fairly equal between man and man, employer and employed. Their teachers in the press don't know it at all times. For example, there was recently a sensational paragraph in the *Star* newspaper in reference to a case which was tried in the Law Courts, the Amalgamated Society of Carpenters and Joiners pleading that the law had no jurisdiction in that particular case.[1] The writer jumped to the conclusion that justice was denied, and that the Unions were under legal disability; whereas

[1] High Court of Justice, Queen's Bench Division, case of Old *v.* Robson, tried before Mr. Baron Pollock and Mr. Justice Wills, January 18th, 1890.

the point of law involved was really in the nature of a concession to the Unions, when the statute was framed, in order to protect them from expensive litigation in Courts of Law. Similar examples could be cited of an apparent inability to comprehend either the exact legal status of the Unions, or the changes effected in the provisions of the laws relating to labour of late years. It is not to be wondered at, therefore, that the workpeople themselves do not fully realize the altered circumstances of the times—legal, political, social, and industrial. But the changes are obvious; they are seen in the more and more perfect organization of labour, and also in the improved condition of the workers. They are even more conspicuous in the character and constitution of the Unions, representing the skilled industries of Great Britain, which have borne the test of time, and have won for their members advantages scarcely dreamed of a half-century ago.

CHAPTER VI.

THE "OLD TRADE UNIONISM."—Part II.

PROVIDENT BENEFITS AND STRIKE PAY.

Provident Benefits formerly commended—Now Attacked by New Trade Unionists—Narrow View of the Objects and Value of Provident Benefits. (I.) Funeral Allowance—Amounts payable at Death of Member, or Wife—Total Amounts in 1869, 1879, and 1889 compared—Aggregate Amounts over Series of Years, Value of Benefit, how appreciated. (II.) Sick Benefit—When introduced—Progress of the Idea of making such Provision—Competition with Friendly Societies—Amounts payable Weekly by Trade Unions—Total amounts paid, 1869, 1879, and 1889 compared—Effects and Influence—Total amounts over a Series of Years—Enormous Advantages of Benefit. (III.) Superannuation Allowance—Age at which it commences, and Weekly Sums assured—The Provision attacked by Enemies of the Unions—Now by their professed Friends—The Strain on the Unions—Successful Working—Growth of this Benefit 1869, 1879, and 1889 compared—Aggregate Amounts over a Series of Years—Immense value of this Provision. (IV.) Accident Benefit—Of more recent Growth—Not so general in its Operation—Sums payable—Amounts paid in 1869, 1879, and 1889—Total Amounts over a Series of Years—Employers' Liability Act, and its Results. (V.) Out of Work Allowance—A unique Provision—Home Donation Travelling Relief—Amounts paid to Members "on Tramp"—Weekly Allowance to Members out of Work—Amounts paid in 1869, 1879, and 1889 compared—Large Totals in one Year, 1879—Aggregate Totals over Series of Years—Value of the Provision—Public Advantages as well as Individual Benefits. (VI.) Other Benevolent Objects—Grants to Members in Distress—Loss of Tools -by Fire—Emigration—Grants to other Trades—The Benefits enumerated are the glory of the Old Trade Unionism. (VII.) Trade Privileges—The Oldest and the Primary Object of all Trade Unions —Its Insufficiency as a Staying Power—Lack of Stability in the older Unions—Strike purposes only in a Union mark an Early Stage of Development—The Addition of Provident Benefits, a Result of Progress and Experience—Fighting Machines, inadequate for present Industrial Warfare—Difference in respect of Weapons not Methods—The New Policy more humane, more enlightened, and more effectual—Unions have never foundered, from overweight; many have been wrecked for want of Ballast—Amounts payable Weekly by Trade Unions—Some additional help from Levies and Grants —Payments made in 1869, 1879, and 1889 compared—Figures incomplete, for reasons given—Total amounts paid over a Series of Years—Timidity in making Full Returns—Why not made. (VIII.) Assistance to other Trades—The Old Trade Unions have given with a Free Hand—Conditionally upon those needing it, asking for it, and helping themselves—Examples of Liberality—Engineers, Ironfounders, &c.—Labourers assisted without Niggardliness— Grants made with open hand and heart in cases of emergency. (IX.) Summaries of Expenditure for Provident Benefits during the last Forty Years—Railway Servants.

SINGULARLY enough, the Provident side of Trade Unions is the one mainly attacked by the apostles of the so-called New Trade Unionism. Yet it was this aspect of Trade Unionism which most helped, in years gone by, to reconcile the public, and English statesmen, to proposals to free Trade Unions from legal restraint, to remove the legal disabilities which continuously hampered them, and to accord to them a rightful place among the recognized lawful institutions of the country. Some of the new leaders seem to be labouring under the hallucination that all was darkness upon the face of the waters in the realm of labour, prior to 14th day of August, 1889. "There's a midnight blackness changing into gray," said one of the dockers' leaders, some two years since. They would have us believe that the " Bird o' Freedom," if not actually hatched at that period, then for the first time fluttered its wings over the dreary waste of labour's chaos.   Probably Mahomet thought that there was no light in Asia before his advent, and that he alone brought light to the Arabs of the desert.   Possibly, also, Joe Smith thought that no real civilization existed in the United States of America before he hoisted the Mormon flag at Utah.   Similarly, in this country, some would have us believe that Industrial England was benighted up to a couple of years ago.   These delusions, like all other delusions, are fading away.   The wonder is that they manage to get a foothold, even for a night and a day.   The organization and management of the Old Trade Unions have been dealt 'with in the previous chapter; in this will be set forth, briefly and succinctly, their provident aspects. Space forbids any elaborate details, and consequently only a few of the larger and better organized Unions will be selected, as types of the rest.   The examples given will be those which most   nearly approximate to the great prototype of what is termed the Old Trade Unionism, namely, the Engineers, in contributions and benefits, and in government.

I. **Funeral Allowance.**—This benefit is one of the oldest in connection with Trade Unions; it is coeval with the establishment of the earliest form of labour combinations. It existed in the earlier guilds, and it ran through the whole system in all its changes.   In Catholic times, masses for the repose of the soul of the departed member were said or paid for, by the guild brethren, the Roman candle being part of the ceremony provided by the guild.   In combinations, where protection of trade privileges constituted their chief object, funeral benefit was included.   It would be difficult to find any trade society, in early or later times, in which some provision was not made for the "decent

H

Christian burial" of its members. The institution has survived to this day. There was hardly a Union in exist-ence which did not make some provision of the kind until a year or two ago. It was probably this feature, in all the pioneer Unions, which gave rise to the notion that Friendly Society objects constituted the fundamental basis of Trade Unions, and that, in later times, they were perverted or diverted from their original purposes by tacking on the pro-tection of trade privileges, as an integral part of their functions. That fallacy has been exposed over and over again, and is now seldom repeated; but judging by the flippant articles and speeches of even a quarter of a century ago, it was commonly accepted. Men unacquainted with industrial history now go to the other extreme, and allege that the Unions have been perverted from their original purpose, and have become "mere benefit clubs." There is about as much truth in the latter as in the former contention—neither of which was or is true. The term " Friendly Society " is used as part of the title of some of the Unions dating back to the beginning of the present century—as, for example, the Friendly Society of Stone-masons, the Friendly Society of Ironfounders, and some others. But the term " Friendly" had often attached to it the meaning of " mutual," in the sense of mutual protection and mutual aid, in whatever form either the one or the other was afforded. Possibly the protection afforded by the first Friendly Society Acts might have induced the workmen in some trades to use the title as a cover to com-bination for trade purposes; but provident objects in some form always formed an ingredient in societies actually es-tablished in connection with labour, except possibly a mere provisional combination for a temporary object.

The amounts payable at death differ according to the

Society. Nearly all Societies provide for the funeral of the member's wife, as well as for that of the member. The highest amount paid on the death of a member appears to be by the London Society of Compositors, which pays £15 at death of a member, and £5 at death of a member's wife. The following are the respective amounts paid by the several societies named :—Engineers, member £12, wife £5 ; Steam-Engine Makers, member £12, wife £6 ; Boiler Makers and Iron Shipbuilders, member £12, wife £6 ; Ironfounders, member £10, wife £5 ; Carpenters and Joiners, member £12, wife £5 ; Stonemasons, member £10, wife £6 ; if the member is killed accidentally while at his work, the wife is awarded £50. Bricklayers, member £10, wife £5 ; Plasterers, member £10, wife £6 ; Tailors, member £6, wife £4. Typographical Association, member £10, wife *nil*. These sums may be regarded as representing the average amounts paid by most of the Unions in Great Britain in all trades. The following table shows the amounts paid for this benefit, in each of the three years given :—

NAME OF SOCIETY.	1869.	1879.	1889.
	£	£	£
Amalgamated Engineers	5,600	7,387	8,289
Steam-Engine Makers	565	617	1,011
Boiler-makers and Iron Ship-builders	1,138	2,379	3,993
Ironfounders	1,355	2,160	2,117
Ironmoulders—Scotland	1,156	1,750	1,827
Associated Blacksmiths	149	170	198
Amalgamated Carpenters and Joiners	829	2,003	2,901
Operative Stonemasons	3,356	4,976	2,175
,, Bricklayers	297	741	1,003
,, Plasterers	581	512	378
Amalgamated Tailors	261	2,515	2,688
London Society of Compositors ...	383	986	1,374
Typographical Association	No benefit	628	718
U. K. Society of Coachmakers... ...	1,471	1,691	996
Totals—14 Societies ...	17,141	28,515	29,868

The increase in the two last years of course indicates the growth of the Unions; to a very large extent it is a natural increase.

The importance of this provision in the poor man's home, in the hour of deep distress, and often privation, is better shown by the totals paid away during the years that the benefit has been operative, than by quoting figures for any one year. The totals, and the yearly amount per member, as the cost of this provision, are as follows :—

NAME OF SOCIETY.	Numb. of Years.	Total Amount.	Approximate average cost per Member per year.
		£	s. d.
Amalgamated Society of Engineers	39	209,917	3 6
Steam-Engine Makers	36	17,825	2 11½
Boiler-makers and Iron Shipbuilders	23	51,579	2 6
Friendly Society of Ironfounders	58	61,541	3 4
Ironmoulders—Scotland	45	44,228	{ Include accidents. 6 5½
Associated Blacksmiths	32	5,203	2 2
Amalgamated Carpenters and Joiners	30	43,729	2 3½
Friendly Society of Stonemasons	50	92,747	4 4½
Operative Bricklayers' Society ...	20	13,616	3 1½
„ Plasterers' Society ...	28	12,804	4 7½
Amalgamated Society of Tailors ...	22	44,081	3 10
London Society of Compositors ...	22	16,098	3 3½
The Typographical Association ...	17	9,227	1 11½
U. K. Society of Coachmakers ...	22	31,148	4 5
Totals—14 Societies ...	—	653,743	— —

In the industrial life of England there is perhaps no point so tender as the idea of being buried by the parish. A pauper's grave and funeral are more repugnant to the sensibilities of the working-class than any other social degradation. This fact is accentuated by the existence of numerous Burial Clubs and Industrial Insurance Societies, which derive a large income from payments for such

benefits. Some of the Socialists and Fabians are endeavouring to familiarize the minds of the poor with the notion
that burial is a municipal duty, and that any provision for
that sad last ceremony is a privation to the living, which
they ought not to be called upon to make. It will take a
great deal of argument to infuse that doctrine into the
minds of the working-classes, and to eradicate their repugnance to parochial burial.

II. **Sick Benefit.**—This provision was introduced at a
much later date. Irregular assistance was often rendered
by voluntary collections, lotteries, raffles, friendly meetings,
and the like, long years before distinctive provision was
made therefor in the rules of any society; and those forms
of help are still resorted to in some trades in which no
relief is provided by the constitution of the Union. But it
is clear that sick benefit was introduced, in some form, long
before the close of the last century. Early in the present
century the practice extended. The Ironfounders' Society
furnishes a continuous record of this benefit from the year
1830, the amount paid in 1831 being £580 10s. 6d. In
the Steam-Engine Makers' Society the records go back to
a date anterior to the "fifties." But, for all practical
purposes, the institution of sick benefit is of modern date;
it belongs to the period of the newer development of Trade
Unionism, commencing with 1850.

To some extent Trade Unions which make provision for
a weekly allowance in sickness come into competition with
the Friendly Society proper. But no man would go to the
Trade Union for this benefit alone, as greater advantages
are offered by several of the large Affiliated Orders, and by
some societies of later date. The weekly allowance during
sickness differs, but the average payments are about ten
shillings per week. In the Amalgamated Engineers the

weekly amount is 10s., in Steam-Engine Makers 10s., in
the Boiler-makers and Iron Shipbuilders 10s., in the Ironfounders 9s., in the Carpenters 12s., in the Masons 10s.,
in the Bricklayers 15s., in the Tailors 10s. The full allowance lasts from thirteen to twenty-six weeks, after which the
amount is reduced for a further period. Some of the older
and flourishing Unions have not yet adopted the system of
sick allowance, being content with the facilities offered to
members in other kindred societies. There can, however,
be no doubt as to the value of this benefit, for it helps to
bind the members to the Union when possibly other considerations might interpose to diminish the zeal of the
Trade Unionist pure and simple, and lead him to neglect
his payments to the society, and thereby become disqualified
from participating in its benefits.

Taking the same societies, and the same dates for comparison, the following are the amounts paid to sick members,
in each year respectively, for this benefit alone :—

NAME OF SOCIETY.	Total amounts paid in each year.		
	1869.	1879.	1889.
	£	£	£
Amalgamated Engineers	17,777	20,514	30,992
Steam-Engine Makers	1,609	2,295	2,802
Boiler-makers and Iron Shipbuilders	5,164	14,729	19,216
Ironfounders	3,734	6,261	6,441
Iron-moulders—Scotland	No sick benefit in this Union.		
Associated Blacksmiths	661	1,074	1,076
Amalgamated Carpenters and Joiners	5,008	11,008	15,822
Operative Stonemasons	2,891	5,842	2,175
,, Bricklayers	272	2,930	4,591
,, Plasterers	Not instituted.	1,707	800
Amalgamated Tailors	901	7,666	8,864
London Society of Compositors ...	No sick benefit in this Union.		
Typographical Association	No sick benefit in this Union.		
U. K. Society of Coachmakers ..	Nil.	612	371
Totals—11 Societies...	38,017	74,637	93,159

The above record shows the value of Trade Unions from the purely provident point of view, quite apart from any other side. It is a record of suffering alleviated, of privation averted, of independence maintained, and of homes kept together, such as to win approval even from the enemies of such societies. But when professed friends, and even some members of those Unions, denounce this, and other provident provisions in the rules of Trade Societies, one cannot help thinking that there is a moral twist in their mental constitution, an absence of the sense of proportion, of means to an end, or that they have some evil design which they dare not openly propound to their admiring audiences, for fear of utter repudiation. The gospel of discontent might do much to unsettle men's minds, but it will not root out the love of manly independence, secured by thrift.

The total amounts paid by the fourteen societies named, during the period sick benefit has existed, will indicate the enormous value of this provision, as a means of self-help, on the mutual principle, by associative effort. The Table on page 104 will show the extent of that help, though no figures are eloquent enough to tell the whole story.

The undermentioned amounts are stupendous, severally, and in the aggregate, especially when it is remembered that the provision is only one of many in the organization of Trade Unions. The record is one of which to be proud. They need not fear the sneers of social innovators, nor be tempted to blush with shame in comparison with other institutions, however laudable their objects. The sick man on his pillow, and the distressed wife by his bedside, have had reason to bless the day when Trade Unions instituted sick allowance as one of the benefits of their organization. It will survive also, notwithstanding all the assaults upon the provision.

Name of Society.	Years.	Total Amounts.	Approximate average cost per member per year.		
		£	£	s.	d.
Amalgamated Engineers	39	680,314		11	10
Steam-Engine Makers	36	60,592		10	5½
Boiler-makers and Iron Shipbuilders	23	291,278		15	7
Ironfounders	59	208,628		10	6½
Ironmoulders—Scotland	No sick benefit in this Union.				
Associated Blacksmiths	32	26,293		12	2½
Carpenters and Joiners	30	239,665		13	2½
Operative Stonemasons	50	120,484	1	6	7
,, Bricklayers	20	54,474		13	10
,, Plasterers	28	21,792		14	9½
Amalgamated Tailors	22	131,631		13	3½
London Society of Compositors ...	No sick benefit in this Union.				
Typographical Association	No sick benefit in this Union.				
U. K. Society of Coachmakers ...	—	5,360		15	8½
Totals—11 Societies...	—	1,840,511		—	

III. **Superannuation Allowance.**—The age at which this benefit comes into operation differs somewhat in the various societies, and also the amounts payable by them to aged members, after a certain number of years' membership. This benefit is one of the latest which Trade Unions have added to their already long list of liabilities, and responsible duties. It is a branch of mutual industrial business often attacked by men who have made the statistics of mortality a special study, and have constructed elaborate comparative tables of the duration of human life, under varying conditions; and doubtless it is the one benefit in the social economy of the Unions which is the most open to criticism on purely actuarial grounds. At one time the hostile attacks upon this benefit were due, not so much to any desire to see the Unions placed upon a footing of permanent security as regards this provision in their rules, and, as such, made part and parcel of their internal economy, constitution, and administration, as to the feeling of repugnance with which Trade Unions were regarded *per se*, whatever their benefits and useful purposes. That feeling has, to a great extent at least, died out. From twenty to twenty-five years ago the attacks were persistent and constant; but as years have rolled on, and the Unions have met all their engagements, and as the beneficial effects of this and other provisions have become more widely known and appreciated, the criticisms have lost their virulence, while the experience gained in the working of this benefit has not been without effect. That the strain on the societies which provide it is a serious one, none can dispute. The additional and accelerated demands made by this benefit on the funds, grows with fearful and fatal certainty year by year, ending only in the one final payment, funeral allowance, at death. But in no case have the drafts upon this fund been dishonoured, when presented for payment, not even in the direst hour of adversity..

In one or two instances disaster was only averted by the most self-sacrificing efforts on the part of the members; but in these cases the fault did not lie at the door of the Union. One example will suffice. After the fearful financial crisis in 1866, and the crash which followed the suspension of payment by Messrs. Overend and Gurney's Bank, trade was at a low ebb, employment was difficult to obtain, sickness had increased in consequence of scarcity and privation, and the demands upon Trade Union funds, for nearly all purposes, were at the highest tension. The Ironfounders' Society felt the strain acutely, but it bravely nerved itself for the struggle. The funds got so low that it became necessary for a stupendous effort to be made to meet the weekly payments. At this crisis every member who could afford to temporarily forego his due, did so, in order that others more pressed by want should not suffer. The members lent their little store to the Union, with no other security than a note of hand, acknowledging the liability. In this way the Union was saved. Every man was subsequently paid in full, back payments and loans. It often happens that a member of a Union does not claim his superannuation allowance at the date when he is entitled thereto by the rules. He prefers to work at his trade at full wages to being relegated to the superannuated list. The amount payable to superannuated members, as before stated, differs; the following examples will, however, indicate the general average in most of the Unions which provide this benefit. In the Engineers the amounts range from 10s. per week, the lowest to 7s. per week; Steam-Engine Makers, 10s. to 6s.; Bricklayers, 9s. to 5s.; Carpenters and Joiners, 8s. to 7s.; London Society of Compositors, 8s. to 4s.; the Typographical Association, 8s. to 6s.; Iron-founders, 7s. 6d. to 5s.; Boiler Makers and Iron Shipbuilders, 7s. to 4s.; Stonemasons, 5s. to 4s.; Plasterers, 5s.; and the Tailors, 5s. to 2s. 6d. per week, according to the period of membership. It will be seen that the higher amounts will suffice in most cases to keep the wolf from the door, and even in the other cases the allowance will help to prevent privation, especially where some additional assistance is rendered by members of the family, and, if at all able to do any kind of work, by the member himself. The value of the benefit is therefore undeniable.

The growth of this benefit in recent years, as compared

with twenty years ago, will be perceived by the following table, taking the same societies as before enumerated :—

NAME OF SOCIETY.	Total amount paid in each year.		
	1869.	1879.	1889.
	£	£	£
Amalgamated Engineers	8,055	17,730	40,170
Steam-Engine Makers	321	870	1,818
Boiler-makers and Iron Shipbuilders	829	1,580	5,017
Ironfounders	1,797	3,727	7,935
Iron-moulders—Scotland	521	1,493	3,252
Associated Blacksmiths	Began to operate in 1876.	46	223
Amalgamated Carpenters and Joiners	60	445	5,026
Operative Stonemasons	985	6,939	4,404
,, Bricklayers	Began to operate in 1882.		204
,, Plasterers	Not instituted previously to 1880.		285
Amalgamated Tailors	Began to operate in 1881.		1,060
London Society of Compositors ...	Began to operate in 1877.	408	1,177
Typographical Association	Began to operate in 1880.		1,612
U. K. Society of Coachmakers ...	1,196	2,787	3,971
Totals—14 Societies...	13,764	35,617	76,154

The three columns of figures above given, clearly enough indicate the growth of claims under the head of superannuation. For example, in the Engineers the payments have increased by £32,125 yearly in twenty years, while the increase in members has been 27,189. The Ironfounders' payments under the same head have increased by £6,138, while the membership has increased by 4,815. Twenty years ago only a few societies had begun to make payments under this head ; now they are numerous. Some had already made provision for the benefit in their rules, but the commencement of payments was deferred. In the

Tailors' Society the period of deferred payment was twelve years. Other Unions prescribed a longer or a shorter period, according to the contributions of the members. The extension of the provision is encouraging, as showing the increased desire to provide for old age, on the mutual principle of thrift, of self-help by associative effort.

The extent of its operation, and the beneficial effects of the provision, will be better understood by the following table, giving the total amounts disbursed under this head, during the time that the members of the several Unions respectively have become entitled to superannuation benefit:—

NAME OF SOCIETY.	Number of Years.	Total Amount.	Approximate average cost per member per year.	
		£	s.	d.
Amalgamated Engineers	39	482,270	13	2½
Steam-Engine Makers	38	22,990	6	2
Boiler-makers and Iron Shipbuilders	23	49,257	3	1
Ironfounders	54	111,268	11	6
Ironmoulders—Scotland	45	38,597	9	6½
Associated Blacksmiths	14	1,989	2	0½
Amalgamated Carpenters and Joiners	30	27,029	2	6½
Operative Stonemasons	5?	84,313	7	6½
,, Bricklayers	8	921	1	6
,, Plasterers	10	3,745	4	3½
Amalgamated Tailors	9	1,744		6
London Society of Compositors ...	13	100,246	3	2½
Typographical Association	10	0,886	3	4
U. K. Society of Coachmakers ...	22	50,821	14	3
Totals—14 Societies ...	—	895,076	—	—

The foregoing totals speak for themselves. They speak eloquently. They indicate succour and sustenance in old age, as the reward of forethought, of thrift, of mutual help, and of consistent conduct. The men who become entitled to this benefit are the flower of the trade to which they belong. Through evil and good report they have stood by the Union; and when the finger of time has written decay upon their foreheads, in so far as physical energy is concerned, they can enjoy, not only without remorse, but with a feeling of pride the provision which the Society has made to smooth the path of the feeble in their onward journey to the greensward of the tomb, where for ever they rest from their labours. To such might be said: Well done, thou faithful servant.

IV. **Accident Benefit.**—This provision is of more recent growth than most of the preceding, though the Amalgamated Society of Engineers made provision for it in their rules, when the reorganization took place, in 1851. This benefit is confined to the more hazardous trades, and therefore some of the societies previously enumerated do not include it in their rules. The amounts payable in the event of injury by accident are usually divided in two classes, the highest being awarded in cases of total disablement from following his occupation in consequence of the injury; the other in cases of partial disablement, when the member is no longer able to take his vacant place at the trade, but is able to follow some lighter occupation. The Engineers, Steam-Engine Makers, Ironfounders, Boiler Makers and Iron Shipbuilders, Carpenters and Joiners, and Masons, give £100 in case of total disablement, and £50 in cases of partial disablement. The Bricklayers and the Plasterers give £50. The Iron Moulders of Scotland only provide for accident in the funeral allowance; while the Associated Blacksmiths give a less amount than the foregoing societies. The Table on next page shows the disbursements under this head at the same dates :—

NAME OF SOCIETY.	Total amounts in each year.		
	1869.	1879.	1889.
	£	£	£
Amalgamated Engineers	1,600	1,800	2,177
Steam-Engine Makers	500	120	200
Boiler-makers and Iron Shipbuilders	240	201	3,155
Ironfounders	32	944	771
Amalgamated Carpenters and Joiners	500	1,500	1,320
Operative Stonemasons	2,787	872	200
,, Bricklayers	Nil.	50	166
,, Plasterers	494	509	195
Associated Blacksmiths	193	Nil.	Nil.
Totals—9 Societies ...	6,346	5,996	8,184

The amounts thus paid have often proved to be sufficient to enable a member to embark in a small business, and thus earn a livelihood, when otherwise he might have been driven to the workhouse.

Although the total amounts paid in any one year may not have been considerable, in comparison with other benefits, yet in the aggregate covering a long period, the amounts reach a large sum, as the following summary will show :—

NAME OF SOCIETY.	Numb. of Years.	Total Amount.	Approximate average cost per member per year.	
		£	s.	d.
Amalgamated Engineers	39	52,630		9½
Steam-Engine Makers	38	8,116		7½
Boiler-makers and Iron Shipbuilders	23	26,660	1	11½
Ironfounders	45	32,830		7½
Amalgamated Carpenters and Joiners	30	25,040	1	2½
Operative Stonemasons	50	31,679		5
,, Bricklayers	20	971		7½
,, Plasterers	28	10,340	2	11
Associated Blacksmiths	32	2,346		5½
U. K. Society of Coachmakers ...	22	4,822		5½
Totals—10 Societies...	—	195,434	—	—

The preceding amounts show that there was some real necessity for the Employers' Liability Act, 1880. Its value is proven by the fact that the amounts have diminished largely since the Act has been in operation. During the last two years there has been an increase, but this has been mainly due to the high pressure speed of production, in which periods neither employers nor employed exercise the same care as they do at other times. Of course many of the claims of members under this head would not in any case be met by the Employers' Liability Act, as the injury might have been caused by pure accident which human foresight could scarcely provide against and prevent. However caused, the recipient of this benefit has reason to be thankful that there is a fund upon which he has claim, without lessening his self-respect, or losing his independence. The presentation of those sums is frequently made the occasion for calling attention to the society and its work; and often some well-known public man in the locality will take the chair and commend the institution. As it is not a commercial speculation, desiring free advertisement, these public occasions do credit to all concerned, besides gladdening the heart of the poor man thus honoured.

V. **Out of Work Allowance.**—This is the one benefit which distinguishes the Trade Union from all other Provident Societies, and renders it unique among the institutions of the land. Donation Benefit, as this provision is usually named, is of comparatively modern date, although the Ironfounders have a record of its existence continuously since the year 1830, in which year a sum of nearly £366 was paid to members out of work. Some years ago, when the Unions were fighting their way to freedom, and to obtain legal recognition, and protection to their funds, no doubt strike pay was given under the more euphonious name of Donation Benefit, the difference being in the amount so paid, which is usually higher in the case of a dispute, than for loss of employment by slackness of trade. The form in which such relief to members out of work was first given, was "travelling relief," vulgarly called "tramp benefit." In those days it was usual for a member to "draw his card," and seek work wherever he heard of a possible chance of employment. This system fell into disrepute, and not without reason. The society man, travelling with his card, was relieved at each lodge-house, or "station." Usually he had bed and breakfast, with perhaps a shilling or eighteenpence to help him on his way. In some societies the relief was paid by mileage. Not unfrequently the travelling member used his privilege by soliciting assistance from those in employment in all the towns he passed through. In later years the system has been abandoned in many of the Unions, in others it is restricted within very narrow limits. Some of the old trampers had a fairly good time of it; they found sustenance and shelter, and often a jolly set to mingle with at the club-house ; but the wife and children at home fared not so well. These were often compelled to seek other relief, not at all creditable to the bread-winner. The system was abused, but, in its early days, it had its uses, and probably it paved the way for a better and a healthier form of relief in connection with Trade Unions.

Travelling relief is still the only form in which many Unions contribute to the support of members out of work. Of those selected as examples of societies paying provident benefits, four still adhere to the old system—namely, the Stonemasons, the Bricklayers, the Plasterers, and the Tailors. One, the Typographical Association, affords relief by mileage to travelling members, and by home donation. The Boiler-makers and Iron Shipbuilders virtually abolished travelling relief in 1880, though it lingered on until its final extinction in 1883. The extent of that relief in this society is seen by the amounts paid in the six preceding years, thus :—1875, £11,043 ; 1876, £13,039 ; 1877, £12,446 , 1878, £19,528 ; 1879, £21,242 ; 1880, £11,078 ; in 1881 it fell to £441. In the six years prior to 1880 the total thus expended in the one society was £88,376, or nearly £14,813 per annum. The practice is falling into disuse year by year, and also into disrepute. The "tramp" is rather avoided than welcomed, even in trades where the system of travelling relief is still in vogue. Several Unions adopt a much better method, namely, of paying the fares of members to situations at a distance, when opportunity offers of work for those signing the "vacant book." Other societies lend the amount, to be repaid by instalments when the member gets his wages at the new place. The Boiler-makers and Iron Shipbuilders have paid no less a sum than £3,307 as "fares to jobs," in twenty-three years. The tendency in this and other changes in the internal economy and management of the Unions is to promote self-respect and independence. The amounts paid to members out of work, or on "donation benefit," varies with the Union. The highest is by the London Society of Compositors, who pay 12s. per week ; the next highest the Boiler-makers and Iron Shipbuilders, who pay 11s. per week ; the Engineers, Steam-Engine Makers, and Carpenters and Joiners, pay 10s. per week ; the Ironfounders, 9s. per week ; the Stone-masons, Bricklayers and Plasterers, 9s. in the shape of travelling relief; and the Tailors 9s. 4d. per week ; while the Typographical Association allow 8s. per week. The

I

higher amounts are paid from twelve to fourteen weeks, after which, for a further period of generally twenty-six weeks, the amount is less by 3s. to 4s. per week, when the amount is further reduced. But, whatever the amount, the allowance helps to keep the family from parochial relief.

The operation and beneficent aspects of "donation benefit," or out-of-work allowance, can scarcely be indicated, certainly cannot be measured by the selection of any one year, though it so happens that one of the years given, that of 1879, shows us distinctly as any one year can, the extent of relief thus given by Trade Unions. It is only, however, by an examination and comparison of a series of years that its full advantages can be estimated and appreciated. The following amounts were paid by the societies enumerated in the three years given for comparison, as in the case of the other benefits :—

NAME OF SOCIETY.	Total amounts paid in each year.		
	1869.	1879.	1889.
	£	£	£
Amalgamated Engineers	59,980	149,931	29,733
Steam-Engine Makers	3,363	8,402	1,300
Boiler-makers and Iron Shipbuilders	1,795	32,027	3,938
Ironfounders	24,887	57,511	5,311
Ironmoulders—Scotland	2,319	15,589	2,141
Associated Blacksmiths	280	3,525	548
Amalgamated Carpenters and Joiners	8,904	27,902	18,805
Operative Stonemasons	4,110	7,213	1,932
„ Bricklayers	34	166	178
„ Plasterers	22	541	60
Amalgamated Tailors	202	1,891	810
London Society of Compositors ...	2,773	5,382	5,275
Typographical Association	1,030	3,934	2,601
U. K. Society of Coachmakers ...	5,288	15,790	3,050
Totals— 14 Societies...	114,987	329,804	75,682

The preceding totals show that even in 1869 the aggregate sum spent by fourteen societies in relieving those out of work was large, but in 1879 it had increased nearly three-fold. In 1889 the amount fell very considerably below the general average of the years immediately preceding, in consequence of the prosperous condition of trade, in most industries. Probably 1890 will show a further decline, as a result of the state of trade. In any case the enormous value of this benefit cannot be exaggerated, whether looked at from an economical, industrial, or national point of view.

The full significance of this provident provision, by Unions which have adopted the system, in whatever form, will be better seen by the aggregate totals of the several amounts so spent over the series of years during which it has been in operation. The following Table exhibits that expenditure, in so far as it can be given, for the whole of the societies named therein :—

NAME OF SOCIETY.	Numb. of Years.	Total Amount.	Cost per member.		
		£	£	s.	d.
Amalgamated Engineers	39	1,492,264	1	8	0
Steam-Engine Makers	38	86,331		18	2
Boiler-makers and Iron Shipbuilders	23	311,814	1	4	4½
Ironfounders	59	709,561	1	17	3½
Ironmoulders—Scotland	48	240,035	2	2	8½
Associated Blacksmiths	32	32,918	1	4	11½
Amalgamated Carpenters and Joiners	30	349,495	1	5	7½
Operative Stonemasons	50	94,763	2		8½
,, Bricklayers	20	3,500	Estimated amt.		
,, Plasterers	28	2,722	Estimated amt.		
Amalgamated Tailors	22	25,166	1	11½	
London Society of Compositors ...	42	92,958		15	0
Typographical Association	27	49,237		7	0½
U. K. Society of Coachmakers ...	23	113,577		18	2
Totals—14 Societies ...	—	3,604,341	—	—	—

In the foregoing amounts are included all payments under the three heads before enumerated, namely, Home Donation, Travelling Relief, and Fares to Situations, except where the latter are in the form of a loan, subsequently repaid. The grand total represents a stupendous sum expended in one benefit alone, out of the seven or eight, provided in several of the societies named. The mere fact that it has stood the test of time, during from twenty-five to nearly sixty years, shows that the provision is workable, at least in several very important industries of the kingdom. Whether it can be made so in all, is a problem which must be left to the future. The experiment has been tried; it has succeeded; it deserves to be extended, wherever possible.

Donation benefit, in connection with Trade Unions, commends itself under three aspects : (1) As it affects the recipients; (2) in its economical aspects; and (3) as it affects the community. In the first place, no one can for a moment doubt its enormous value to workmen engaged in occupations where employment is liable to fluctuations. In most cases, when work ceases, privation begins. The margin left after the expenses of the home are met, is not great at the best, even in the better paid trades. And where employment is not constant all the year through, the struggle to make both ends meet is continuous. The Out-of-Work provision is a great help where thrift and temperance are characteristic qualities of the bread-winner; and where these do not exist, the amounts paid by the Union week by week at least keep the wolf from the door. The weekly allowance saves the home, and preserves the independence of the workman. He is not humiliated in accepting what he himself has helped to create and accumulate, because it is rightfully his own. Secondly, it is important from an economical point of view. The provision relieves the labour market. The workman is no longer forced to accept any terms offered through the pressure of hunger. He can wait. He has helped to institute a fund for the purpose of enabling him to wait. This fund tends to, and really does, keep up wages. The competition of labour is lessened in proportion to the ability of workmen to refuse to work under the current rates. Strikes become less frequent in such cases, because the employers know that reductions can be, and will be resisted. Thirdly, the community is largely benefited. The members of the Unions providing such relief are kept from the parish. The rates are relieved to that extent. Such men keep their own poor, and contribute towards the relief of the less provident in all trades and occupations. The influence of this provision is wholesome in all respects, not less in its moral than in its material aspects. It deserves commendation and encouragement from all classes, and should command the support of all workmen by reason of its uplifting power, amid the depressing conditions of industrial life, ever tending to intensify the struggle for existence.

VI. **Other Benevolent Purposes.**—The five benefits previously dealt with do not exhaust the list, though they constitute the principal ones in operation. The Unions have others, however, which need not be dwelt upon at length, as they do not require the same detailed explanation and elaboration : (1) Several of the Unions have what is termed a Benevolent Fund, out of which sums are from time to time granted towards the relief of distressed members, in cases of prolonged sickness, out of work through depression in trade, and other causes. These benevolent grants amount to a considerable sum in the course of a year in several societies. In the year 1879 the Engineers disbursed under this head £6378. The amounts usually expended reach from £2000 to over £4000 a year. (2) Loss of tools by fire is also provided for in several Unions. The Carpenters and Joiners have expended over £24,000 in this benefit during its existence. (3) Emigration benefit used to be provided in several cases, but this has been discontinued in many unions of late years, in consequence of the changed conditions, cheapness of transit, and other altered circumstances. (4) Grants to other trades come more properly under the head of strikes, but such assistance is provided, and ought therefore to be noted.

The nine benefits enumerated, leaving out the last one, constitute the chief glory of the Old Trade Unionism. With such a record they may well despise all attacks, from within and without. They can afford to treat even with contempt the sneers of those who call them " mere benefit clubs," for " the relief of the rates." The work done, however imperfectly recorded, tells its own tale ; not adequately perhaps, but sufficiently to indicate its character, scope, and extent. A careful and thoughtful student will also be able, in some degree, to appraise its value, as an element of importance in the organization of labour. At the base of this monument of provident provisions, and on the panels of its pedestal, are written : Self-help, mutual aid, and associative effort. The words are graven in eternal brass, and the structure is of adamant ; neither need fear being defaced by time, or by malice.

VII. **Trade Privileges.**—The maintenance of trade privileges doubtless was, and is, the primary object of every Trade Union. For that purpose they were originally instituted.

This is indeed the essence of the Old Trade Unionism. The earlier Unions were merely fighting machines, and nothing beyond. Some of them made a splash, rose to the surface, and sank to rise no more. It was at best a kind of guerilla warfare, in which an irregular force harassed the enemy, captured an outpost, took a few spoils, and retired. There was no element of stability in these earlier Unions, useful as they were in their day and generation. The men who talk about the New Trade Unionism appear to be totally ignorant of its meaning. In so far as they seek to restrict Trade Unions to the one object, strikes, they are simply "progressing backwards," towards the infancy stage of trade organizations. Trade Unionism has advanced beyond that elementary stage of being. In its evolution from the lower forms of organism, it has risen step by step, if not to the perfect maturity which we hope to see, yet to a high state of development. The New Unionism may attempt to arrest that development, and for a time it might even retard its growth, but there is no such thing as going backwards; the only things left are—decay and death. Whether these are things devoutly to be wished, is possibly a matter of opinion. But if Trade Unions are to be destroyed, let us at least know, before decay sets in, and death writes its sentence on the lintel, what is to be substituted in their place. "Anarchy," exclaim some; the "Social Democratic Revolution," shout others; meaningless words, even by the lips of those who use them; more meaningless still to the poor struggling workman who wants to know, at once, where he can get the wherewithal to purchase a dinner. It is cruel mockery to pull down the shelter, with the bare promise of a possible mansion at some distant date. Work for the utopian mansion if you like, but let the shelter remain, as a refuge, until some better is provided to take its place.

In so far as the maintenance of trade privileges, and the advancement of labour generally, are concerned—as regards wages, hours of labour, and the like—whatever difference exists, if any really does exist, is in respect of the weapons used, or rather the methods of warfare. The difference is, however, more nominal than real when analyzed, and resolved into its elements. The "Old Unions" seek to maintain every privilege which they have won, and to secure permanently every advance made in whatever direction. They, moreover, endeavour to obtain other advantages, as occasion may arise and opportunity offers. In this, and all other matters affecting the interests of the members, there has been no retrogression, no desertion of first principles. The utmost that can be rightfully urged against them is that recently they have been extremely cautious in all their movements, and possibly even, in the opinion of some, a little slow. But each Union is its own best judge in these respects. Social innovators from the outside are not qualified judges. The caution complained of really means prudence, an evidence of a higher state of civilization. It is not Falstaffian prudence, devised in order to cover cowardice; in such a case it would not be the better part of valour. Prince Rupert was perhaps a brilliant exploiter on the battle-field, but he was no general. Cromwell's genius was of another kind, and he won Marston Moor, and other victories. Trade Unions have imitated the old Romans in their methods of extending empire, securing and consolidating as they conquered, rather than the French, who achieved many brilliant victories, and founded many colonies, but lost them speedily afterwards. The one method might be thought by raw recruits to be slow; but it should be remembered that the slow-going tortoise in the fable reached the goal before the swifter hare. A *coup-de-main* is sometimes very successful; so also has been a *coup-d'état;* but, as a matter of general policy, neither can be elevated into the dignity of a system in the polity of nations, or of communities.

Probably the provident benefits in the better class of Unions have helped to steady the organization, to ballast the ship in the trough of the sea. But the vessel is less likely to founder by overweight, than it is to be driven on the rocks and be wrecked by reason of its lack of cargo or ballast to steady it in the storm. It is a singular and significant fact that no Trade Union has ever foundered as a result of excessive overweight in the matter of benefits; it is equally significant that the coast-line is dotted with records of wrecks in consequence of the lack of such benefits. If, however, Trade Unions had really abandoned their primary purpose, and had become Friendly Societies and nothing more, there might be some reason for thus attacking them. But they have not, as the following facts abundantly prove. Usually the amount of strike-pay is larger than for any other benefit, than for out-of-work from any other cause. Taking the societies previously named we find that the Compositors allow 25*s.* per week to members on strike; the Typographical Association 20*s.* per week; the Stonemasons 15*s.* per week; the Bricklayers 15*s.* per week, to full wages in certain cases; the Plasterers 15*s.* per week; the Tailors 15*s.* per week; the Carpenters and Joiners 15*s.* per week; the Boiler-makers and Iron Shipbuilders 12*s.* per week; the Ironfounders 11*s.* per week; the Engineers

and the Steam-engine Makers 10s. per week. The two
latter societies add 5s. per week by levy, so that their
payments are 15s. per week also.   In other cases additional
sums are given where there are children under working-age,
of 1s. to even more per week for each.   In many cases the
above amounts are supplemented by grants, collections,
levies, &c., so that the actual fighters engaged in the battle
shall not unduly suffer, certainly not in the matter of
provisions.   The provisioning of the forces is usually well
attended to by the commissariat of the Union ; and their
efforts are frequently supplemented by voluntary assistance
by a "strike committee," often quite outside the Union.
All this is done with regularity, the result of proper
forethought and organization.

The payments for this benefit cannot be accurately guaged
by any one year's expenditure, and least of all can it be
guaged by a table constructed upon the lines of those
previously given.   But for the sake of uniformity the same
rule is here followed, the same years being given.   Strikes
occur at irregular intervals, whilst the other benefits are
tolerably regular in their recurrence, year by year.   Strikes
occur most frequently either when trade is in a flourishing
condition, at which times the men seek to share the
prosperity, or when trade is slackening off, or during
depression, in opposing reductions in wages.   The payments
in the years selected were as given in Table on the following
page.

The undermentioned figures are necessarily incomplete,
for two reasons : (1) The Engineers', and perhaps one or
two other societies, include strike-pay in out-of-work benefit ;
(2) the amounts given take no account of amounts expended in strikes other than those paid directly out of the

society's funds. But the table is otherwise as complete as the reports and balance-sheets of the several societies enable any one to compile the figures. That is to say, the amounts are accurate as far as they go.

Name of Society.	Payments in each year for Strikes.		
	1869.	1879.	1889.
	£	£	£
Amalgamated Engineers	50	20,576	1,920
Steam-Engine Makers	Not distinguished.	1,225	121
Boiler-makers and Iron Shipbuilders	27	7,109	4,450
Ironfounders	187	5,386	151
Ironmoulders—Scotland	Included in unemployed benefit.		
Associated Blacksmiths	Included in unemployed benefit.		
Amalgamated Carpenters and Joiners	588	10,558	2,299
Operative Stonemasons	7,995	9,971	289
,, Bricklayers	147	1,174	169
,, Plasterers	460	121	97
Amalgamated Tailors	45	1,411	541
London Society of Compositors ...	448	1,700	624
Typographical Associations	193	991	245
U. K. Society of Coachmakers ...	Included in unemployed benefit.		
Totals—14 Societies...	10,140	60,222	10,906

There used to be some timidity in making known the exact amounts spent in strikes, in support of trade privileges, advances in wages, reductions in working-hours, and similar objects. This was at a time when the Unions were denounced and persecuted. Now they are abused for spending so little for these purposes. Truly the fable of the man with the ass might here be quoted, to show how impossible it is to please everybody. The Unions may not have spent enough, or they may have spent too much, upon objects once deemed to be in restraint of trade. That is, of course, a matter of opinion. The Unions best know whether they have discharged their duties to the members. One thing is certain, namely, that the members have annually endorsed the action of their councils and officers, and have generally voted aye or nay to a strike. They may therefore disregard the carping criticism of outsiders, and take at its value the conceits of new men, two-year-old members of Trade Unions.

The total amounts expended in support of trade privileges, that is to say, in strikes and disputes, in so far as they are separately given in the annual reports of the several Unions, are as under :—

NAME OF SOCIETY.	Numb. of Years.	Total Amount.	Cost per Member.
		£	s. d.
Amalgamated Engineers	39	86,664	2 5
Steam-Engine Makers	38	3,982	1 2½
Boiler-makers and Iron Shipbuilders	23	70,255	2 4½
Ironfounders	53	30,167	7½
Ironmoulders—Scotland	Included in donation benefit.		
Associated Blacksmiths	Included in donation benefit.		
Amalgamated Carpenters and Joiners	30	87,094	3 0
Operative Stonemasons	50	112,103	5
,, Bricklayers	20	5,160	3¾
,, Plasterers	28	7,250	1 6
Amalgamated Tailors	22	20,973	2 10
London Society of Compositors ...	42	22,313	5
Typographical Association	40	16,860	1 9
U. K. Society of Coachmakers ...	Included in donation benefit.		
Totals—14 Societies...	—	462,818	—

VIII. **Assistance to other Trades.**—One of the complaints urged against the Old Trade Unionists is that they have not sufficiently assisted those below them in the ranks of labour. But it must be remembered that the funds of Trade Unions belong to those who contribute to them week by week, year by year. The councils have only a very restricted power of voting money, and rightly so. The funds so accumulated are the outcome of self-sacrifice very often, always the result of self-help. Usually the one condition of obtaining help from the Unions is that those seeking it shall have done something to help themselves, or at least that they are endeavouring so to do, when assistance is solicited. It is seldom that the request is denied, if the men asking it can make out a good case. The record of that help is very incomplete in most cases. The Unions do not parade it in public as a rule. But it is well known that the Engineers vote their thousands in aid of struggling labour, upon good cause shown. The most complete record of votes of this kind is preserved by the Ironfounders' Society, the reports of which show that £3640 4s. 8d. have been so voted in sums varying from £5 to £500 at a time, the latter being given to the National Union of Agricultural Labourers in 1874. Between £6000 and £7000 were voted by various Unions in aid of British Sailors in 1874. There has been no lack of generous assistance in times of need when those soliciting it manfully strove to help themselves. Would it not be mere madness, sheer waste of money and strength, to make grants to an unorganized mass, upon the request of an unrepresentative committee, or body of individuals, to be recklessly spent in an impossible contest, possibly entered upon without rhyme or reason? The Unions are not to be bullied out of funds, nor will they be cajoled. But they have an open hand and heart when capital tries to clutch labour by the throat, as the history of the last half century shows. There is no lack of sympathy, and help is given with no grudging hand.

IX. **Summary of Amounts paid as Benefits.**—It might be extremely useful and convenient for reference, if the whole of the foregoing benefits were presented at one view, in order to see in what way, and to what extent, Trade Unions, of the most advanced type, seek the welfare of their members, and endeavour to promote their interests. For reasons before given, the record is not so complete as could be desired; but it presents the general aspects of the Old Trade Unionism in such a form as will enable the public to understand how the vast funds of labour organizations are expended, and for what purposes. The following aggregate amounts have been disbursed by the several societies named :—

NAME OF SOCIETY.	Aggregate amounts expended for :—			
	Funerals.	Sick-pay.	Superan-nuation.	Accidents.
	£	£	£	£
Engineers	209,917	680,314	482,270	52,630
Steam-Engine Makers	17,825	60,592	22,290	8,116
Boiler-makers, &c. ...	51,579	291,278	49,257	26,660
Ironfounders	61,541	208,628	111,268	32,830
Ironmoulders	44,228	Nil.	38,597	Sick & Funerals
Blacksmiths	5,203	26,293	1,989	2,346
Carpenters and Joiners	43,729	239,665	27,029	25,040
Stonemasons	92,747	120,484	84,313	31,679
Bricklayers...	13,616	54,474	921	971
Plasterers	12,804	21,792	3,745	10,340
Tailors	44,081	131,631	1,744	Nil.
Compositors—London	16,098	Nil.	10,246	Nil.
Typographical Asso.	9,227	Nil.	9,886	Nil.
U. K. Coachmakers...	31,148	5,360	50,821	4,822
Totals—14 Societies...	653,743	1,840,511	895,076	195,434

It will be seen that the benefits are adjusted to the trade, in so far as Accident benefit is concerned; in some Unions sick-pay is not adopted, while funeral allowance is general, and superannuation allowance for aged members is becoming customary in most Unions, of the type here more particularly described.

NAME OF SOCIETY.	Aggregate amounts expended for —			
	Donation.	Benevolent Grants.	Loss of Tools, &c.	Strikes.
	£	£	£	£
Engineers	1,492,264	70,598	—	86,664
Steam-Engine Makers	86,331	1,606	—	3,982
Boiler-makers, &c. ...	311,814	—	—	70,255
Ironfounders	709,561	3,549	—	30,167
Ironmoulders	240,035	—	—	{Included in Idle Benefit.
Blacksmiths	32,918	—	—	
Carpenters and Joiners	349,495	18,005	24,113	87,094
Stonemasons	94,763	7,902	—	112,100
Bricklayers	3,500	929	—	5,160
Plasterers	2,722	—	—	7,250
Tailors	25,166	2,165	Nil.	20,973
Compositors—London	92,958	13,272	507	22,313
Typographical Asso....	49,237	—	—	16,860
U. K. Coachmakers ...	113,577	—	702	(Donation.)
Totals—14 Societies...	3,604,341	118,025	24,822	462,818

The aggregate totals under each head, as above given, speak for themselves. The significance of the grand totals, under the respective heads of Provident Benefits and expenditure for strike purposes, is still more imposing, and appeals to a wider circle than Trade Unionists alone. The aggregate amount devoted to what might be called the constant and permanent requirements of workmen, namely, pecuniary assistance in cases of need, over which they have little control, reaches the grand sum of £7,331,952; while the total ascertained amount expended solely on strikes was only £462,818. It is not intended to deprecate expenditure

under the latter head ; for the most part, doubtless, it has
been a necessary and a wise expenditure, and an excellent
investment from a mere commercial and material point of
view.   But indirectly the other and larger amount expended
has had a similar effect, by lessening the pressure of that
competition which is superinduced by hunger, and which
has been, in all ages, the most fruitful cause of low wages
and social discontent.

Amalgamated Society of Railway Servants.—The great
Railway strike in Scotland has brought to the fore the above-
named society.   It had not been long enough in existence
to include it with the others, as it did not exist, on its
present basis, in 1869.   The society was instituted, as now
constituted, in 1872.   It had 33,000 members on the 7th
of October last.   This is its record of work in 18 years:
Paid to members out of work £12,054 14s. 6d.; to superannuated members £21,627 ; to orphans £7,369 18s. 6d.;
for legal assistance to members £11,583 19s. 4d.; and for
trade protection £10,272 4s. 0d.; total £63,507 16s. 4d.
Its balance in hand at the end of 1889 was £81,713 11s.
6d.   It has recently given £6000 to the Scottish men on
strike, besides taking care of their own members in that
struggle.   Its income in 1889 was £17,969, and its
expenditure £9,939 5s. 3d.

CHAPTER VII.

THE "NEW TRADE UNIONISM."—Part I.

CHIEF CHARACTERISTICS OF THE NEW TRADE UNIONS.

Review of the Organization of Labour, in various stages, for many Centuries. (I.) Protective Power of Combination—The Old Trade Unionism assailed from within—Attacks were formerly mostly from without—The Solidity of the Old Trade Unionism—Trade Unions a Sanctuary for the Persecuted and Oppressed—A Fortress of Defence, and a Protection for Pioneer Workers in the Cause of Labour—Its Battles and Victories—The Adjustment of Differences not yet Finally Settled—The New Foes in the Garrison—Wager of Battle, Courting a Conflict, and Risking Defeat. (II.) Conduct of the New Leaders—Attacks upon their Officers, and upon the System—Sowing the Seeds of Discontent—Slander and Calumny—Labour Members—Endeavour to Weaken the Labour Army by Dissension—Progress of Labour during last Fifty Years—Conduct of New Unionists at Liverpool Congress, Vulgar Abuse—Treatment of Strangers and Guests—Misbehaviour during Discussion, and Concurring to ensure a Temporary Triumph by a "Snatch Vote." (III.) Fighting Machines—Condemnation of Provident Benefits—The Railway Workers' Union and the Amalgamated Society of Railway Servants, compared—Benefits of the Latter, and its Expenditure over a series of Years—Unionism for mere Trade purposes not a new feature, it is the old feature Revived. (IV.) Antagonism to Non-Union Workmen—The Use of Force, a remnant of old forms of Antagonism, which had practically died out—Repeal of Criminal Law Amendment Act gave scope to Moral Suasion, not power to Compel—Little Violence, 1875 to

K

1889—Reverted to in 1889-1890—Examples cited—Aversion to
Non-Union Workmen no new feature—Some Excuses for the
Aversion—Freedom must be Respected—Objection to " Blacklegs,"
"Scabs," &c. (V.) Ticketing and Coercion—Action of Trades
Congress—The Law therein cited —The Plymouth Case. (VI.) The
Law of Libel. (VII.) Closing the Ranks—Attempt to Create a
Monopoly of Labour at the Docks, under Authority of Dockers'
Union—Failure of the Manifesto to achieve its Object. (VIII.)
The Dockers' Union—Earlier Struggles—Men engaged in the
Work of Organization—Attacks upon the Leaders—Progress of the
Union—The Dockers' Strike—The Constitution of the Society—Its
Objects—Sub-contracts—Essential character of the Union. (IX.)
The Sailors' and Firemen's Union—Early History and Progress—
Great Strikes—Its Numerical Success—Objects of the Union enu-
merated — Their Reasonableness. (X.) Other New Unions —
General Objects, mainly commendable—Success of the New
Unions. (XI.) Outrages in connection with Labour Struggles.

IN the preceding chapters we have indicated the rise, and
traced the growth, of Trade Unionism from the earliest
times down to the present, even this year of grace, 1891,
when it might be thought that the organization of labour, at
least on present lines, is approaching to something like
completeness.   It has been shown that the Trade Unionism
of to-day, in all its main features of organization, only dates
back some forty years, in so far as many of its chief characteristic benefits are concerned.   The germs existed at a much
earlier date, but, as a living organism, Trade Unionism was
only in a chrysalis state during the first half of the present
century.   Yet this essentially modern institution, as we now
see it, and as before described in these pages, is now somewhat rudely and impertinently, not to say ignorantly,
denominated the " Old Trade Unionism," and is sneeringly
pointed at as being effete ; just as some rude boy not out
of his teens is often heard speaking irreverently of his father
as the old gov'nor, whose exit from the world's stage is

contemplated with a kind of philosophic indifference, with possibly a calculation as to who shall inherit the accumulations of a lifetime, and the amount. Old! yes, perhaps, as we move nowadays. But in its old age, even in its ruins, perchance, the Old Trade Unionism is not unlike some of the old mediæval structures, worthy of veneration by reason of its age and its present uses. As we contemplate some of the old edifices we are struck with wonder at their grandeur, their geometrical proportions, their perfect symmetry, their noble elevation, their vastness, their marvellous fitness for the purposes for which they were designed; their architectural and artistic beauty, in design and execution; and also the solidity of the work, from the foundations to the topmost pinnacle. Some of them approach to sublimity in their wholeness and perfection. If Trade Unions do not approximate to those for complete- ness in all details, it must be remembered that the architects, artists, builders, and workmen were hampered step by step; that their designs were called in question, that the materials supplied for the structure were faulty, that ignorant legislators interposed with impossible conditions, at every stage in the progress of the building; and that, moreover, those engaged in the undertaking went in fear of their lives, and were nearly always in danger of forfeiting their liberty. Considering all these and other circumstances, it is really wonderful that the edifice rose to any height at all, and still more wonderful that it should have attained to complete- ness in any of its parts. That Trade Unionism was able to build up such a system, however imperfect, shows that it had in it all the vitality of enduring life; it was the survival of the fittest, in an age when every effort was made to strangle associations of all kinds at their birth.

I. **Protective power of Combination.**—Trade Unions have been to the workmen of this country both a sanctuary and a fortress, except that in the former case those who took shelter within its precincts were denied " benefit of the clergy," a protection afforded by ancient law to the persecuted, and sometimes, often even, to criminals. Still, combinations did afford some protection in those evil days, when the law pressed with unusual severity upon labour. To that extent they were a sanctuary to the pioneers of labour, fighting for freedom from restraint, and suffering, and enduring rather than yield the right of association, for mutual protection and advancement. As a fortress Trade Unionism shielded the old Unionists, and protected them when attacked. Under cover of its battlements they were able to sally forth and worry the enemy, taking an outpost here, and an outpost there, and sometimes even venturing on a vigorous assault upon their enemies in their own entrenchments. After long struggles, some hair-breadth escapes, many defeats and occasional victories, one strong-hold after another was taken, until at last the citadel surrendered, and it has been held ever since. But the victors were not vindictive ; they recognized existing rights, they gave quarter to all in arms, only maintaining that henceforth there must be equality of rights between the combatants, each having duties and responsibilities, as well as rights. The equality of rights was a question which could not be settled in a day ; time was required for adjustment, so many and diversified were the interests involved, most of which had been the creation of quite another order of things, and for which neither party could be properly held responsible. The adjustment is not yet completed. Complications of long standing can only be solved by mutual

arrangement, and some concessions, perhaps, on either side.
But, though the final settlement has not been effected,
negotiations, expressed or understood, have been going on,
even at accelerated speed, during the last few years, the
victorious army scoring concession after concession. Im-
patience at delay is natural, though it is mostly manifested
by those who had no share in the prolonged struggle.

In all the earlier battles of Trade Unionism the fighting
garrison had this advantage, they were fighting an attacking
or besieging army from without. Foes within were not
absolutely unknown, but they were infrequent. Now the
entire line of battle seems changed. The attacks come
from within, more than from without; from those who
ought to be brave defenders, not implacable foes. Some
of these men have been braying upon the battlements,
calling aloud to the forces outside, for the most part long
quiescent, to resume the conflict. They have done more;
they have tried to spike the guns, and damp the powder,
to prevent anything like capable resistance, should a long
and stubborn battle ensue. These are grave charges; the
facts that follow will show whether or not they are well
founded. The points of difference between the New and
the Old Trade Unionism are not always so clearly drawn
that the run-and-read people are able to see the distinction;
but a careful examination of the speeches of a few of the
" new leaders," and the action of some of the New Unions,
will help to elucidate the matter. These will be referred to
in turn, under their heads following.

II. **The Conduct of the " New Leaders."**—The distin-
guishing trait in the conduct of prominent " new leaders "
has been, and is, their persistent, cowardly, and calumnious
attacks upon the old leaders, upon men who have borne the

brunt of labour's battles, many of whom are still the trusted officials of the several Unions. For several years some of those men have attacked such representatives as Thomas Burt, Charles Fenwick, and John Wilson, in the mining districts of their own constituencies; to such an extent was this pursued that Mr. Burt offered to place his resignation in the hands of his council, and of his constituents. Mr. Broadhurst was attacked so vehemently and persistently that he retired from the post of Secretary to the Trade Union Congress, a post held by him for about fourteen years. An effort was similarly made to get rid of Mr. Shipton, Secretary of the London Trades Council, a post he has held for nearly twenty years. The attacks upon Mr. C. J. Drummond, the Secretary of the London Society of Compositors, were of such a character that he also resigned, but in this case he was entreated to withdraw the resignation, and continue at his post as secretary. Mr. Robert Austin, the Secretary of the Amalgamated Society of Engineers, has been subject to similar attacks, though he has not gone so far as to tender his resignation. The same remarks apply to Mr. James Swift, of the Steam-Engine Makers' Society, and Mr. E. Harford, of the Amalgamated Society of Railway Servants. There is, indeed, scarcely a secretary of long standing who has not had to endure abuse, misrepresentation, and calumny from some of the new leaders, or their satellites. This condition of things has become almost unbearable in many instances, for, besides having to endure the abuse, their labours have been correspondingly increased by the necessity of replying to animadversions, and by other work consequent thereupon. Singularly enough the extreme violence of the abuse has been reserved for the Labour Members in Parliament. On the platform, in the press, and at hole-and-corner meetings, the poison of calumny has been distributed freely, in some instances so freely that it has become its own antidote. None have been spared, although the virulence has subsided in the case of Mr. B. Pickard and Mr. W. Abraham, in consequence of their having consented to promote and support an eight-hour day by Act of Parliament.

The effect of slanders, so ruthlessly and persistently circulated, has been to foment discontent among the members of societies represented by those named, and others occupying official positions in other Unions. Some of the new leaders have openly proclaimed that their mission is to preach the gospel of discontent. Of course there is discontent, *and* discontent. In so far as discontent leads to emulation, to vigorous effort to better the condition of the workers, it is healthful; it stirs the stagnant pool. But there is discontent of another kind, which aims at lawlessness and license; we have seen examples of it during the last few years, in strikes, without reason; in the exercise of brute force, without compunction; and in capitulation without honour. Violent methods are, or rather, they should be, things of the past. They belong to an age when freedom of association was denied; when persecution drove men to something like frenzy; when long hours, low wages, dear provisions, scarcity of work, and demoralizing conditions, had degraded the working classes almost to the level of brutes. Things are bad enough now, in all conscience; but it shows an utter ignorance of history, especially of the history of labour, not to know that the working classes of to-day are immeasurably better off than they were forty or fifty years ago. Let them who doubt it turn to the Reports [1]

---

[1] Gibbin's *Industrial History*, pp. 192, 193.

of the Royal Commissioners and Select Committees, from 1832 to 1850, on the Factory System, on Mines, on Agriculture, and the like; and also to the Health of Towns Commission, and the Reports on the Sanitary Condition of the Labouring Population in England and Wales, and Scotland, 1838 to 1842. The improvement effected, in all respects, is enormous; had it not been, then the labours of our forefathers have been wasted, and of non-effect. The results of their labours embue us with courage and hope that the amelioration of the condition of the masses of our population will be continued and accelerated under newer and better conditions. To ignore the labours of those who have gone before shows base ingratitude, the offspring at once of ignorance, envy, and perversity.

Perhaps the culmination of vulgar abuse, and of overbearing behaviour, was reached at the Liverpool Trades Union Congress; and of shameless misrepresentation subsequently, in the reports and speeches made thereupon. According to one "leader," tall hats and black coats, and also the size and stature of the delegates from the old Unions, were indications of a frightful state of decay, in the policy and management of the Old Trade Unionism. The delegates who happened to be the happy possessors of these obnoxious characteristics of decayed manhood, as regards membership of Trade Unions, were sneered at as "Aldermanic." Rudeness to "visitors" was exemplified in the treatment of the Mayor of Liverpool, who had entertained the delegates, and also of the representatives of Co-operative Societies, who had come to the Congress by invitation to explain the uses of the co-operative system to the Trade Unionists present. A loud voice, impatient gestures, and persistent interruptions were in strong force at the Trades Union Congress of 1890. The exhibition was sad and pitiful to behold.

III. "**Fighting machines.**"—This aspect of the New Trades Unionism is pithily expressed in the resolution of the Railway Workers' Congress, held at the Hope Town Hall, Bethnal Green Road, on Wednesday, November 19th, 1890, as follows : " That the Union shall remain a fighting one, and shall not be encumbered with any sick, or accident fund." The society calling that Congress, namely, " The General Railway Workers' Union," must not be confounded with the " Amalgamated Society of Railway Servants," which has been in existence for many years, and is organized on a basis something like that of the Engineers' and other societies, whose benefits have been enumerated in the preceding chapter. The former is indeed one of the New Unions, originally designed apparently to compete with the Old, possibly to overthrow it, but now to some extent co-operating with it. Its weekly contributions are less in amount, while the benefits are 15s. per week strike-pay, for the first ten weeks, and 7s. 6d. the week for a further ten weeks, then to cease. Strikes have been known to last more than ten weeks, or twenty weeks ; some very recently have extended to eighteen weeks, and others even longer. What is to become of the strikers after the expiration of twenty weeks is not vouchsafed to us in the resolutions of that Congress. In comparison with the above, let us see what the Amalgamated Society of Railway Servants has done, and is doing. It provides for the unemployed—£2068 was so expended in 1887 ; for the sick, accidents, superannuation, orphans, legal defence, and strike-pay £10,902. For those and other purposes the society had disbursed £96,742 by the end of 1888, and its balance in hand at the close of 1889 was £81,764. By its quiet persistent action, it has done much to better the condition of railway employés all over the kingdom. As a Union, it has made less noise, perhaps, than some of the new ones; but its influence can be traced in concessions made by the different Railway Companies during the last year or two, and its influence is extending. There might be room for both, but prudence would suggest friendly co-operation, if amalgamation is not possible.

But, as before pointed out, the militant side is no new feature in Trade Unionism. Militant purposes only means the old phase revived, which the better Unions had minimized if not discarded. Many of the Old Unions have never been able to see their way to such a revision of rules and re constitution, as regards objects, as would enable them to embark on the wider scheme exemplified in the policy of the several Unions previously adverted to. The more experienced of their officers and members, however, in most cases regard this as a misfortune; in no case do they sneer at the type of Union before described. Herein they differ from the "New Unionists." Those commend, where they cannot imitate; these condemn, as not worthy of imitation. Many of the older Unions have done useful work in their more limited sphere, are doing good work still; some of the New Unions may survive and do useful work also. They have, however, to stand the test of experience; it is too early to estimate their strength, or appraise their efficiency; it would be presumptive to attempt to forecast their future. As regards provident benefits, they glory in the fact that they leave off where they ought only to have commenced; they even make a boast of it, as though they had entered upon an entirely new stage of Trade Unionism, which was at once its Alpha and

Omega. It might be, often is, desirable to limit and restrict the scope of a newly-formed Union; to temper the wind, as it were, to the shorn lamb. But why expose the lamb to the inclemency of the weather any longer than need be; and why mock the lamb by declaring that he is fully covered with fleece sufficiently to resist any and every kind of weather! However useful such Unions may be in their degree, it is obvious that they have not, cannot have, the staying power of organizations constituted on a wider basis, having the recuperative power and sustaining force of Unions such as those enumerated in the previous chapter. It needs no argument to uphold this view, the facts of industrial history prove it incontestably, but it is necessary to assert it, because of the obliquity of some of the new leaders in labour movements.

IV. **Antagonism to Non-Union Workmen.**—This is no new feature in the history of Trade Unionism. Unfortunately it is one of the oldest difficulties which Trade Unions have had to deal with. The greatest misfortune of all is that the New Trade Unionists have to some extent revived the violence and intimidation of by-gone times, when we had hoped that intemperate heat, as a mode of industrial motion, had well nigh died out. When the Unionists of the United Kingdom were demanding the repeal of the Criminal Law Amendment Act, they pleaded that they did not desire to coerce, or to compel, but to persuade and induce. The law was repealed with the view of giving free scope to moral suasion, but not with the view of conferring a license to intimidate by force. And it must be admitted that for several years, from 1875 to 1889, the conduct of the Trade Unionists of Great Britain justified the legislature in repealing that Act, and also several other Acts in 1875.

Their conduct, indeed, was such that the late John Bright, one of the stoutest opponents to the repeal of the Criminal Law Amendment Act, up to 1874, admitted that the repeal had been justified by the results. During the last two years we have seen a recurrence of violence to non-Unionists, for which we can only find a parallel in the earlier years of Trade Unionism, prior at least to the Inquiry instituted in 1867. In a few isolated instances there was a partial revival of personal encounters between that date and the final repeal of the old laws; but these occurred at times of great excitement, when feeling ran high, and labour struggles were acute. It was reserved for the recent development of the New Trade Unionism to systematically revert to terrorism, and brute force, to compel non-Union hands to leave their employment. Examples of this kind of militant Unionism were found in connection with the Dockers' strikes in London, Liverpool, Cardiff, Southampton, and other places; also in connection with the Gas-stokers strikes in South London, Manchester, and other places; and in connection with the Seamen and Firemen's Union, in several cases. It is lamentable that this revival of an old and a bad practice should have taken place; but it is gratifying to find that the use of force and violence is being discontinued.

The aversion of Trade Unionists to work with non-members is as old as the Guild system. And, so long as Trade Unionists abstain from violence and intimidation, much can be said in excuse if not in favour of their contention and action. The members of a Trade Union point to the fact that they have fought for every privilege, have suffered and endured in many a long struggle, have made great sacrifices, and have won many victories; they also point out that non-Unionists enjoy all the advantages which have been won, without contributing to the victory; and further, that when they suffer defeat, it is by the aid of, if not always at the hands of, non-Unionists. The latter will neither sow the seed, nor promote its growth and maturity; will not even help to reap, or gather in the harvest. But they are ever ready to eat and enjoy the fruits of others' labours. It is sad that it should be so. Unfortunately, however, that is the case. But this is a free country; and a man must not be compelled to join a Union any more than he should be compelled not to join a Union. The State must preserve equal liberty to all, as it has at length done in matters of conscience. Nevertheless, within certain tolerably defined limits, Trade Unions have the power to put on social pressure, even to a high degree of tension, to induce non-Union men to take their share of duty, and of responsibility. And so long as they do not overstep the boundary line, few will be disposed to complain of their action. The chief cause of strife, in connection with non-Union workmen, is not however by reason of their not joining the Union, strong as this often is. The wrath of Trade Unionists is mostly concentrated upon men who, in the event of a strike, go in to take the places of those who come out—the "blacklegs" as they are termed, or "scabs," or by some other epithet, to describe their perfidy. Honourable men will feel little compunction for such traitors to their own order, but the law must not permit lynching, even in the case of foul murder; and in those cases violent hands must not be laid on the men who skulk work in ordinary times of pressure, but swarm like vultures to a carcase when the battle is raging fierce, even to feed upon their own comrades.

V. Picketing and Coercion.—For many years the Trade Unions of England sought to free themselves from statutory enactments, and more especially from decisions in the Courts, which rendered picketing illegal, and punishable as a criminal offence. Their efforts were crowned with success in 1875, when the "Labour Laws" were passed, repealing not only the Criminal Law Amendment Act, 1871, but provisions in other Acts which remained in force; and also by the abolition of the law of conspiracy, as applied to labour disputes. The legislation of that year was hailed by the Trade Unionists of the country as the "workmen's victory," the Acts of that year being regarded and spoken of as the "Workmen's Charter." All through that long and arduous struggle, fought with determination and prudence by the leaders of the Unions, and resisted by all the means at their command by capitalists and employers, the workmen pleaded that they did not seek to "coerce," but to persuade; not to use force or exercise terrorism, but to exert moral pressure upon those in their own ranks who would not otherwise join or help the Unions. The law as it now is gives considerable latitude to Unionists in the exercise of their right to induce, by all lawful means, non-Union workmen to join the Union, or at least to abstain from injuring the cause of Unionism, by working contrary to its tenets. The law stopped short at compulsion; a man may not compel another man to do, or abstain from doing, what he has a lawful right to do, or abstain from doing. It guards personal liberty; and Unionists, above all men, should guard it also as the sure foundation of all rights of citizenship. During the fifteen years that have since elapsed, no serious complaints have ever been made against the law, and very little against its administration, until within the last twelve months, when some of the new Unionists found that they could not do just as they thought fit, regardless of the consequences to other men who did not think exactly with themselves. The extent of the reaction against law, by those who so vigorously demand more law, will be understood by what follows.

The Parliamentary Committee of the Trades Union Congress had been instructed to consider the question of picketing, in view of the complaints recently made. The Committee accordingly did consider the matter, with the following result : They reported to the Liverpool Congress, September 1890, that they had given careful attention to this subject ; and they stated that "the law is perfectly clear, and cannot be mistaken, in the permission it gives to peaceful picketing." The report goes on to say : "If those engaged in trade disputes, necessitating this means of pro-tection, would only obtain the information which they could easily get before undertaking the work, there is no reason why they might not conduct picketing successfully and without any liability to prosecution." The Committee then refer to the "judgment given by Mr. Justice Cave at the Bristol Spring Assizes, in which he clearly upheld the rights of workmen in this matter." This conclusion of the Parliamentary Committee accords with the views held by Trade Unionists generally, and agrees with the reasons stated for a change in the law during the fifty years of agitation, which preceded the repeal of the old laws. The report of the Committee did not appear to give complete satisfaction, for the following resolution was proposed and seconded later on, when that portion of the report was reached :—

" That, in the event of any member of a Trade Union

represented at this Congress being convicted of picketing without violence, under the Conspiracy Act, 1875, the Parliamentary Committee be instructed to take steps to have the Act more clearly defined." This sensible and moderate resolution was rejected, by 154 votes to 9, in favour of the following amendment: "That we instruct the Parliamentary Committee to have the clause making picketing illegal entirely repealed." The absurdity of this amendment is that there is no clause in the Act which makes picketing illegal. But another resolution of the Congress throws some additional light on the subject. The resolution referred to is :—

"That we instruct the Parliamentary Committee to abolish clause 7 of the Conspiracy and Protection of Property Act, and to amend such other clauses as are dangerous to the liberties of the working-classes." The mover said that "one of the anomalies of the Act was that, though picketing was allowed in one clause, in clause 7 it was made penal under some conditions." The seconder, however, said he had not so much fault to find with the Act itself as with its interpretation. "The resolution was adopted without dissent." It is rather lamentable that this was so, for none of the speakers seem to have had any accurate knowledge of the Act in question. What they meant no doubt was section 7 of the Act, the whole of which is so important that it is here given *in extenso*. Section 7 says :—

" Every person who, with a view to compel any other person to abstain from doing or to do any act which such other person has a legal right to do or abstain from doing, wrongfully and without legal authority—

1. " Uses violence to or intimidates such other person or his wife or children, or injures his property; or,

" 2. Persistently follows such other person about from place to place ; or,

" 3. Hides any tools, clothes, or other property owned or used by such other person, or deprives him of or hinders him in the use thereof; or,

" 4. Watches or besets the house or other place where such other person resides, or works, or carries on business, or happens to be, or the approach to such a house or place ; or,

" 5. Follows such other person with two or more other persons in a disorderly manner in or through any street or road,

" Shall, on conviction thereof by a court of summary jurisdiction, or on indictment as hereinafter mentioned, be liable either to pay a penalty not exceeding twenty pounds, or to be imprisoned for a term not exceeding three months, with or without hard labour.

" Attending at or near the house or place where a person resides, or works, or carries on business, or happens to be, or the approach to such house or place, in order merely to obtain or.communicate information, shall not be deemed a watching or besetting within the meaning of this section."

One would think that this section was sufficiently clear for any ordinary citizen to understand ; certainly there is no excuse for any intelligent delegate at a Trades Congress mistaking its purport and effect. The whole of the sub-sections are governed by the words " to compel," and therefore the vote of Congress means, if it means anything at all, that a Trade Unionist shall have the power to do all the things mentioned in the five sub-sections, " with a view to compel " another person to abstain from doing or to do any act which such other person has a legal right to do or

L

abstain from doing. Instead of those "clauses" being dangerous to the liberties of the working classes, they are a protection ; the danger would commence with their repeal. It is advocating an appeal to brute force, to demand a repeal of this part of the Act of 1875. And the men who demanded the repeal of this section are the foes of order and progress, enemies to their class, and supporters of a tyranny even more crushing than that under which Trade Unionists suffered from the bad old Combination Laws of a bygone age.

By way of contrast to the demand for the free use of violence, intimidation, persistently following, rattening, watching, and besetting, and following, with others, in a disorderly manner, the following resolution was unanimously agreed to by the Congress :—

"That this Congress is of opinion that the action taken by the Irish Constabulary in shadowing Trade Unionists during the strike of tailors in Londonderry is contrary to the repeated statements made by the Chief Secretary for Ireland, that the law is the same, and that, with a view to the better organization, and assisting those already organized, it be an instruction to the Parliamentary Committee to use every effort possible to secure for Ireland the same protection and privileges to Trade Unionists that are allowed in Great Britain." The mover, seconder, and supporter of the resolution stated that the matters complained of "in Ireland would not be tolerated anywhere else in the British Isles."

In this resolution we have a protest against watching and besetting, and following about from place to place, the term used to designate these practices being "shadowing." But the Congress had already passed a resolution in favour of shadowing—by Trade Unionists—when it proposed to abolish Section 7 of the Conspiracy and Protection to Property Act, 1875, and after the resolution above quoted was passed a further resolution was adopted, by 154 to 9, to have the clause making watching and besetting and following, otherwise "shadowing," repealed. That is to say, shadowing by Trade Unionists is to be lawful, but shadowing by the Royal Irish Constabulary, or other accredited officers of the Crown, is to be unlawful. A Congress which could pass such utterly opposite and contradictory resolutions must have become thoroughly demoralized, forgetful of its past history and notable achievements in the cause of individual liberty and industrial progress.

The foregoing pages were in the printers' hands before Mr. H. M. Bompas, the Recorder of Plymouth, had given his decision in the case of Regina *v.* Curran and others; or before public attention had been called to Judge Seymour's decision at Newcastle-on-Tyne in November last. The remarks previously made need, however, only to be modified thus far : The two decisions referred to were based upon a strained interpretation of the term "intimidates," an interpretation never before given in any similar or analogous case. The validity of those decisions is open to question, and it is altogether doubtful if either would be upheld on appeal to the higher Courts. If intimidation is construed to mean any kind of "moral pressure" which one man, or several men, may bring to bear upon another, or other persons, rendering them liable to a criminal prosecution, then no man is safe. But the decisions referred to are explained by the fact that they apply only to pressure brought to bear by workmen in connection with labour disputes, and are not

equally applicable to employers under analogous circumstances. It is a class interpretation of a class law. Were
the law general in its application to all citizens alike, in the
exercise of all social pressure, then the word "intimidates,"
as used in the Act, would be interpreted to mean such
intimidation as is contemplated by the Summary Jurisdiction Act, 1879, namely, such as would justify a Justice of
the Peace binding the person guilty of the offence over to
keep the peace. In neither of the cases named was there
any intimidation in that sense. There is a danger to liberty
when the law allows such latitude of interpretation as might
lead to license; there is equal danger when the lines of
legal restraint are so narrow that a man is liable to break
the law if he moves to the right hand or to the left. If
the decisions are ultimately held good, the Act of 1875
is simply a trap for the unwary, and ought to be amended.

VI. **The Law of Libel.**—Another rather extraordinary
resolution was passed by the last Congress, held at Liverpool, in September 1890, namely, one relating to the
Law of Libel and Trade Unionists. The resolution was
as follows :—

"That, in view of the verdict against Mr. John Judge,
at the recent Yorkshire Assizes, in the action for slander,
'Andrews v. Judge,' it be an instruction from this Congress to the Parliamentary Committee to obtain the best
legal opinion upon the laws affecting Trade Union officials
in any action they may take against those persons whom
the members and officers of the Union consider do not
conform to the rules of the trade, and circulate such
opinions, and any advice the Committee may think proper
to give amongst the Trade Societies of the country."

An addendum was subsequently moved to the effect that

the Committee use their influence with members of Parliament to get the law of libel so altered, "that when persons were trying to inflict hardship, or injury upon any portion of the community, they might be exposed without fear of prosecution, provided the statements made were true, and without malice." The resolution and the addendum were adopted and carried unanimously. The Congress did not seem to be aware of the fact that a defendant can plead justification, that the libel was true, and that it was published for the public benefit. Besides which, the mere fact of damages being cast in the case cited, proves that the term "scab," or other similar term, is one of opprobrium, consequently the act described by the expression is, inferentially, condemned as an unworthy act, and, as such, carrying with it a stigma and a disgrace. Trade Unionists had better leave libelling to the scum of the press in this country, and to the disreputable cliques and coteries whose only chance of a hearing in public is by reason of the malicious slanders and calumnies they circulate with the view of discrediting honest workers in the cause of human progress.

VII. **Closing the Union Ranks.**—This is quite a new feature, in so far as Trade Unions are concerned. It was reserved for the Dockers' Union to institute this modern monopoly in the labour market. But even here they cannot claim credit for invention. It is merely a revival of the ugliest and worst feature of the more degenerate guilds. They might, indeed, have borrowed the idea from the City of London Guilds, institutions which have faithlessly betrayed their trust, have ceased to represent the industries for whose benefit they were instituted, and have become monopolies, in so far as Trust Funds are concerned, even if they have ceased to be monopolies in matters industrial.

The leaders of the Dockers' Union, who initiated that preposterous and restrictive policy, proclaimed to the world their unfitness for leading a great labour movement, and most of all for solving the labour problem. The resolution which recorded this stupendous act of folly was passed by the Executive of the Dockers' Union in August 1890, and was widely circulated throughout the metropolis; it deserves to be quoted, if only that it might be preserved as an historical curiosity. It was as follows :—

"That, recognizing that our Metropolitan membership is quite equal to the labour requirements of London, resolved that instructions be sent to each branch secretary in the Metropolitan area, that no candidates for membership be accepted after August 13th, 1890, except by special sanction of the district committee, and each district committee to be informed that no men known to be physically weak or otherwise incompetent are to be accepted under any consideration. Special arrangements are to be made for the enrolling of those engaged in special industries, such as brewery men, sawyers, &c. &c." This attempt to create a virtual close monopoly of all dock and riverside labour has of course failed, as it deserved to fail, but the failure to enforce the resolution does not diminish its absolute stupidity; on the contrary, it stamps with the stigma of incompetence the authors and abettors of the manifesto, proclaiming them to "be physically weak or otherwise incompetent."

If one class of labour, or those for the time being employed in any industry, can claim the right to close a trade or occupation against all comers, why not all? It is generally alleged, except perhaps in the case of domestic female servants, that each branch of industry is overstocked.

Even in times of prosperity, like those of the last two years, we hear complaints of men being out of work; ever so slight a slackening off will increase the number, and with it the relative proportion to the total employed. Supposing, then, that all the Unions closed their ranks—what is to become of the redundant population? And, as to the future, are those who come into the world to be strangled, or what? " Welcome, little stranger," will have to be effaced from our nursery prattle, there being no longer any room for additions. If the dockers claim the right to regulate the number who shall be allowed to work at dock-work, had we not better re-endow the City Companies with all their original privileges, and give them the power to turn adrift, out of the city, all who have not fulfilled the conditions of their early charters and ordinances. They at least can claim prescriptive rights. Why also may not employers claim that the market is overstocked—that any additional number will so increase competition that prices will go down; and that it is necessary to restrict the number in order that profits shall be augmented. Or shopkeepers, that they are being ruined by further competition. Publicans, it is true, exercise a kind of indirect controlling power, by bringing influence to bear upon licensing magistrates to refuse further licenses. But of course these exercise that power in the interests of public morality, so careful are they of the common weal. Railways and Water Companies spend a good deal of money in "maintaining their acquired rights," and in preventing further competition; but these methods are not generally commended. In any case the public regard with suspicion all and every of such devices to create monopolies, or to perpetuate them; it will scarcely welcome any new departure in this respect, not even in the interests of labour.

VIII. **The Dockers' Union.**—The story of the original formation of the Dockers' Union has not yet been adequately told, not even by the founder. He has probably thought it prudent to omit particulars of its early struggles, but they should be made known. Another "leader," who essayed to tell the story of the Dockers' Strike, in the *New Review* for October 1889, discreetly began at a subsequent period of its history. The dock and riverside labourers had been for some years the toys of a small knot of professional agitators, by whom they were used to promote all sorts of schemes, from man-holes on the Metropolitan District Railway to bridges across the Thames; and from the abolition of sugar bounties to the incorporation of South London as a separate municipality. Mr. Ben Tillett had seen something of this kind of work, and he conceived the idea of instituting a regular Union, on *bonâ-fide* lines. For a long time attempts were made to thwart him. By degrees, however, he managed to get a committee together, and the rules were drafted for the "Tea Operatives' and General Labourers' Union." It was then determined to register the society as a Trade Union. The present writer was more than once appealed to, to assist in getting the rules passed by the Registrar. This was at last accomplished. The work of organization was extremely slow, and efforts were persistently made to prevent the growth of the Union. But the secretary was not the man to be pushed on one side easily. During two quarters the income barely sufficed to cover the expenditure, and the accounts which he manfully published were laid hold of by his opponents and were sent to the *Star* newspaper, by which paper Mr. Ben Tillett was several times severely handled. Mr. Tillett again sought the services of the present writer, who went to the *Star* and explained matters, and begged that they would not strive to strangle this young, feeble, and struggling but *bonâ-fide* Union. The appeal was successful, and the secretary was left in peace. Throughout 1888, and down to the 13th of August, 1889, Mr. Tillett had no help from the men who now claim to have originated the Dockers' Union.

The secretary of the Union partly tells the tale in the *English Illustrated Magazine* for November 1889, according to which he had never even seen, and had never spoken to, the other claimant to the honour of having founded the Dockers' Union. Yet several large meetings had been held, one at least in the great Assembly Hall, Mile End, attended by some thousands of people in 1889. In his original conception of forming the Union, Mr. Tillett had no notion of founding a new Trade Unionism. He merely wished to go on the old lines, but not to embark upon provident benefits, as the wages of the men would not permit of a contribution sufficient to run the risk. The contributions were fixed at twopence per week. A strike at Tilbury Docks, for an advance of one penny per hour, from 4*d*. to 5*d*., took place soon after the Union was formed; it dragged on for a month, and then flickered out. The labourers lost heart, Tillett was ill from exposure and overwork, and, when he recovered, the Union had dwindled down to a few hundreds again, from about 800 to 300 men. A new move was made in the spring of 1889, when the Gas-workers' Union was formed, the first move of which was attended by some success. An attempt to establish a new Union, for the permanent hands at the docks, seems to have revived hope, and infused new vigour into the small Union of Tea Operatives and General Labourers.

A dispute on August 12th at the South West India Dock was a prelude to the more formidable strike on the following day—henceforth renowned as the Great Dockers' Strike. The demands made were for 6*d*. per hour, time of hiring not to be less than four hours, 8*d*. per hour for overtime, and the abolition of contract work and piecework. The letter making those demands was sent on August 13th, requesting an answer by noon the following day, and soon the men themselves were on the road to the Dock House to ascertain the answer. The story of the strike need not be told—it was however successful.

The Dockers' Union as now constituted was created out of the strike. It was then called the "New Dockers' Union." It does not profess to be anything more than a Trade Union "for the protection of trade interests," except that it provides " for the recovery of compensation in cases of accident." The strike-pay is 10*s*. per week. The other objects are to control the system of boy labour; abolish present system of contracts; regulate hours of hiring; enforce minimum of four hours; minimum rate 6*d*. per hour, overtime 8*d*. per hour; in stream 7*d*. per hour, overtime 9*d*. per hour; to abolish extra work and overtime, and to establish a labour bureau. These objects are, with the exception of the last one, similar to those in other Unions; there is nothing new in them whatever. They accord with those of the earlier Unions, where no provident benefits are attached. The Dockers' Union seems, however, to have abandoned its attitude of resistance to sub-contracts, but it calls them by another name—co-operation, which is but a revival of the gang-system. Of course this system is co-operative, and if properly worked out might be a useful form of labour in some industries. It was the system under which English navvies cut and embanked our English railways, a system brought almost to perfection by the late Mr. Brassey. The New Unionism is therefore not to be sought in the rules of the Dockers' Union. Certainly nothing new is to be found there. The exceptional feature in the management of the Union is that the president, and leading spirit, is not a docker, but an engineer. In no other Union hardly would this be tolerated, for Trade Unionists are most conservative in this respect; they say "let the cobbler stick to his last." However, there are precedents even for outside help. William Burn, a shoemaker, was for years the secretary of the Brickmakers' Union, as that body had no one within its ranks capable of keeping the books, and conducting the correspondence. But such instances are rare, and with the spread of education are not likely to happen again.

IX. **The Sailors' and Firemen's Union.**—Perhaps the most striking experiment in the organization of what is termed "unskilled labour," is the formation and growth of the Sailors' and Firemen's Union. The men constituting this Union cannot, however, in any proper sense, be termed unskilled, except in comparison with the highest skilled trades. The movement took shape in 1888, and at the Trades Union Congress, held in September of that year, the Union was represented by its secretary, the numbers stated in the credentials being 500 members. In a few months it was stated that the membership had risen to 40,000; at the Congress of 1889 the members were returned as 65,000 members. In January and February 1889, extensive strikes were organized for an advance of wages in many of the chief ports of the kingdom. Those strikes, if not in all cases successful, resulted in very substantial advances in wages, and what is perhaps of almost equal consequence, in better conditions of hiring, and of living on board ship. The income for 1889 amounted to £26,600; and the expenditure to £18,915; the balance being £7,685. This Union does not pretend to be based upon what is called the " New Unionism " principle. That it is a fighting Union none will dispute. Its strikes have been nearly, if not quite, as numerous as the Dockers' Union can boast of, and in some contests quite as many if not more men have been engaged. In one conflict alone 35,000 men were said to be involved, but fortunately it lasted only a short time. The benefits provided for the members are more varied than in most, sickness and accident being included. Altogether the objects are commendable. If any complaints arise, they have reference to the means adopted for effecting those objects, they cannot fairly be made against the objects themselves. Attempts had been made previously to create Sailors' Unions, but they mostly failed until Mr. J. H. Wilson took the matter in hand. The success of this Union is absolutely phenomenal in the history of labour.

The Union includes foreign as well as British seamen, but there is nearly a prohibitive tariff in the shape of a heavy entrance fee for foreign sailors. Briefly stated, the objects are : (1) To improve the condition and protect the interests of all seafaring men. (2) To establish homes for seamen in all places where required. (3) To make advances to members on security of wages and allotment notes. (4) To obtain reasonable hours of duty, maintain fair wages, and promote Parliamentary representation of the seafaring classes. (5) To assist men victimized for belonging to, or rendering services to, the Union. (6) To afford legal assistance to members for recovery of wages, compensation for injuries, or in cases of prosecution for breach of contract, &c. (7) To provide for safety of men when on board ship, and prevent loss of life at sea. (8) To provide an efficient class of able-seamen, and see that they are in a fit condition, and ready as to time, for service. (9) To provide assistance for shipwrecked mariners. (10) To assist men travelling in search of work. (11) Granting of privilege cards to non-members willing to join the Union. (12) To provide sick benefit, accident benefit, and funeral benefit. (13) To provide a fund for Parliamentary representation. (14) To provide a fund for the support of men on strike. With such excellent objects as these, it is "a thousand pities" that shipowners cannot see their way clear to co-operate with the Union in order to secure them. Were this the case, difficulties as to the means for securing their adoption would vanish. At the recent Congress in Glasgow (1890), in the revision of rules, expressions were often used in the discussions which meant, if they meant anything at all, a manly determination to fulfil their duties, and to obey and support the captains, masters, and officers in authority. This is quite consistent with the assertion of manhood, and independence of character. The better the man, the more amenable is he to discipline; duty and obedience are high qualities, to be developed and trained. Brute force develops resistance, which only needs the opportunity to display itself. The Seamen and Firemen's Union may have erred in policy, but it has in it the elements of great good for the brave crews who man our mercantile marine.

X. **Progress of other New Unions.**—These two Unions are but samples of those called into existence during the last two or three years. The Railway Workers' Union has been already adverted to; it is constituted upon the basis of the Dockers' Union. The Gas-workers' Union is similar, in most respects. The same may be said of the Carters' Union, the Tramway Men's Union, and many others, including the Women's Unions recently established. The objects in all cases are the improvement of the condition of the workers in the particular industry, or industries, for some recent Unions are not confined to one industry, but include workers of various kinds. Those are rightful objects, and commendable in all respects. Men may differ as to the means adopted, the policy pursued, the action of some of the members, or the tone and attitude of the leaders, but the amelioration of the condition of the working classes is an object worthy of the highest praise.

Nor can it be said that the efforts made during the last two or three years have been unattended with success. Immense progress has been made, progress so vast that it seems as though we were reaping the harvest of a whole century's work, in the course of a single season. Year by year the seed has been sown, and the land tilled and manured; the weeds also have been plucked out by the roots, and the growing crops have been watered by diligent hands. But it seemed as though the grain would never come to maturity. Suddenly, as it were, the sky cleared, the sun shone brightly, warming with its rays the backward crop, soon to rise to almost meridian splendour, ripening with its heat the harvest for the sickle. The ingathering was with a rush; the garnering was done in haste; and there was a danger of the corn being injured by the too hasty conduct of the harvestmen. If some has been spoiled, much remains; sufficient perhaps to give succour and support, should scarcity again arise, until a further seed-time and harvest have again provided for the pressing needs of our population.

XI. **Outrages in connection with Trade Unionism.**— Although personal violence, intimidation, and coercion have not wholly disappeared in connection with labour disputes, they are less frequent, indeed it might be said they are infrequent now, in comparison with the past. During the last twenty years, since the inauguration of juster laws by the Trade Union Act, 1871, there has not been much to complain of in any respect, in so far as unlawful interference is concerned. On the great strike of cotton operatives in 1878, against reductions in wages, there was an outbreak of violence, reminding one of the labour struggles of a century ago. Some 300,000 persons were, it was alleged, affected by the strike and lock-out; feeling ran high, the workpeople were goaded into desperation, and some misguided men gave vent to their bitter exasperation against the enforced reductions in wages by violence. Some mills were set on fire, the house of Mr. Raynsford Jackson in Lancashire being also set on fire and destroyed; and a man who had been formerly secretary of his own trade society, the Ironfounders, and likewise secretary to the Blackburn Trades' Council, was blinded by some corrosive fluid, which was thrown in his face. No fewer than sixty-eight persons were tried and convicted for the violence and outrages committed in the course of that disastrous dispute. But the cause of labour suffered more than the capitalists by the deplorable occurrences of that date. It was ever so—ever will be so; if on no higher grounds than those of "policy," such violence must be avoided. Otherwise than the above, the history of industrial warfare has been singularly free from actual outrage for a period of twenty years.   It was hoped, nay, it is hoped, that it is now a closed page in that history.   The revival of stories current a quarter of a century ago in the drama called the *People's Idol*, at the Olympic, was scarcely justifiable, was certainly not in good taste at a moment when the relations between labour and capital are sufficiently strained, and need no stimulus to accentuate or intensify them.   Industrial strife is even now bitter enough in all conscience ; but for intensity and bitterness it pales before the political strife of to-day in which all the worst passions of human nature are brought into play, and hatred is preached unblushingly on the platform, in the pulpit, in the press, and in Parliament, without even shame.

The only excuse that can be offered for the dynamite scene in the *People's Idol*, was its effectiveness as a scenic display, in which attribute it was perhaps unrivalled for stage effect, in so far as the mere explosion was concerned.   Its moral effect is, however, questionable ; and the figment of truth in the dramatic conception does not justify the lesson it conveyed.   The only plea that can be urged in extenuation of the representation there made is to be found in some sentences from recent articles in the *Nineteenth Century*, in the form of a dialogue by a "champion" of labour, one of the leaders of the New Trade Unionism.   In the October number, 1890, under the title of " A Multitude of Councillors," Blake, the "people's representative" in those dialogues, tells "one little incident," which, he says, " may help" one of his listeners "to form an accurate opinion without undergoing an experience which might deprive the House of Lords of the chance of ever hearing him again."   Listen !

"One night it was ascertained that a train full of

'blacklegs' was to be run into the docks without stopping at any of the places at which, on previous occasions, the pickets had been able to get at the new-comers and cajole or intimidate or bribe them into refusing to work. This was a serious matter, for if it had been found that this experiment was successful it would have been repeated, and train after train would have run into the docks the thousands of men all over England who were eager to accept any work at a pound a week. It was as though an army that had invested a fortress, and knew that its garrison was on the point of capitulating for lack of food, suddenly heard that the besieged had cut through the lines at a place from which they could draw supplies sufficient to enable them to hold out for months.

"Luckily, the train never started, as the 'blacklegs' were dissuaded from coming before they left the town where they were enlisted. But, had it come down the line, I have reason to believe that it is probable that it would have left the metals at the top of a steep embankment." ! ! !

This learned labour leader and advocate of mob-law, argues that "strikes can only be successful in the present condition of the labour market when the strikers can prevent 'blacklegs' taking their places. And that means the use of force and violence." And this force and violence is to be used to " prevent a starving man from taking employment." How the editor of the *Nineteenth Century* could so far forget himself as to insert, or allow to be inserted, in a respectable magazine, such diabolical street-corner clap-trap passes comprehension. The moral sense of the editor must have been twisted in some way by political obliquity to permit such an insult to his readers, or base calumny to the working men of England, to be published under his

M

authority. There is no justification for wholesale murder, "in the present condition of the labour market," even if Unionists can only "enforce a sufficiently deterrent punishment on those—'blacklegs'—who accept work." The writer alluded to professes to believe that strikes can only be successful in the present condition of the labour market when the strikers can prevent "blacklegs taking their places" by "the use of force and violence;" and he asserts that this can only be prevented by the Commonwealth enacting that "work shall not be done except on the strikers' terms." It is nothing less than a foul slander upon working-men to allege that they depend upon the use of force and violence; and it shows an utter ignorance of industrial history to contend that strikes cannot be carried out and won without the use of the kind of force and violence here indicated. The writer elsewhere says: "It is not I, but you, who advocate the settlement of these disputes by such primitive if effective methods;" but such advocacy belongs only to that select circle who now and for some time past have sought to turn Trade Unions into political machines, for the purpose of promoting a bastard socialist propaganda.

CHAPTER VIII.

THE "NEW TRADE UNIONISM."—Part II.

STATE AID, STATE REGULATION, AND STATE CONTROL.

In what consist the New Trade Unionism—Labour Bureaus—Decision of Congress thereupon — Municipal Organization of Workers, Factories and Workshops—France, National Workshops—Opposed in principle to Trade Unionism—Eight Hour Day by Act of Parliament—For Government Employés—Miners—Shop Assistants —Early Closing of Shops—For all Trades—Decision of Congress—Demands of Public Servants—Of Miners—Proposals of the Latter—The Eight Hours Bill—Reasons therefor, Examined—Statistical Report of Working Hours in Mines—Government Return on same —Analysis of the Return—Accidents in Mines and Long Hours—Synopsis of Return—Universal Eight Hour Day—Origin of the Demand—May-day Demonstrations—Continental—London Demonstration—Bradford and Dundee Trades Congresses—Votes of Trade Unions—Liverpool Congress—Members represented, Analysis of Vote—Exaggerations—Value of the Vote—Dockers' Decision—Engineers' Decision—Textile and other Trades—Attitude of the Parliamentary Committee—The Eight Hours Bill.

THE elements composing what is termed the New Trade Unionism are not to be found in the constitution, organization, and rules of the Unions started within the last two or three years. In these respects they either conform to the experience of modern Unions, or they revive the practices of the older Unions. There is scarcely a feature in which any of them differ from types of Unions long in existence.

In what, then, consists the "New Trade Unionism," of which we hear so much? Mainly in the aspirations, conduct, modes of advocacy, and methods of procedure of, and also in the expressions used, and principles inculcated by, the new leaders in labour movements, in their speeches, and by their acts. This New Unionism has been formulated and promulgated at Trades Union Congresses, at other Congresses and Conferences, and at the meetings held in various parts of the country; and in letters and articles which have appeared in the newspaper, press, and public journals from the pens of the new leaders. Only the more important of these pronouncements need be examined and commented upon in this chapter.

I. **Labour Bureaus.**—The institution of Labour Bureaus, or the establishment of Labour Registries, is one of the acknowledged objects of the Dockers' Union. Singularly enough this is the first time that any such project has had the sanction of a *bonâ-fide* Trade Union. All the older Unions repudiate every such scheme. It has hitherto been regarded as opposed in principle to Trade Unionism. When Mr. Alsager Hay Hill endeavoured to establish such a bureau, he was assailed and denounced on the ground that it was a blow at Trade Unions. On the other hand, employers have often favoured the idea, but it has not been persisted in by reason of the opposition of the Trades.

At the recent Trades Union Congress held in Liverpool, September 1890, the following resolution was moved by one of the London delegates representing the "South Side Labour Protection League"—

"That, in the opinion of this Congress, in order to carry on more effectually the organization of the large mass of unorganized labour, to bring into closer combination those sections of labour already organized, to provide means for communication and the interchange of information between all sections of industry, and the proper tabulation of statistics as to employment, &c., of advantage to the workmen, it is necessary that a labour exchange, on the model of the Paris Bourse des Travail, should be provided and maintained by public funds in every industrial centre in the kingdom."

The above resolution was seconded by another London delegate. It was urged that the Paris Municipality paid for a similar institution £120,000 per year, and that its control was entirely in the hands of delegates of trade organizations. The mover said that "not a single delegate could deny the necessity for such an institution, in every industrial centre." The Congress evidently thought otherwise, for only 74 voted for the resolution, while 92 voted against it. As there were 457 delegates present, no fewer than 291 delegates did not even care to vote on the question at all. How, indeed, could it be otherwise? All Trade Unions of any stability act as their own labour registry; they keep a "vacant book," in which are entered the names of the members out of work, and each member in work is supposed to exert himself to find an opening for un-employed members. A Labour Exchange, such as that indicated, would, it is thought, rather tend to destroy than promote Trade Unionism. This evidently was the opinion of the Congress. A registry for unorganized labour might be useful, though all past experience points the other way. The proposal, however, shows to what an extent the New Trade Unionism seeks for Government aid, or municipal assistance, in labour movements.

II. Municipal Organization of Workers.—The most astonishing resolution carried by the Congress was the following—

" Whereas the ever-changing methods of manufacture affect large numbers of workers adversely, by throwing them out of employment, without compensation for loss of situation, and whereas those persons are in many instances driven to destitution, crime, and pauperism : Resolved, that this Congress is of opinion that power should at once be granted to each municipality or County Council to establish workshops and factories under municipal control, where such persons shall be put to useful employment, and that it be an instruction to the Parliamentary Committee to at once take the matter in hand."

The foregoing resolution was proposed by the president of the Dockers' Union, and was seconded by the Secretary. The resolution, said the newspapers at the time, was carried "to the astonishment of everybody" present. To the resolution was added : " That Trade Union wages be paid." Neither the resolution, nor the proposer or seconder, attempted to indicate the kind of business to be carried on in municipal workshops ; the omission was a prudent one. At the same Congress the following resolution was also carried—
" This Congress strongly protests against all parochial bodies using pauper labour to the detriment of the firewood-cutting trade, it having been most conclusively proved that such labour is carried on at a loss to the ratepayers, and we call upon the Parliamentary Committee to use their influence with the Local Government Board with a view to stopping this unfair system." Pertaining to the same subject this further resolution was moved—" That this Congress regrets the Parliamentary Committee have not succeeded in carrying

out the instructions of the Congress, given by unanimous votes during the last three years, with reference to prison labour, and hereby instructs the new Committee to at once take steps to induce the Government to stop prison-made goods coming into the open market." In support of the first of the last two resolutions, it was urged that there was a loss of 59 per cent. to the ratepayers; that a strike cost £950, whereas but for pauper labour it would only have cost £200; and that, in one case, the painting of a workhouse was deferred until pauper painters enough were in the house to do the necessary work. Subsequently the resolution was carried with an addition forbidding "the employment of pauper labour generally by all public bodies." In support of the last it was stated that the mat-makers, of all the 150 trades carried on in prisons, suffered most. That portion reflecting upon the Parliamentary Committee being omitted, the resolution was carried. Those resolutions plainly indicate that pauper labour and prison labour must not be brought into competition with non-pauper and free labour; the reasons are obvious; all such competition tends to press down wages in the trades affected. But what of labour performed in municipal workshops? If the persons so employed are put to some "useful employment," and the goods so made or manu-factured are to be sold in open market, will not such labour come into competition with outside labour? How is it to be avoided? Supposing that the price of the goods were fixed by Act of Parliament, or by the municipal authority, one of two things would probably happen; either that prices would be fixed so high, that the goods would not sell; or be fixed so low, that dealers would purchase them in preference to other goods made elsewhere, provided that

they were of equal quality.   In any case, competition would
be inevitable; unless, as is most likely, the articles were of
such a character that they would be practically useless, as
marketable commodities; in which event the loss would
not be the fictitious 59 per cent., but a hundred per cent.,
and possibly something more.

It is generally supposed that the idea of national workshops originated with M. Louis Blanc, in 1848, when he
was President of the "Government Labour Commission."
He states that he "had absolutely nothing to do with the
*most absurd and fatal establishment of these national work-
shops,*[1] which were nothing better, and nothing else, than the
regimental embodiment of thousands of workmen of different trades, aggregated pell-mell, and set upon a kind of
labour not less unprofitable than ridiculous."   He goes on
to say that "public opinion in Europe has been brought to
father upon me the 'national workshops,' in spite of official
documents, and of the very confessions of the real contrivers,
all proving, beyond possibility of dispute, that the 'national
workshops' were established by my adversaries in the
council, notwithstanding my resistance in direct opposition
to my views, and for the express purpose of counter-
balancing my influence, is one of the most striking illustrations on record of the power of calumny."   M. Louis Blanc
has rightly indicated the nature of such workshops.   There
would have to be either separate workshops for every
industry, the workers at which are liable to reverses through
lack of employment; or the workers would be turned pell-
mell into such workshops, without regard to fitness, training,

---

[1] See M. Louis Blanc's Letter, giving "an Account of the Legislation affecting Labour in France, 1860;" also his *Historical Revolutions*,
Chapter IX.

or competency at any given work. In the first case, there would have to be separate provision for dockers and clerks, engineers and scavengers, building operatives and, chimney-sweepers, textile operatives and pitmen, shoe-makers, tailors, hatters, dressmakers, washerwomen, and all other classes of workers without exception ; in the latter case, all kinds of workers would have to be located in one place under overlookers, probably as ignorant of the re-quirements of industry as the workers were incapable of performing the tasks allotted to them, individually and collectively.

The absurdity of the position in which Trade Unions find themselves by the passing of such a resolution is this : Municipal workshops and Trade Unions are incompatible ; the one would inevitably destroy the other, the weakest going to the wall. The movers of the resolution apparently did not see this, and the delegates who voted for it did not seem in the least to care about it. One solitary protest only was raised in Congress against this preposterous reso-lution. Municipal workshops must be either one thing or the other. They cannot fit in with the present conditions of industry and trade ; they would obviously be an in-congruity in existing industrial economy. Socialists favour the notion of handing everything over to the State—pro-viding work, doling out payment, furnishing provisions, re-lieving sickness, and burying the dead. They believe that the State should do everything for the individual, transacting all business, carrying on all trade and industry, holding in the palm of its hand, so to speak, all capital and all labour. They seem to think that men can be rounded off by a lathe, to a fixed quantity, to the gauge of State calipers, so that none shall be bigger or less than others. In such a process the calipers must be fixed to a small diameter, thus levelling down, not up, as most sensible men hope to be possible. That Trade Unionists, and above all, delegates at a Trades Congress, should vote for such a resolution is incomprehensible. The new leaders went to Congress to give guidance; they led Congress into a quagmire, from which the Parliamentary Committee will find themselves unable to extricate the Trade Unions of England—except they totally disregard the proposition to hand over all industry to municipalities.

III. **Eight Hour Day, by Act of Parliament.**—The proposal of all others which the new Trade Unionists sought to ingraft upon, and had determined to carry as a portion of the programme of the Trades Union Congress, was the "legal Eight Hour day;" and they actually succeeded in their design after a stormy battle. The new leaders, with their socialist allies, had been working to that end for over two years. At the Dundee Congress, in 1889, the note was sounded, and, in the interval between that date and the Congress of 1890, an active propaganda was carried on in various centres and at Trade Union meetings. The advocates of legislative action, in regard to the hours of labour, differ somewhat in their proposals. It will be necessary, therefore, to refer to several measures put forward for limiting the hours of adult-male labour in various directions.

(a) The proposal which first found acceptance to any large extent, was an Eight Hours Bill for all Government employés. This was enlarged so as to include all persons employed by municipalities and all other local bodies— County Councils, Vestries, Boards of Works, School Boards, Sanitary Authorities, and all other similar bodies. The plea put forward is that the State and Local Authorities, being employers of labour, should show a good example by starting an Eight Hour day as the normal and recognized working day for the whole of their employés. There can be no possible objection to any public body fixing the hours of labour at eight per day, provided that it is done by its own act, as employers of labour. The objection is to legislative action, whether by an Act of Parliament or by a resolution of the House. In either case it becomes a decision of the State, and is therefore an interference with the hours of adult male labour, which is outside the domain of law.

(b) The next proposal was that there should be an Eight Hours Bill for miners. This was sanctioned and promoted by the " National Federation of Miners," called into existence in 1889. The Bill is now supported by the coal-mining population in most districts, except Durham and Northumberland. In so far as legislative action is concerned, it is opposed by Durham and Northumberland, in which counties the actual working-day is already less than seven hours in most cases. The proposal does not extend to all workers in and about the mines, being mainly confined to hewers, men working at the face. The demand is that the time shall be reckoned from " bank to bank," that is, from the moment they descend into the pit to the moment they reach the top again. Recent statistics seem to show that the actual working time rarely exceeds 8 hours and $25\frac{1}{2}$ minutes on the average, even in collieries where the demand for an Eight Hours Mines Bill is most pronounced. To put into motion the elaborate machinery of Statute Law for the purpose of cutting off $25\frac{1}{2}$ minutes of working time in a day seems preposterous, especially in view of the fact that coal-miners have shown a capacity for organization and self-help by mutual effort, far surpassing any other body of men in the kingdom. So well organized are they that their will is practically law, in so far as any reasonable proposition is concerned. That eight hours in the mine is long enough, none will dispute ; that six hours of continuous work would be sufficient, few will deny. In seeking a further reduction in working hours, most will wish the miners God-speed. But the mischiefs of State regulation are such that some of their best friends hesitate to commit themselves to any measure, the principle of which involves a return to the darker days of labour struggles, when industry was fettered and shackled by State control, and men were denied the right to combine for mutual protection and assistance.

(c) The Shop Assistants' League demand a Twelve Hours' Bill and a weekly half-holiday. But at a meeting held at Toynbee Hall in London, on Sunday, February 9th, 1890, "an Eight Hours proposal was only rejected by a small majority." The motion, however, for eight hours did not come from a shop assistant, but from one who has no kind of connection with the business in which shopmen are engaged. But a large minority of the men present seem to have swallowed the bait, without apparently stopping to inquire what would result if such a measure were carried. It is true that women and girls are employed in establishments where it is proposed to institute shorter hours by Act of Parliament, but many of these dread any action which might further interfere with their right to live by labour. That the hours in shops are, as a rule, too long, no one will deny ; but an Act of Parliament to regulate the number of hours would probably be equally disastrous to the shopmen and shopwomen and to the shopkeepers.

(d) Singularly enough, some shopkeepers are themselves

favourable to an Eight O'Clock Closing Bill. Sir John Lubbock brought in Bills in 1888, 1889, and 1890 for this purpose. He proposes that all shops (with exceptions) shall be closed, in any local or municipal boundary, by a vote of two-thirds of the resident shopkeepers affected. The majority proposed is large, but is it right to compel one-third of the shopkeepers in any locality to close against their will? Without saying one word against the general principle of the majority ruling, there are cases in which no majority, however large and powerful, has the right to coerce the minority. In connection with these two proposals (c and d), the fact that shops are kept open later in poor districts than in more wealthy localities, proves that there are great if not insuperable difficulties in the way of legislative action, restraining men from doing what they have a perfect right to do.

(e) The culminating proposal is that there shall be a universal Eight Hour day for all trades and industries. The resolution upon this subject, carried by the Trades Union Congress, being as follows—

"That, in the opinion of this Congress, the time has arrived when steps should be taken to reduce the working hours in all trades to eight per day, or to a maximum of forty-eight hours per week; and while recognizing the power and influence of trade organizations, it is of opinion that the speediest and best method to obtain this reduction for the workers generally is by Parliamentary enactment. This Congress, therefore, instructs the Parliamentary Committee to take immediate steps for the furtherance of this object."

To the foregoing resolution, the representative of the Durham miners moved the following amendment—

" 'That, in the opinion of this Congress, it is of the utmost importance that an Eight Hour day should be secured at once by such trades as may desire it, or for whom it may be made to apply, without injury to those employed in such trades; further, it considers that to relegate this important question to the Imperial Parliament, which is necessarily, from its position, antagonistic to the rights of labour, will only indefinitely delay this much-needed reform."

The issue was thus clearly put—whether the Eight Hour day shall be obtained by voluntary effort and mutual arrangement, or by legislation, with the following result— 173 voted for the amendment, and 181 against; majority against the amendment, 8. For the original resolution, 193; against it, 155; the majority in favour of the resolution, as a substantive motion, was therefore 38, in a Congress of 457 delegates.

With respect to the several before-mentioned proposals, it is not possible to gauge accurately the *bonâ-fide* character of the demand, or its extent. Two things are, however, clear, namely, that many have, by popular demonstrations and otherwise, declared for an Eight Hour day, and also that the distinctive votes of the Unions where taken have been, for the most part, adverse to legislative action. The actual position seems to be this—

(1) Government employés are probably generally in favour of eight hours, in preference to nine, or any other number, provided always that the rates of pay remained the same. In all Government Departments and elsewhere the desire is doubtless for the maximum amount of pay for a minimum amount of work, reckoned by time at least. No fault can be found with this. It is the commercial principle which underlies the entire industrial and trading system,

from the sale of apples to traffic in securities—the highest price or rate for the fewest rosy-cheeked apples or the least quantity of scrip. This is the system that rules in every transaction in commerce, trade, industry, and finance, from dealings in a huckster's shop to dealings on 'Change. If, therefore, public servants, whether under the State or the Local Authority, seek maximum wages or salaries for shorter working hours, they are not to blame. The Executive Government, or the Local Authority, stand in the position of employers of labour to the employés, and they are also the guardians of the public purse. They have the right to bargain with those they employ for the benefit of the public service, always with due regard to the rightful claims of their servants and workpeople, both as regards payment and hours of work. The country is never disposed to grumble at generous treatment ; it is indeed rather lenient in that respect. The objection here taken is to the doctrine that the State, whether by an Act of Parliament, or by motion, should take a step which would have the effect of fixing rates of wages or pay, and limiting the hours of labour in the various industries of the kingdom, by an act of executive authority, the effects of which might be far-reaching, beyond calculation, upon the entire commercial, trading, and industrial system of the country. At the same time, any sweating, lowering of wages, or extension of working hours by the State or Local Authority, in the capacity of employers, deserve the severest condemnation, as a matter both of policy and principle.

(2) The mining population are not wholly agreed upon the question of a legal Eight Hour day; but it is asserted that some 212,000, or nearly one-half of the total number, have declared in its favour. Durham, Northumberland, and

probably parts of Cumberland and Cleveland rely upon
voluntary action.   In the two former counties the miners
have won not merely an Eight Hour day, but seven, or even
less than seven hours, in some cases.   With the commencement of the present year (1891) the drawers and others
have had their hours reduced to fifty per week, with an
advance of wages into the bargain, owing to the self-denial
of the miners in accepting five per cent. advance in lieu of
twenty per cent. demanded.   This concession will probably
affect the two adjoining counties in the immediate future.
The National Federation of Miners, representing about one-
half the total in the United Kingdom support the legal
Eight Hour day.   About this there is no doubt, and their
views demand a respectful hearing.   The fact, however, that
a majority supports this or that policy is by no means
a conclusive argument in its favour.   Majorities are sometimes apt to go wrong.   In this case we think they are
wrong as to the means, though they are right in the object
they seek.   The miners sigh for shorter hours—more ·
leisure ; the aspiration is a good and noble one ; but there
is grave danger in the remedy they propose as a cure for
the evils complained of.

The National Federation of Miners support two Bills
relating to this subject.   The one prepared under the
auspices of the Federation, entitled—"A Bill to amend the
Coal Miners' Regulation Act, 1887," which provides that
(§ 5), " No person under the age of twenty-one years shall
be employed, or allowed in any mine below ground for the
purpose of employment, for more than eight consecutive
hours in twenty-four hours ; " § 6 provides also that " no
woman or girl shall be employed in manual labour above
ground in connection with any mine."   This Bill, therefore,

only deals with persons under the age of twenty-one years, and not generally with all adult males. The proposal to abolish female labour on the pit-brow was stoutly opposed in 1887, and was defeated because of the opposition of the women themselves whose right to labour was sought to be interfered with. The growth of opinion in this direction is, however, a healthful sign of progress.

The Miners' Eight Hours Bill did not originally emanate from the National Federation of Miners, but it has been adopted by that body. The Bill of this Session (1890-91) is backed by two out of the five miners' representatives in the House of Commons—Mr. Burt, Mr. Fenwick, and Mr. Wilson being opposed to its provisions. It provides that— " A person shall not, in one day of twenty-four hours, be employed underground in any mine for a period exceeding eight hours from the time of his leaving the surface of the ground to the time of his ascent thereto, except in the case of accident or other emergency." § 3. "Any employer or agent of any employer, employing or permitting to be employed, any person in contravention of this enactment, shall be liable to a penalty not exceeding forty shillings for each offence, to be recovered in the same manner in which any penalty under the Acts relating to factories and work-shops is recoverable." The entire onus and responsibility are thus thrown upon the employer or his agent, these alone being held liable for the penalties. It is passing strange that the men who clamour for the Bill should seek to shirk all responsibility in the event of non-compliance with section 2 of the measure. It looks as if the men were conscious of the fact that they required an active agency outside themselves to prevent them from violating their own law. This is rather a reversal of procedure. The men demand

N

class legislation for themselves, for their own protection, and yet are not willing to share the responsibility for any breach thereof, committed possibly without the consent or even the knowledge, at the time, of the employer or his agent. The proposal is monstrous; there is no reciprocity or mutuality in it. Even if the provisions of the measure were otherwise just and reasonable, the penalty clause is outrageous. Men who shirk the penalties will not be over particular in offending against the law should circumstances permit.

The demand for legislation has led to inquiry into its reasonableness, and the grounds upon which this exceptional measure for a legal Eight Hour day are supported. Four authentic documents have been issued throwing light upon one or another aspect of the question, each of which deserves a brief examination. They are as follows—

I. **The Annual Report of the Yorkshire Miners' Association.**—This report states officially the Miners' own reasons "why they want the Eight Hour Day," thus—

a. (1) Because of the unhealthy and unsanitary condition of our mines;

(2) Because the work is laborious and dangerous;

(3) Because we want more time for recreation, rest, and leisure;

(4) Because we want to work more uniformly.

b. The report proceeds to state the reasons why Miners desire "to obtain the Eight Hours by legislative enactment," thus—

(1) Because it will be done most effectively;

(2) Because we want uniformity, and if secured by law, we shall have a uniform Eight Hour Day throughout the length and breadth of the land;

(3) Because it will lessen unhealthy competition in the coal

trade, and thus bring about quietude at our collieries, and anxiety for the safety of the mine, instead of increased output.

(4) Because it will bring about a better feeling between working-men and their employers, and prevent the possibility of strikes and lock-outs, as no doubt such would obtain if sought by the rough-and-ready means suggested by some of our advisers.

c. Having stated their reasons for the Eight Hour day, and also for the attainment of that object by legislative enactment, they go on to give a " list of examples where the State has interfered" in support of their contention, thus—

(1) Closing of public-houses on week-days and Sundays ;

(2) Child and female labour in Mills and Factories ;

(3) Dealing with female and boy labour in Mines;

(4) Church and State (Ireland) and the Truck Acts, and what is further intended, by interfering with tenant-farmer and landlord in Ireland, half-holiday for workers in shops, and other matters of a like character. The report adds—" We know the law steps in between the man who strikes another on the jaw, and sends him to gaol."

Here, then, we have the miners' case stated in full by their own able and accredited representatives. They know all the facts, and are as capable of defending the position they have taken up as any men are in the country. With no disrespect to those men, without calling in question their ability, their judgment, or their conscientiousness, we venture to assert that a weaker case for instituting great legislative changes was never submitted to the public. (1) The question of unhealthy and unsanitary conditions belongs to quite another sphere of legislation, namely, the Public Health Acts, and it behoves the Government to do all in their power to improve those conditions, and to see

that every reasonable precaution is taken to prevent injury
to health in all occupations alike, whether in the mine or
elsewhere. (2) That coal-mining is both laborious and
dangerous, all will admit; so also is the work of blast furnace-
men, railway employés, sailors and firemen in the Mercantile
Marine, and other workpeople in various industries. It is
a question of degree—where we are to stop? The Miners
think, apparently, that the legislation proposed should begin
and end with mining. Other trades do not think so; nor
could it stop, if once initiated. (3) More leisure and rest are
required by the vast majority of workers; and, if this plea
is to have weight, those who work the longest hours first
need legislative interference. (4) Uniformity in working
hours is scarcely practicable, even in mines. If uniformity
be desired, then those who work less than eight hours must
conform to the Eight Hour law—what would Durham and
Northumberland say to this? Uniformity in conditions
would mean equality in wages also; do the miners plead
for a uniform wage as well as uniform hours? (5) The
lessening of "unhealthy competition" by law is a wide
subject; must it not also involve interference with the prices
of commodities as well as rates of wages? (6) The "list
of examples" given can hardly be said to be quite on all
fours with the legislation proposed, not even in a single
instance. (7) The prophecy that an Eight Hour law would
"prevent the possibility of strikes and lock-outs" is not
likely to be fulfilled, judging by the rather plentiful crop of
strikes in the mining industry during the last two years.
If strikes did not take place on the question of hours, they
would arise in the adjustment of rates of wages to the hours
worked, which would practically mean the same thing.
On their own showing, the case, in the language of the

Scotch Courts, is not proven ; and, if it be true, as one of the ablest miners' delegates recently stated, that the mine-owners rather forced on than resisted the shorter hours in Durham and Northumberland, the miners will not need legislation to secure to them eight hours as the normal working day in the mining industry.

II. " **Statistical Report** supplied by Checkweighers and District Secretaries, of the hours worked at collieries in every mining district in Great Britain, except Durham, North-umberland, and Cleveland." This Report, dated October 1890, is very elaborate, comprising thirteen columns in which details are recorded. No totals and no averages are given or attempted, although the words " total average " are printed at the foot in each case. The object of this statistical report is to furnish support to the advocates of the Eight Hours Bill. To what extent it is relied upon for that purpose, is not very clear ; nor is it possible to test the accuracy of any of the figures, or appraise their full value. Taking the figures as they stand, it appears that at 223 collieries the working hours were 8 per day or under; at 240 the hours were from 8½ to 9 per day; and at 121 the hours were above 9 per day. Those were the hours supposed to be worked at the face ; but whether those hours were worked every day, or only 4, 4½, 5, 5½, or 6 days per week, is not stated. As this is the only test by which we can ascertain whether the maximum of 48 hours per week is actually worked, the report does not help us much.

On Monday, November 3rd, 1890, the *Star* newspaper published what purported to be a condensed summary of this lengthy official report, in which it is stated that the figures given showed " that the average time worked at the face was 8 hours 25½ minutes ; boys 8 hours 48 minutes ;

and labourers 8 hours 49 minutes." That paragraph, which had the appearance of being an official statement, or of being inspired, said—"This does not take into account the time occupied in travelling underground, which must be reckoned in the miner's day, and which averages 39 minutes." It further stated that "183,720 miners concerned in the Return would be reduced by 65 minutes," under an Eight Hour day. No such calculation appears in the report; the accuracy of the above description is not therefore vouched for. There is no possibility of ascertaining from the Return whether, upon their own showing, the miners at the 584 collieries specified work 48 hours per week, on the average, or not. The Return is therefore defective, to this extent, as positive evidence of the actual working hours, however valuable it may be in other respects. The two reports named may be taken as the official statement of the miners for the Eight Hour Bill; it is their brief—their advocates must make the best of the materials there presented.

III. **Hours of Labour in and about Mines.**—This is a Government Return, granted on the motion of Mr. Provand. It is important in many ways; it is official; it gives the actual number of hours daily worked by miners and others at all the mines throughout Great Britain, together with the intervals for rest and meals, the total number of days per week usually worked, &c. The details furnished are so varied, and the time worked in the several mining districts is so different, that a tabular synopsis of the whole Return is not practicable in a brief form. The following summary will, however, give a tolerably accurate view of the general features of all the tables in their bearing upon the Eight Hours Question. The figures here presented refer, in all cases, to the coal-getters, and give the actual working hours at the face, deducting the time for meals and rest, and also the time occupied in descending the pit, travelling to the workings, and returning again to the surface. The whole is divided into fourteen districts, over which the Mines' Inspectors have jurisdiction, the totals and averages being found by adding the total number of hours worked at the face in the several sub-districts, and dividing the total hours by the number of sub-districts. The same process is gone through with the number of days usually worked at the pit in each case. The result is given in the form of the average number of hours and decimals of 100 ; and of days, decimals of 100, or fraction of a tenth, as the case may be. The average usual working hours are then found, as subsequently given. The method of procedure is thus explained at length in order that the reader, who may not be able to get the Return, shall feel that the figures are not cooked to support a foregone conclusion. The following then are the net working hours of miners at the face—

District.	Average number of hours per day worked in the pit.	Usual number of days actually worked in each week.	Number of hours actually worked per week.
I. East Scotland ...	7·52	5·3	40·10
II. West Scotland ...	7·54	5·44	41·42
III. Newcastle... ...	6·61	5·31	32·20
IV. Durham	6·27	5·66	34·00
V. Yorkshire ...	7·4½	4·9	35·20
VI. Manchester ...	7·82	5·53	42·00
VII. Liverpool	7·58	5·61	43·00
VIII. Midland	7·64	5·36	40·00
IX. North Wales, &c.	7·4	5·80	43·50
X. North Stafford...	7·47	5·8	37·50
XI. South Stafford...	7·62	5·15	38·50
XII. South Western	7·42	5·65	39·50
XIII. South Wales ...	8·6	5·7	46·00

In the Cornwall and Devon district (XIV.), the usual

number of days worked are not stated, but the figures given would indicate that the men work about 40 hours per week. If the figures given be at all correct, and they have not been challenged, though the Return has been out a considerable time, it would appear that in no district, save South Wales, would the men working at the face average more than 48 hours per week, allowing 39 minutes as the average time for descending, travelling underground, and returning to the surface. This calculation would make the time, from bank to bank, 49½ hours in South Wales. North Wales on the same calculation would be about 47 hours, the Liverpool district about 46½ hours, and Manchester district 45½ hours; in all other cases the actual number of hours worked per week, from bank to bank, would be very much under 45 hours per week.

To make matters still more clear, it appears that the total number of hours in the mine, from bank to bank, including meal times and rest, per week were approximately as follows— East Scotland, 47 hours; West Scotland, 47½ hours; New-castle, 42½ hours; Durham, 43 hours; Yorkshire, 42·8 hours; Manchester, 49½ hours; Liverpool, 47 hours; Midland, 47·10 hours; North Stafford, 44·3 hours; South Stafford 39½ hours; South Western, 48·10 hours; South Wales, 51½ hours. Thus in the South Western district an average of 8 hours per day was exceeded by 10 minutes per week, or under 2 minutes per day; Manchester district by 90 minutes, or 15 minutes per day; and South Wales by 3½ hours per week, or 35 minutes per day. In another form the facts seem to be these: 18,352 men worked on an average two minutes per day beyond eight hours, or 48 hours per week; 19,203 men worked 15 minutes per day over that maximum; and 31,432 men worked 35 minutes per day in excess of 48 hours per week. It seems, therefore, that

under 69,000 men work in the mines beyond an average of
an Eight Hour day, or 48 hours per week, while the majority,
according to the Return, work less than that number of
hours. Is it right, or reasonable, to ask Parliament to
interfere with adult male labour, to enforce an Eight Hour
day under such circumstances? Can it be contended that
a case of great hardship is made out to justify such interference? The want of uniformity might be a deplorable
thing ; but there is a remedy for it, if remedy be at all
possible. The men have the power in their own hands to
effect it by combination.

· IV. **Coal Mines, Explosions.**—This Return (No. 6, 1890)
was granted on the motion of Mr. Charles Fenwick, one of
the miners' representatives in the House of Commons, and
the Secretary of the Trades Union Congress Parliamentary
Committee. It had been alleged that explosions in mines
were often due to the long hours worked, and it was contended that an Eight Hours Bill would diminish such catas-
trophes. The Return in question covers nominally a period
of ten years, but in reality it extends to nearly twelve years,
1879 to 1890, inclusive. No summary is given, but the
present writer has tabulated the whole of the figures, the
following being the result :—Within the period covered by
the Return there were a total of 202 explosions, the number
of lives lost being 1,951. The hour of the shift in which
these 202 explosions occurred, and the total number of
deaths resulting therefrom, in each case, were as follows—

The Hour of the Shift in which the explosion occurred—

	1st.	2nd.	3rd.	4th.	5th.	6th.	7th.	8th.	9th.	Totals.
Total number of explosions	47	22	29	26	24	17	11	16	10	202
Do., of deaths	130	322	278	521	334	69	183	60	95	1951

The foregoing effectually disposes of any argument in support of the view that an Eight Hour day by legal enactment would materially diminish the number of fatal accidents, for if the two last hours were cut off, the total number of accidents, in the dozen years, would only be decreased by 26, and deaths by 155.

The case for legislative action and interference by law cannot be said to be conclusive, even in so far as the miners are concerned. Nevertheless, few will deny that eight hours, seven hours, or even six hours' hard work in the mine is exhaustive enough, in an occupation at once laborious and dangerous. The miners deserve every concession they can obtain as regards pay, leisure, and better conditions, by combination, conciliation, and the force of public opinion. But to resort to legislation is too dangerous an experiment, the perils of which would more than counterbalance any possible or conceivable advantages which it might confer upon those who seek it. For this reason, it is a project of law to be opposed.

UNIVERSAL EIGHT HOUR DAY FOR ALL TRADES.

The aspiration for an Eight Hour day is by no means new; it is the revival of a sentiment long associated with labour movements, but recently intensified by the action of the Social Democrats. The demand for a universal Eight Hour day by Act of Parliament is, however, new in this country. To quote the words of the late John Bright, it is "the offspring and spawn of feeble minds," transplanted from the continent of Europe into this country by men who have misappropriated to themselves the name of Socialists. Even the Anarchists, who denounce all law, and by implication all regulation, are infatuated enough to desire a "legal Eight Hour day." Few of them seem to have any respect for law as it is, whatever they may profess with regard to law as they would have it be. The advocates for the legal regulation of the hours of labour appeal to America and Australia in support of their contention, forgetful of the fact that the industrial conditions are not the same, not even approximately similar to those in Great Britain. But fitness is not their forte. With an utter incapacity to invent any new phase, and apply it to labour movement, some of them show a wonderful capability for appropriation, only they dignify the act by giving it another name. The varying phases of the legal Eight Hour day agitation will be understood by a brief review of its recent history.

(a) The sole honour of instituting and leading off the agitation for a legal Eight Hour day, belongs to the Social Democratic Federation—a body which prides itself upon being non-political, in the party sense of that term, but which, curiously enough, usually confines its operations to attacks upon Liberals, and especially upon the Labour Representatives in Parliament. For some time the "Eight-Hour Day," and the "Social Democratic Revolution," were the two chief cries of the insignificant knots of listeners from time to time addressed at street corners, in Trafalgar Square, Hyde Park, Clerkenwell Green, and other places. Gradually the expression, "Social Democratic Revolution," dropped out of the programme, or it was less distinctly heard. The Eight Hours became more and more the war-cry as new adherents threw in their lot with the movement. The subject was mooted at meetings, then at Conferences, then at Congresses, until at last a pronouncement was made in its favour by an "International Congress," when the demand was tacked on to the Labour programme. There was little difficulty in getting the two International Congresses, which met in Paris on October 29th, 1883, and the later one on August 23rd, 1886, to endorse the Eight Hour movement. It was much more difficult to get a pronouncement in its favour on November 6th, 1888, at the International Congress held in London. A resolution was however carried, by a fluke, towards the end of the Congress, in spite of the protest of the majority of the English delegates. To the Socialists, the manner of its adoption was immaterial; the fact, to them, was sufficient; and it was followed by efforts to secure the adhesion of the London Trades' Council, and other Trades' Councils in the kingdom; and also of the Trade Unions, and subsequently of the Trades Union Congress. The Social Democrats were certainly active, most active; their activity fanned into a flickering flame the submerged elements of discontent, and they gave ready utterance to the despairing cry of the slums of London, so long a disgrace to our boasted civilization.

(b) In 1889 the idea was conceived of making "a great demonstration in favour of an Eight Hour day." The date selected was the 1st of May, 1890. The intention was that there should be simultaneous gatherings in all the chief centres of industry, "to demand an Eight Hour legal working day." The meetings accordingly took place, and resolutions to that effect were carried. In London the demonstration was a fiasco, for the trades did not turn out. The first of May was specially selected by the "Socialist League"; the time fixed was 4 p.m.; the place Hyde Park. In the evening there was to be a torchlight gathering on Clerkenwell Green. The demonstrators were to assemble on the

Thames Embankment at 2·30 p.m., and march to the Park, avoiding Trafalgar Square. The resolution prepared by the Socialist League was to be submitted at those meetings, and at all the provincial gatherings. The oddest thing about it was that it contained no reference whatever to an Eight Hour day. The resolution ran as follows—

"That this meeting hails with joy the awakening of labour, which is taking place throughout the civilized world ; declares the necessity for the union of workers in all countries to obtain complete freedom from the monopoly of capital; asserts that the only possible remedy for the poverty and misery of the workers is the free access to the resources of nature, and the management by the workers of the organization of labour; and calls upon all workers to accept the task of bringing about this freedom as a necessary duty, paramount over all others."

This remarkable resolution was duly proposed, seconded, supported, and carried at the " May-day demonstrations all over the country." The newspaper reports on the following day tell us that the Socialists' demonstration in London, organized by the " National Federation of all Trades and Industries," was attended by about 2000 persons ; a reporter, who states that he timed the procession, said that it took exactly five minutes to pass a given spot *en route* to the Park, and that the spot selected was near the Park, so that it had gathered in force after leaving the Embankment. In London, and in various parts of the country, the gatherings were described as " demonstrations in favour of the solidarity of labour ;" of " an Eight Hours Bill " ; and " the union of the working-classes of all countries in order to secure freedom from the monopoly of capital." In Hyde Park, the advice given was to embark in " a universal strike," on the grounds

that "there could be no reconciliation between the working
and the idle classes," and that "the relations between master
and servant must be set aside." In a few provincial towns,
such as Liverpool, Manchester, &c., there was a kind of
demonstration or celebration of May-day as a labour-day;
but there was no general cessation of work, and the demonstrations were, in most instances, very poor affairs. "The
National Federation of all Trades and Industries" did not
long survive the ordeal of organizing these demonstrations;
but the "Socialist League" and the "Social Democratic
Federation," seem still to be distinct, if indeed they ever
had an independent existence. In so far as this country
is concerned, the May-day demonstrations evoked no sort
of enthusiasm in favour of a universal Eight Hour day;
indeed, they showed a want of faith in the movement, and
also a disposition to mistrust the active promoters of an
agitation which promised the emancipation of labour only
by legislative enactment. With all their tendency to believe
in quack remedies, when bawled out at a street corner by a
big voice, accompanied by declarations of the wonderful
cures effected, the masses hesitated to believe in the uni-
versality of an Eight Hour day, as the sole remedy for all
the ills that industrial flesh is heir to in the world of
labour.

(c) On the Continent of Europe the demonstrations
seem to have been more real and effective; continental
workmen believe in the State, at least theoretically. If
they were as ready in their obedience to law, as they are to
extend its domain, one might be disposed to anticipate
some good from its extension. But they are not, and those
in this country who agitate for "labour laws" are the first
to complain of and set at naught those in existence. It is

another illustration of the fact that persons often find more pleasure in the pursuit of an object than in its attainment. It is more than probable that, if the Eight Hour law were enacted, the first to rebel against its iron provisions would be the very men who most clamoured for it. Judging by reports which came to hand, the largest demonstrations were held in Vienna, where it is estimated that 80,000 persons took part, meetings being held simultaneously in forty halls, in addition to those held in the open air. In Berlin and other parts of Germany, in France generally, in Italy, in Spain, in Austria and Hungary, in Belgium, in Holland, in Switzerland, in Portugal, in Denmark, in Sweden and Norway, there were May-day celebrations in favour of the "solidarity of labour," Eight Hours and other idealistic proposals. Fortunately all passed off quietly, except at Buda-Pesth, where a disturbance took place, and some blood was spilt; but even there the affair was not very serious. But enormous military preparations were made "in case of emergency." The Emperor of Germany appears to have shown at once his faith in the people, and in the social programme by sending troops, supplied with ball cartridge, to every provincial town. In Rome the troops were similarly equipped and supplied; in Paris, and other parts of France, preparations were completed to put down disturbance should any occur. All this, because the people wanted more law! Strange comment this, at once upon the demands made by the "people," and upon the attitude of Governments towards those who seek an extension of the law. It ought to be an object lesson to British workmen bearing upon the same subject.

(d) Goaded by the attacks of the Socialists and New Trade Unionists, and possibly stimulated by emulation, the

London Trades' Council was prompted to take an active part in the Labour Demonstrations ; but it steadily refused to connect itself with the demand for a legal Eight Hour day. The Council however decided to hold a demonstration in favour of Eight Hours on May 4th, in Hyde Park. Most of the London trades took part in that demonstration. These were divided into eight groups, as follows—(1) The Leather trades, (2) Metal trades, (3) Cabinet and Fancy trades, (4) General trades, (5) Shipping trades, (6) Clothing trades, (7) Printing and Paper trades, (8) the Building trades. In addition to the foregoing, any branches of trade not included in the above eight sections, and the different bodies of labourers were organized as a contingent, under the guidance of the Socialist League. In all, about ninety branches of industry took part in the demonstration in favour of Eight Hours as the normal working day. The failure of the Socialists, and of the "New Trade Unionists," to enlist the great body of the organized London workmen in the "May-day demonstration," led them to manœuvre in all sorts of ways to gain admittance to the delegate meetings of the Council, and they so far succeeded that some of them were admitted at a later stage. The effect of this was that the scope of the resolution, as prepared by the Council, was enlarged at the final meeting, when it was adopted. The resolution submitted by the Council to the delegate meeting was as follows—

"That this vast meeting of workers of London, knowing that the excessively long hours of labour being worked in many industries cause irregularity of employment, resulting in much misery and social demoralization, believes that the best way to mitigate such evils is by reducing the working hours to a minimum of forty-eight hours per week, heartily congratulates our fellow-workmen in other countries in demanding these hours of toil, earnestly urges our fellow-countrymen to be unceasing in their efforts to successfully establish this limit by every legitimate means in their power, and as a first step calls upon the Imperial Government and all local bodies to at once fix these hours in all departments of labour under their control."

The influence of "the aggressive party" is seen in the above resolution as finally adopted by "the trades"; it is further seen by the two following "riders," which were added at the last delegate meeting—(1) "We further earnestly request workmen in the various constituencies to demand the best efforts of their Members with a view to the reduction of hours in Government and local employments;" and (2) "That the Government should be requested to insert a clause in all Railway, Tramway, and Canal Bills, enforcing an Eight Hours' working day." Thus the London trades practically abandoned the position they had previously taken up, and allowed themselves to be dragged into the whirlpool of State interference, although in a somewhat modified form. The leverage obtained by these concessions was subsequently used with effect inside the Council, and resulted in the adoption of a resolution pledging its delegates, at the Trades Union Congress, to vote for a legal Eight Hour day. Other Trades' Councils, in various parts of the country, were similarly used to forward a movement wholly opposed to Trade Union principles, namely, an application to Parliament to do for labour what the Unions had always asserted labour could do for itself, if it were freed from the trammels of legal enactment. A more utter abdication of their own functions, by Trade Unions, was never witnessed in this country—and this, too, by the Councils called into existence to promote and protect their interests, locally and generally.

(*e*) Simultaneously with the movements outside the Unions previously adverted to, but prior to the "May-day" and other demonstrations, efforts had been made to induce Trade Unions to throw their influence into the scale in favour of an Eight Hour day by legal enactment. For the most part the movement was in the direction of influencing the Trades Union Congress, and, through the Congress, the Trade Unions of the country. At the Bradford Congress, in September 1888, there was a heated discussion upon the subject, which eventuated in a vote of the societies being subsequently taken upon the question. The result of that vote was communicated to the Trades Union Congress which met in Dundee, in September 1889. The report of the Parliamentary Committee stated that 1200 circulars were addressed to the various trade societies of the United Kingdom. The delegates at that gathering (the Dundee Congress) represented over 885,000 members of these societies. Yet only thirty-seven societies replied to the circular, the total membership of which was 178,376. The actual voting as tabulated in the Congress report shows that 67,390 declared against an Eight Hour day, and 39,656 in favour; majority against an Eight Hour day, 27,734. But upon the question of Eight Hours by Act of Parliament the order was reversed, thus: In favour, 28,511; against, 12,283; majority in favour, 16,228. If the votes are added together we find that 79,673 voted against the Eight Hours, and 68,167 in favour; majority against, 11,506. But then the total falls short of the entire number by 30,536. Such a vote could not, by any stretch of the imagination, be con-

sidered conclusive, in any sense, for 1,163 societies sent no
returns, while only thirty-seven responded. But negatively
it shows this: That the majority of the societies took no
interest in the question; some of them voted by resolution
all one way; in others the proportion of votes was small;
in one only fifty-one voted out of 10,000, and in another
case no actual vote is recorded. If the subject had taken
the intense hold of the workmen which some had asserted,
the voting would have been altogether different.

The promoters of the legal Eight Hour day now directed
their energies to a further test of strength, at the next
Congress, fixed for September 1890. In many respects
the advocates of legal enactment were favoured by circumstances. In the first place, the miners of Lancashire, Yorkshire, the Midlands, and South Wales gave in their adhesion
to the movement, though *only for miners*. In the second
place, the May-day demonstrations were deemed to be
favourable; and, in the third place, the New Trade Unionists
threw in their lot heartily with the movement for a legal
Eight Hour day. The advocates of legal restriction and
regulation were active in all directions, beating up recruits,
and preparing for the battle at Liverpool. They appear to
have come to the conclusion that if a resolution could only
be carried at the Trades Congress, the question was settled.
A supreme effort was therefore made to secure that vote.
The advocates of a "legal Eight Hour day" succeeded.
They achieved their object. In what way, and with what
results, will be seen.

The Trades Union Congress held in Liverpool, in
September 1890, consisted, according to the official report,
of 457 delegates from 311 societies, representing a total
of 1,810,191 members; or, excluding the federations, which

were supposed to represent 340,000, the approximate number of persons represented was said to be about 1,470,191. Accepting those figures as correct, and they are based upon the returns of the societies sending delegates, as stated in the credential forms, the last Congress was by far the largest gathering of the kind ever held. But its composition was in many respects different. Previously some of the largest societies were only represented by one or two delegates; in some instances this was also the case at the last Congress. But in other instances the number of delegates from certain bodies was large beyond all precedent. As some rather wild statements have been made with respect to the representative character of the Congress, and also as regards its "decisive vote" on the Eight Hour resolution, an analysis of the representation will help to clear matters up a little, and enable us to understand the real value of that vote. The several industries have been grouped, for the purposes of comparison; the numbers represented are those stated in the Congress Report.

The miners were represented by 67 delegates, representing a total, as stated in the official report, of 412,430 members. The Dockers, Carters, Labourers of all kinds, Gas-workers, &c., 32 delegates, 412,485 members. Seamen and Firemen, 26 delegates, 143,197 members. The other Shipping trades, exclusive of the Iron Shipbuilders, 39 delegates, 27,819 members. Railway employés, 8 delegates, 99,845 members. The Textile trades, 65 delegates, 150,350 members. The Iron, Steel, and Metal trades, including the Engineers, Boiler Makers and Iron Shipbuilders, Iron-moulders, and the Sheffield trades, 54 delegates, 196,072 members. The Building trades, 24 delegates, 64,221 members. The Printing trades, 21 delegates, 32,842 members.

The Boot and Shoe trades, 8 delegates, 56,800 members. The Clothing trades, tailors, hatters, working-women, &c., 15 delegates, 28,071 members. The Cabinet trades, 4 delegates, 6809 members. Colliery Mechanics, 4 delegates, 8486 members. The Bakers, 4 delegates, 5780 members. The Coopers, 4 delegates, 4954 members. The Glass trades, 3 delegates, 3354 members. Pottery trades, 2 delegates, 1200 members. Salt and chemical workers, 6 delegates, 9614 members. Miscellaneous trades, Coachmakers, Cigarmakers, Gold-beaters, Agricultural Labourers' Union, &c., 14 delegates, 27,483 members. Trades' Councils, 60 delegates, and 337,778 members.

The aggregate totals do not quite correspond with the summary given in the Congress Report, even as regards the number of delegates, for 460 are printed in the returns, whereas 457 were said to be present. But that is a small matter, the three might not have attended. But the total number said to be represented shows even greater disparity. A cursory glance at the returns show that there were gross exaggerations. The Dock Labourers are credited with 56,000 twice over, making 112,000, besides other duplicates; the Gas-workers with 60,000 twice over, making 120,000, besides duplicates. Again, the Dock Labourers' General Union stands for 50,000 men, in addition to the above. The Railway Workers' Union is credited with 40,000, and again with 20,000, exclusive of the Amalgamated Societies representing England and Ireland, and Scotland. Then the National Federation of Miners is put down for 120,000 members, the Lancashire Federation for 30,000, the North Wales for 10,000, the North Stafford for 9,500, and the National Union of Miners for 50,000, besides the representation from the different Unions. Then there was the National

Labour Federation, 60,000, and the National Labour Union, 40,000, total 100,000. These may not have been intentional exaggerations, but as the total has been quoted with approval, in order to show the weight of the Eight Hour vote, it is essential that the actual voting power of the Congress should be examined. No exaggeration of numbers is needed, nor can it be of permanent avail in labour struggles. The power of Trade Unions consists in their actual numerical strength, not on paper, but of *bonâ-fide* members in benefit; and in the aggregate funds available in case of a dispute. Their success depends mainly upon the way in which that power is used, and in the ability of the several Unions to support their members when work is slack, so that they shall not be compelled to accept the first offer of employment, if the terms are below the standard Union rates. The Congress of 1890 was the largest ever held, in spite of all deductions for duplicates and exaggerations. Supposing the actual strength was reduced to about three-quarters of a million, it would still be a splendid army of workers, capable of doing great things for labour. The decisions of such a body, if given with due deliberation, and accompanied by the sense of responsibility which should always co-exist with strength, and would, if guided by intelligence and prudence, deserve grave and careful consideration at the hands of the public, in all cases. It is to be feared that those elements were to some extent absent at the last Congress; hence the decisions have failed to exert the influence which had been expected. The voting was singularly defective also, in many respects, as the following, on the Eight Hour question, incontestably shows.

The total number of accredited delegates at the Congress, as reported, was 457. Of those only 354 voted on Mr.

Paterson's amendment to the Eight Hour resolution. For the amendment, 173; against it, 181; majority against, eight only. Then came the original resolution, in favour of an Eight Hour day for all trades, by Act of Parliament, as the substantive motion, when only 348 voted, or less than on the amendment by six delegates. But the result was different. The number who voted for the resolution was 193, or twelve more than voted against the amendment; against the resolution 155, or eighteen less than supported the amendment, the majority for the resolution being 38. The result of the voting is so very curious that the two methods in which the vote was taken deserve to be quoted side by side, for the purposes of comparison—

For the Amendment	...	173	For the Resolution	...	193
Against the Amendment	...	181	Against the Resolution	...	155
Majority against	...	8	Majority for ...	...	38
Total votes given ...	...	354	Total votes given ...	...	348
Abstentions	...	103	Abstentions	...	109

In what way the voting as above shown can be said to be conclusive, in favour of an Eight Hours Bill, as claimed by its supporters, it is difficult to conceive. It rather appears to be the other way, for the advocates of an Eight Hours Bill exerted all their power and influence to swell the vote, whereas those opposed to legislation seem not to have regarded the matter very seriously. It is not possible to apportion the relative weight of the votes on either side of the question, as no record is preserved of the voting which will justify any absolute decision thereon ; but this fact is apparent from the subsequent action of some of the delegates, namely, that the textile trades voted against the proposed Act of Parliament Eight Hour day. The Miners were somewhat divided—Durham, Northumberland, and Cleveland going against the resolution, other mining localities for it. The Boot and Shoe trades voted against the resolution, as indeed all "season trades" were bound to do, unless they meant to cripple the industries they represented. The most prominent, persistent, and overbearing advocate of the legal Eight Hour day, at the Congress and out of it, has stated, in an elaborate address, revised, printed, and extensively circulated, that 900,000 voted for the resolution, and only 540,000 against. The value of that contention is seen by the statement before given of the composition of the Congress. It is a bad cause which requires to be bolstered up by exaggeration and fiction. That a large number voted for the resolution is not denied, and the fact must stand for what it is worth ; but even if the majority voted in its favour, it does not prove that the policy shadowed forth therein is practicable, or desirable. The value of the vote is still further diminished by reason of the fact that the miners declare themselves only to be in favour of a Mines' Eight Hour Bill.

The foregoing observations refer solely to a reduction of working hours for adult males by Act of Parliament. In no case do they refer to any reductions of working hours, in any industry where the workers can by com-bination or conciliation effect a reduction. Every such reduction, or proposed reduction, will in that case be taken on its merits, and the time asked for and conceded will bear some relation to the conditions of the particular industry, what hours have been customary in the trade, and what further reductions it can stand, without serious injury to capital and labour. Such reductions in working hours constitute a kind of natural process, by selection.

But an Act of Parliament, making eight hours a maximum days' work for all classes and all industries, would be a wrench which trade and commerce could not possibly bear, under existing conditions, and would not be able to survive the strain thus suddenly made upon it. Some of the industries of the country could perhaps, with little inconvenience, so adjust its own labour that eight hours would suffice for the normal day's work. Let each trade, for itself, aspire to, and work for, an Eight Hour day. Public opinion, if not wholly favourable, is converging to that view. Sympathy will be evoked by every reasonable effort towards that object. But the attempt to effect it and enforce it by law will be regarded with disfavour more and more as the real issues and consequences are understood, and as the .inevitable results are estimated and appreciated. The worst enemies to an Eight Hour day. are those who demand it by legislation.

The Dockers and the Eight Hours.—The New Trade Unionism is remarkable for its surprises. "The unexpected happens," once said a statesman, who for a considerable time occupied a prominent position in English politics, and who was himself a master in the art of surprising. The aptness of the phrase was oddly enough illustrated by the action of the Dockers' Union almost immediately after the great fight, and signal victory of the " Legal Eight Hour " men at Liverpool. At the " Dockers' Congress " subsequently held the subject was discussed, where one might have supposed that the victory would have been suitably celebrated ; instead of which the Congress passed a resolution declaring that the Eight Hour day was unsuitable to dock-work. When, after mature deliberation, the assembled delegates and officials representing the Dockers' Union found that the introduction of an Eight Hour day would be disastrous to dock labourers, and disadvantageous to the kind of work performed at the docks, they deserve credit for the declaration embodied in that resolution. But what a curious commentary upon the conduct and action of their leaders and representatives, to whose activity and advocacy the passing of the Eight Hour resolution at the Trades Union Congress, in Liverpool, was mainly due. The victory was achieved amid almost wild shrieks of applause ; and when the victors announced their triumph to the body of men by whose aid it was chiefly secured, these declared that it was not for them, the conditions of their industry rendering the terms thereof unsuitable. Had the delegates of the Dockers' Union authority to pledge the members to an Eight Hour day for all trades? Or was it another instance of sudden conversion? Or did the delegates vote first, and commit their body to a given policy, and think afterwards and repent? It is difficult to assign any satisfactory explanation for such conduct. The fact, however, remains that the Dockers' Union has officially declared against a compulsory Eight Hour day for dock-work, the action and votes of its accredited representatives at the Trades' Congress, and at the London Trades' Council, notwithstanding. This fact must be borne in mind in estimating the value of the great victory scored at Liverpool.

The Engineers and the Eight Hours.—The Secretary of the Amalgamated Society of Engineers was taunted at the Trades' Union Congress with not carrying out "an imperative mandate from the Executive Council of their society," which, it was alleged, was "to vote for a Legal Eight Hour day." The Secretary replied that the society had taken "no vote direct or indirect to obtain the opinion of the Amalgamated Society of Engineers on the Eight Hours Bill." He further stated that it was not true that he and his colleagues had a mandate to vote for the Eight Hours' Bill. He was then challenged to appeal to the society for its collective opinion upon the subject. This was done, apparently, for in the November report of the society, the following appeared—

"**Eight Hours and Federations.**—This month we publish some information for our members on the above questions, which, up to date, gives a reflex of the opinions of those who have chosen to express them." A "summary of votes and results on the Eight Hours Question" is then given. From the table given it appears that the "total number of branches that gave returns on the subject" was 17 out of a total of 415 branches in the United Kingdom, exclusive of branches abroad. Of the 17 branches which took the trouble to vote, 13 were unanimously in favour of voluntary action, and only two in favour of legislation. In the two remaining branches, 25 was in the favour of legislation in the Battersea Branch, and 20 in favour of voluntary action; while in the Woolwich Third Branch 21 were in favour of legislation and one against. Another Woolwich Branch was, however, opposed to legislation, and in favour of voluntary action. Aberdeen and Glasgow Sixth Branch were in favour of legislative action, whilst the Glasgow Branch and Greenock Second were in favour of voluntary action. In reviewing the returns sent in the report says—" From these brief and incomplete returns you will see that 204 votes have been given in favour of eight hours per day, and five against. On the other hand, 46 votes have been given in favour of such being obtained by legislative action, and

148 by voluntary efforts. Again, four branches are in favour of the former, and 13 for the latter." The absurdity of the Trades Congress vote could scarcely be accentuated in a more emphatic manner.

The Textile Trade and the Eight Hours Vote.—The representatives of textile industries of the United Kingdom were firm in their attitude, and strongly pronounced in their opinions, in opposition to the Congress resolution in favour of an Eight Hour day by Act of Parliament for all trades. Their position in relation to the question was considered by the delegates from the several branches of that industry, with the result that Mr. Thomas Birtwistle, J.P., resigned his seat on the Parliamentary Committee, though he stood second on the list. Subsequently, Mr. J. Maudsley, J.P., though third on the list, also resigned; Mr. Henry Slatter, J.P., having refused to accept the seat vacated by Mr. Birtwistle, it fell to the next lot of the delegate on the list, one who, with all his exertions in favour of a legal Eight Hour day, had failed to secure sufficient votes to place him on the Committee, his position being thirteenth in the ballot. Other secessions were, it appears, threatened, but have been averted.

The Parliamentary Committee and the Eight Hours Bill.—The Bill for the attainment of the Eight Hour day for all trades, according to the resolution of the Congress, was issued in February 5th, 1891. The Secretary to the Committee refused to take charge of or back such a Bill in the House of Commons. Notice of such Bill was given, and in dummy it was brought in on November 26th, by the hon. member for Lanarkshire, Mr. W. Abraham, a miners' representative, but no other Labour Member's name being on the back of the Bill. There was no kind of competition for the honour of introducing such a Bill; it seems to have been a case of "Hobson's choice," so little favour was shown towards the measure by members of Parliament. To this absurdity then is reduced the barren victory achieved at Congress—not a single Labour Member will undertake the responsibility for such a Bill, and one only has his name on it. Its proposals are repudiated by the Textile trades, by the Engineering trades, by the Boot and Shoe trades, and by the Dockers, whilst not one of the thirty-seven trades which voted on the question, to which allusion has already been made, has shown any sign whatever in favour of such a Bill. It stands condemned therefore by the very men in whose favour it is said to have been formally introduced.

The Eight Hours Bill having been issued as the preceding pages were being finally corrected, its chief provision is here given. It is as follows—

§ 1. "On and after the first day of January 1892 no person shall work, or cause or suffer any other person to work, on sea or land in any capacity, under any contract or agreement, or articles for hire of labour, or for personal service on sea or land (except in case of accident), for more than eight hours in any one day of twenty-four hours, or for more than forty-eight hours in any week." The penalties and fines are to be inflicted upon the "employer, manager, or other person subject to his or her authority or commands, or in his or her employment," the minimum penalty for such offence being £10, and the maximum penalty £100. The Bill speaks for itself; it is brief, drastic, concise, and universal in its application. There are no exceptions of any kind except "accident," as before mentioned in § 2 of the measure.

CHAPTER IX.

THE MATERIAL FORCES AND RESOURCES OF TRADE UNIONISM ; ITS STRENGTH AND WEAKNESS, SUCCESSES AND FAILURES.

Early Struggles of Trade Unions—Recent growth—Public recognition —Patronage of Trade Unions —Numerical Strength — Table of Members—Stimulus by New Unionism—Amalgamated Unions and Branches—Yearly Income—Table of, at periods—Annual Expend- iture—Totals of, at periods—For Benevolent and Strike Purposes —Cash Balances—Table of, at stated periods—Weakness of Trade Unionism—Inability to solve Labour problem—Fruitless Disputes —Popular Demonstrations—Federations—Trades' Councils.

As intimated in the earlier chapters of this work, Trade Unions struggled into existence about a century ago. For a long period they were little more than mere " fighting machines," combinations for certain specific purposes, but with no staying power, being temporary devices rather than permanent institutions. They were illegal associations, *per se*, and their objects were construed as being unlawful, by reason of their being, in the language of the law courts, " in restraint of trade." When the legislature repealed the statutes which declared combinations to be unlawful, the right to combine was still hampered by the laws of conspiracy, and the legal fiction of " restraint of trade " ; practically the objects of Trade Unions were regarded as unlawful, the members of such Unions being often punished for acts which, if committed by persons other than Trade Unionists, would not have been a punishable offence. Up to 1825 there was

very little Trade Unionism in existence ; it was mainly combination, for specific or general purposes, as occasion arose.
During the next twenty-five years some progress was made
in the way of effective organization, the foundations being
laid for future developments.   The modern Trade Union
may be said to have commenced its active career about half
a century ago ; before that date its activity was mostly
manifested by way of experiment and preparation.   During
the first thirty years of this period it was still under the ban
of the law, outlawed in reality, for it had no recognized
status as a corporate body, its funds and property being
absolutely without legal protection.   As a lawfully recognized
institution, its history only dates back twenty years ; but
even of these the first five years witnessed a determined
effort to still brand Trade Unionism as criminal, in its
intent and *modus operandi*, the stigma being only removed
after a persistent struggle, in which Trade Unionists alone
found the sinews of war, the active forces for the battle, and
the officers by whom the campaign was planned, and by
whom the victory was at last achieved.

The growth of Trade Unionism was for a long time
rather slow, often fitful and spasmodic, but, nevertheless, it
made progress.   Within the last twenty years it has advanced
steadily, and it has even found favour with the thinking
portion of the public, at last.   Instead of being tabooed, it is
flattered ; and this flattery has rather tended to develop its
vices than promote its virtues.   Trade Unionism is, in its
very nature, self-sustaining and self-supporting.   It lives by
the contributions of its own members.   So jealous are the
Unions of all outside help that no one is permitted to attend
the Trades Union Congress whose expenses are paid by any
body of persons other than by the *bonâ fide* Trade Union

which he represents as a delegate, and any individual help in the way of expenses would disqualify the delegate from sitting and voting. Some expulsions have taken place on these grounds, and the experiment is not likely to be repeated. Its value as an institution depends upon its own initiative, and its own support. No Trade Union started under patronage has long survived. The saddest instance of the kind is the Agricultural Labourers' Union, which once boasted of some 50,000 members, but which has now dwindled down to less than a fifth of that number. Encouragement and help have been similarly extended to other bodies of workmen, and latterly to workwomen also, with the view of instituting Trade Unions in particular trades and occupations. Such encouragement and assistance are commendable in the initial stages of the movement; but a Trade Union must run alone. It must be self-governed, self-supporting, self-sustained, and self-contained, to be of real practical value in labour conflicts in the industrial world. Upon no other basis can it exist and prosper. As well attempt to make a pyramid stand firmly upon its apex, as to start a Trade Union by patronage, and expect it to attain the ends, and accomplish the work for which such an association is designed. It is certain to wither and die, sooner or later; therefore all such societies must be taught to run alone, depending only upon their own strength and resources.

I. **Numerical Strength.**—The proportions to which Trade Unionism has extended are indicated in the previous chapter, by the number of societies, and of numbers represented, at the Trades Congress, held in Liverpool in September last. Yet the 311 societies said to have been there represented, merely indicate their probable strength.

It is supposed that there are at least four or five times that number of societies in the United Kingdom, many of them having never been represented in these Congresses. But the number of societies is no longer a gauge of numerical strength. In 1861, when the first Trade Union Directory was compiled, there were at least 2000 trade societies; the computed strength at that time being at least from 1,000,000 to 1,250,000 members. At that time there were numerous local bodies belonging to the same trade, all independent of each other. What is now called amalgamation was then in its infancy. The Engineers led the way in this direction, in 1850-51, when the workers connected with the various branches of engineering merged their local unions into one large association. From 1850 to 1860 they stood almost alone in this respect. In the next decade, however, 1861-70, several other bodies of Unionists followed their lead, and formed what are now called amalgamated societies. But several Unions had, even previous to 1850, extended their organization beyond a given locality, in spite of the legal and other difficulties with which they had to contend. The provisions of the Corresponding Societies Act prevented the formation of associations with branches in various parts of the kingdom, at the commencement of the present century, and for a long time subsequently; and its effects continued to operate even when its provisions were no longer in force. Notwithstanding which, some few trade societies established branches early in the century, two or three of them surviving to this day. During the last thirty years the tendency has been to merge local Unions into one large association, for the entire trade; and where this was not quite practicable, a new Union has been instituted, which has so extended itself as to absorb local Unions,

P

ultimately constituting them a branch of the association thus formed. There are consequently fewer separate Trade Unions to-day than there were in existence thirty years ago, but the strength and vigour of Unionism have increased, and not diminished, thereby. Centralization has taken the place of diffusion, amalgamation has been substituted for isolation.

It is not necessary to give any extended list of examples of the numerical strength of Trade Unions to-day, as compared with twenty years ago; a few examples will suffice, and those mostly of such bodies as have branches in various parts of the country. At the dates given the membership stood thus at the end of each year—

Year ending Dec. 31st. NAME OF SOCIETY.	1869. Members.	1879. Members.	1889. Members.	1890. Members.
Amalg. Engineers ...	33,539	44,078	60,728	67,800
Steam-Engine Makers	2,805	4,071	5,500	5,822
Boiler-makers, &c. ...	6,298	16,988	29,993	—
Ironfounders	8,990	12,276	13,805	14,821
Ironmoulders (Scotland)	2,432	4,519	5,992	6,198
Blacksmiths	1,509	2,118	2,077	2,323
Carpenters and Joiners	9,305	17,034	26,472	31,784
Stonemasons	23,036	15,350	11,306	—
Operative Bricklayers	2,020	5,874	8,189	—
Amalgamated Tailors	3,994	13,888	15,276	—
Compositors—London	3,300	4,930	7,955	8,910
Typographical Asso.	2,266	5,150	8,388	—
U. K. Coachmakers ...	5,719	6,908	4,985	5,367
Totals—13 Societies...	105,216	155,184	200,666	—

The membership of the above thirteen societies presents a progressive development from 1869 to 1879, in which decade the increase would have been more marked had it not been for the deplorable depression in trade from 1875 to 1879 inclusive, the latter year being unprecedented in its severity, in so far as Trade Unions are concerned. The Stonemasons had also to face the greatest defeat they had ever sustained, by the strike of 1877, a strike which, in its ultimate results, lost to the society nearly 10,000 members. The progress has been most marked in those societies which are constituted on the widest basis, like the Engineers, Steam-Engine Makers, Ironfounders, Boiler-makers, Carpenters and Joiners, Tailors, and Compositors. The out-of-work provision is undoubtedly one of the mainstays of the modern Union, though the tax to keep it up is often a deterrent to the less thrifty of the men constituting the trade. A glance at the above table will show that several societies doubled their members in twenty years; in one case they were trebled; in another the increase was nearly five-fold. All this was accomplished ere the " New Unionism " asserted itself, and threw down the gauntlet to the old.

The " New Unionism " has, however, stimulated the older Unionism into greater activity, in some cases at least. Some of the old Unions had unwisely abstained from missionary propaganda; they had practically abandoned that kind of work; with the result that the mass of the workmen in a trade reaped the benefits, while a proportion only fought the battles which won and maintained the accruing advantages. The movement in the less skilled, and among the unskilled, trades, gave an impetus to the more staid, prosperous, and long-existing organizations which had done excellent work, but now seemed to rest on their oars, being apparently content to drift with the stream. There was a shaking among the dry bones; new life was infused into stagnant institutions, and a revival set in which is destined probably to leave its mark on this and a future generation. The result of this awakening is seen in the last column of the table, giving the total membership of such of the Unions whose returns are available, thus bringing the figures down to January of 1891. These figures are approximately correct; but, in a few cases, the final corrections in the next annual reports may show a small increase over and above the totals above recorded.

With respect to other Unions, not mentioned in the table, the figures given in the preceding chapter sufficiently indicate their position and progress. The most marked progress has been with the Miners, the Seamen and Firemen's Union, whose latest returns show a total membership of 110,000; the Dock Labourers, whose membership is said to be 50,000; the Gas-workers, the Railway Employés, and various other bodies of workmen, many of whom are now organized for the first time. Probably the total number of workpeople connected with Trade Unions at present will approach to two millions of persons. This force, if efficiently and prudently utilized and managed, is capable of doing great things for labour, for workmen in each trade so organized, and in all trades. Animated by high aims, inspired by loftly aspirations, and working together for objects at once good and attainable, there is scarcely any demand, founded in reason and justice, which could be long denied to the organized skill and industrial energy of such an army of workers.

II. **Branches, or Lodges.**—All the "amalgamated" societies and general Unions are divided into branches, or lodges, the government being in the hands of a Central Council, or committee, elected by the members. The branches meet weekly, or fortnightly, as the case may be, and receive subscriptions, vote monies, and discuss matters pertaining to the society.   They are governed by the general rules ; the bye-laws, as to which so much has been made by malevolent persons, or those hostile to the Unions, generally consist of mere lodge regulations, for the proper conduct of business.   In many of the Unions the funds are equalized every year, so that each branch is neither richer nor poorer than another, in proportion to members.   In other cases the federal principle operates ; the Union being governed by general laws, the expenses of management being equally distributed, the officials being elected by the general body.   Otherwise each lodge or branch controls its own funds.   The branches are held responsible for the proper use of the funds according to the rules, and they select their own auditors to examine the accounts. But the executive has the power to hold a special audit, and to enforce the repayment of any monies wrongfully applied.   The London Society of Compositors is an instance of a local body without branches.   It is metropolitan, the members assembling quarterly to discuss and decide matters of policy and management.   The Engineers have at the present time (January 1891) 497 branches ; of these 418 are in the United Kingdom, 42 in the United States, 32 in British Colonies, and the rest in foreign countries.   The Ironfounders have 116 branches; the Blacksmiths 42 branches ; the Boiler-makers and Iron Shipbuilders 238 branches; the Carpenters and Joiners 501 branches ; the Tailors 355 branches ; and other societies in proportion. In the metropolis, and other large towns, there are often several branches of the same Union, the members having the right of visiting and being present during business, but not of voting.   The several lodges send monthly to the Council a report of their doings, and also the state of trade; from the latter returns, which are published by the society, the Labour Correspondent to the Board of Trade compiles his monthly statement for the *Board of Trade Journal.* These monthly reports are of great value to the members of the several trades, and they have acquired a much wider interest now that they are officially summarized and published. The information given is valuable and generally reliable; it is the best record we have as to the actual condition of industry periodically in this country.

III. **Financial Strength—Yearly Income.**—The annual income of some of the larger Trade Unions is an evidence at once of their strength, and, to a great extent, of their popularity with the more intelligent and thrifty of the working-classes. The weekly payments which make up those large annual amounts show that the members are prepared to make present sacrifices for a future benefit. The total amount of the weekly and other contributions will average quite one shilling per week in numerous societies, while in others the average will be much higher. In some others the total is a trifle less; in the " fighting Unions," as they are called, the weekly contributions scarcely exceed one-fourth of the above amount ; but, then, the benefits are practically nil, except in the event of a strike or labour dispute. The older and better class of Unions provide for the latter liberally; they also provide benefits of a more permanent and far-reaching character, all of which exert a lasting influence upon existing relations between capital and labour, though its effects are less obvious to the uninformed. Taking the same dozen societies, as before enumerated, the total yearly income, in the same years, was as follows :—

Year ending Dec. 31st. NAME OF SOCIETY.	1869. Total Income.	1879. Total Income.	1889. Total Income.	1890. Total Income.
	£	£	£	£
Amalg. Engineers ...	82,406	135,267	183,651	—
Steam-Engine Makers	7,091	10,618	15,303	15,849
Boiler-makers, &c. ...	—	46,974	104,523	—
Ironfounders	33,513	43,104	39,800	—
Ironmoulders (Scotland)	6,478	14,123	20,983	22,164
Blacksmiths	2,181	3,352	4,585	—
Carpenters and Joiners	21,802	39,854	75,069	—
Stonemasons	21,835	31,213	19,043	—
Operative Bricklayers	1,909	8,270	12,696	—
Amalgamated Tailors	—	17,517	20,953	—
Compositors—London	4,366	7,712	14,242	16,533
Typographical Asso....	—	6,616	9,667	—
U. K. Coachmakers ...	10,206	30,699	10,971	11,963
Totals—13 Societies ...	192,787	395,319	531,486	—

The foregoing totals manifest a good deal of staying power, and this power is capable of increase by levy if circumstances so require.   This was the case in 1879, in many instances the drain on the funds being excessive, more particularly for out-of-work benefit, sickness, super-annuation, and benevolent grants.

IV. **Yearly Expenditure.**—It is but natural, in view of the numerous and important benefit provisions in these societies, that the expenditure should be correspondingly large.   Frequently the expenditure exceeds the income, when of course the accumulated balance has to be drawn upon, to make up any deficiency.   For example, in 1879, scarcely a society was able to pay its way out of revenue, so peremptory and continuous were the calls for relief, under all heads.   A similar strain had to be endured in 1866, but it was more confined in its operations, and did not last so long.   In point of fact, the year 1879 was but the culmination of four or five years of continuous pressure, especially upon those societies which make provision for their unemployed members. Lack of work means also lack of means, and the sick list increases in proportion, telling the tale of privation and want. The annual expenditure is indicated by the three years selected, in two of which it might be termed normal, while the third (1879) might be said to be abnormal. The following are the amounts :—

Year ending Dec. 31st. NAME OF SOCIETY.	1869. Expenditure.	1879. Expenditure.	1889. Expenditure.	1890. Expenditure.
	£	£	£	£
Amalg. Engineers ...	104,929	245,598	132,642	—
Steam-Engine Makers	6,006	8,761	19,357	10,553
Boiler-makers, &c. ...	—	66,299	56,655	—
Ironfounders	34,991	80,089	26,005	—
Ironmoulders (Scotland)	6,072	21,530	15,133	10,297
Blacksmiths	1,792	5,570	2,892	—
Carpenters and Joiners	21,355	62,446	59,824	—
Stonemasons	32,833	37,466	14,060	—
Operative Bricklayers	1,990	7,677	10,188	—
Amalgamated Tailors	—	19,519	19,836	—
Compositors—London	4,577	11,084	11,502	12,377
Typographical Asso.	—	6,537	9,253	—
U. K. Coachmakers ...	10,923	41,841	10,707	9,841
Totals—13 Societies ...	225,468	614,417	388,054	—

The above figures show how enormously the expenditure exceeds the income in some years; that of the Engineers in 1879 amounted to no less a sum than about £100,000, that of the Ironfounders being about £40,000. Some societies felt the pressure longer than others, but generally it was felt from 1875 to the end of 1879 very acutely by many trades.

The pressure of expenditure is naturally felt mostly in

regard to the provident benefits. This fact no doubt has inspired some ill-informed leaders of the New Unionism with the notion that if those benefits could be got rid of, and societies were constituted for fighting purposes only, greater benefits would immediately accrue to labour. The facts, however, all point the other way. Strikes form a very small part of the economy of a strong Trade Union. The Stonemasons' Society is as good an example of this as could be quoted, for it was almost always in the forefront of a fight; yet its expenditure, over a long term of years, shows that it has spent on benevolent objects, sick, super-annuation, out-of-work, medical assistance, accidents, gifts for charitable purposes, subscriptions to hospitals, donations to orphan children, and the like, £435,862 12s. 6d., whilst in the same period it only spent £108,404 18s. od., though the period covers the most militant years of modern in-dustrial warfare. The proportion spent on strikes was less than 25 per cent., while the expenditure for benevolent purposes was over 75 per cent. Then, as regards manage-ment expenses, the total does not often exceed from 10 to 12½ per cent. of the total income, including all costs for all the branches, as well as the central office. In the case of the Engineers, and Carpenters and Joiners, where they have about 500 branches each, the cost would include pay and allowances to about 2000 officers of all kinds, in each of those societies, besides rent, printing, stationery, postages, and all other incidental expenses. All the other Unions would be in proportion, four or five officers being the general rule in each branch, such as president, secretary, treasurer, tyler, stewards, the auditors and trustees. The allowance is however very small in most cases, the honour and earnestness in the cause being generally the chief

inducements to take office, and run the risk of being
displaced in the shop or firm in which they are employed.
It might be truly said that, as a rule, the work is done
economically and efficiently by officers of Trade Unions,
much to their credit.

V. **Cash Balance at end of the year.**—The actual
material resources which denote the fighting force of a
Union, consists of the immediately available funds at its
disposal, in the event of a conflict. This, however, may
not be the full measure of its force, scarcely more than a
mere indication to the beholder outside the Union, of its
war-footing strength. It is often said by politicians that
the best way to ensure peace is to be prepared for war;
without unreservedly assenting to that proposition, the
principle foreshadowed in it finds some justification in the
policy of Trade Unions. The mere knowledge, on the
part of employers, that a Union had large material and
available resources, ready at almost a moment's notice,
would have a tendency to deter any one of them from
risking a prolonged struggle, in which the issues would at
least be problematical and doubtful. Fortunately, the
accumulation of large funds has not been provocative of
industrial war, on the part of Trade Unionists; on the
contrary, it has tended rather to moderation and caution.
This arises from a sense of responsibility, rather than from
any trace or notion of weakness, though the latter interpretation has apparently been given to the possession of a
large accumulated capital, by some of the newer men of
light and leading in the Trade Union movement. Extreme
caution might be a bad thing, both in military affairs and in
industrial warfare; but rashness, a declaration of hostilities
in a state of unpreparedness, with raw recruits, no sinews of

war, no properly organized commissariat, and with weapons of doubtful calibre and make, will but invite defeat, and precipitate disaster. Battles have been won by dash, by a sudden attack, before the enemy could marshal its forces; but the risk is always great, and a general who so conducted a campaign might almost be accused of massacre, so nearly may it resemble that mode of slaughter, instead of lawful war, even according to the barbaric code still obtaining in civilized communities. Some recent industrial battles have been sudden, both in respect of a declaration of war, and the commencement of hostilities; but the successes have not been sufficiently great to commend the practice, even from the stand-point of success, all other considerations apart at the moment.

Some idea of the financial condition of the better class of Trade Unions may be formed by the following table, comprising the same list as before of Unions whose benefits are not only commensurate with the contributions of the members, but, in the estimation of actuarial experts, above and beyond what, from a statistical and actuarial point of view, the Unions can permanently carry out, and still maintain themselves in a solvent condition. Inasmuch as the societies here given have a continuous record for from thirty to forty years, and some even much longer, the cash balances at the present time ought to satisfy the most sceptical as to their soundness. (See Table next page.)

The significance of the figures given is that the Unions, with one or two exceptions, which provide the largest benefits, have increased their balances in a greater ratio than those which have the fewest and least benefits, an evidence of the fact that overweight, in the shape of provident benefits, is not a source of weakness.

NAME OF SOCIETY.	Cash Balance in Hand at end of the Year :—			
	1869.	1879.	1889.	1890.
	£	£	£	£
Amalg. Engineers ...	76,176	141,116	209,780	—
Steam-Engine Makers	6,006	8,761	19,357	24,654
Boiler-makers, &c. ...	5,253	9,195	100,896	139,147
Ironfounders	650	1,909	33,888	47,855
Ironmoulders (Scotland)	556	4,821	13,624	25,492
Associated Blacksmiths	1,789	3,226	4,864	—
Carpenters and Joiners	17,626	53,596	58,922	—
Stonemasons	3,496	978	4,559	—
Operative Bricklayers	4,770	20,392	30,590	—
Amalgamated Tailors	765	13,809	16,043	—
London—Compositors	4,449	10,727	25,432	29,587
Typographical Asso.	—	4,295	16,613	23,000
U. K. Coachmakers ...	4,886	580	6,668	8,786
Operative Plasterers ...	—	11,850	2,064	—
Railway Servants ...	—	24,118	81,764	—
Totals—15 Societies	126,422	309,373	623,064	—

The fighting strength of the Unions, in men and material resources, would seem to indicate a capability and preparedness for almost any emergency, or contingency. But the more experienced officers know that there is no room for waste, no overplus for wild experiments. They recognize the fact that trade fluctuates, that after the spring-tide will come the neap-tide, that we are subject to waves of depression, as well as tidal waves which carry us beyond the high-water mark of previous experience. In view of these facts, some of the Unions have been preparing, in the hour of prosperity, for the adversity which will probably come, sooner or later, so that the aged and infirm shall not possibly suffer for lack of sustenance and support. With true Roman prudence, they have endeavoured to secure the conquests already made, before they push on to other possible conquests. It is the slower method, but the safest.

It is often more easy to win a battle, than it is to permanently secure the objects for which it was fought; this fact is only learnt by actual experience; or by a wide range of knowledge, gleaned from the experience of others. It is, however, the one fact which is obvious in the history of nations, of public movements, and in the biographies of notable men. The history of industrial disputes is studded with instances which point a moral that all who run may read, if they only take the trouble to examine its pages, and note its lessons. There is, moreover, another fact which, though less obvious, is none the less certain, namely, that the strength of Trade Unions, representing the cause of labour generally, does not wholly depend upon the number of members, and the total available funds. They have a great moral power and influence, the force and weight of which depend upon the justice of their claims, and the way in which those claims are put forward and pressed. These factors are increasing in importance, and will increase by a rightful use of means to the end, provided that the end itself be just. Labour has now its allies; it is no longer the Ishmael of the desert; but it must respect its friends, if it would succeed in its trials of strength, and din of battle.

VI. **Weakness of Trade Unionism.**—The weak side of Trade Unionism may be viewed from various standpoints; accordingly it may seem to have many aspects. Some of these are not pertinent to the objects comprised in the preparation of this work. It is not contended that Trade Unions are capable of solving the great industrial questions which agitate the public mind, and which probably in the near future will occupy a good deal of attention, not only in this country, but in all parts of the "civilized world."

Their work is, at best, only a temporary expedient for dealing with labour questions as they arise. They enable their members to effect a bargain upon more equal terms than they could command if they were not in union standing isolated and alone. And, in this respect, their strength is only equal to the weakest link in the chain. What is that weak link? It does not consist in any theoretical defect in policy, nor in its composition or constitution. The defect arises from the fewness of its numbers, compared with the mass of the workers in any particular trade. A Trade Union is strong in proportion to its total membership to the aggregate number working at the trade. The best evidence of this is to be found in the almost supreme power wielded by the Boiler·makers and Iron Shipbuilders, perhaps the strongest of all Unions, representing a great national industry. The miners of Durham and Northumberland occupy a similar vantage-ground. When any Union can boast of having within the pale of its influence two-thirds of the entire workers at the trade, its power is almost paramount ; with a less proportion the struggle is continuous, persistent, and anxious, because at every step it has to consider what the non-Unionists might possibly do, in the event of a dispute. The Unions might well consider how best to promote the spirit of Unionism all over the country, by missionary enterprise and otherwise ; and strive to infuse some self-respect and patriotism in the minds of those who are ever ready to reap where they have not sown. Every workman in a trade owes a duty to the Union in that trade for fighting the battle of labour, and mere theoretical differences of opinion as to the methods or means does not absolve him from that obvious duty. The great source of weakness is abstentions on the part of the workmen in their own real work.

The Unions have other weaknesses, some of which might be avoided. Money is frequently wasted in fruitless and trifling disputes. More irritation is often caused by some foolish strike than by a gigantic struggle, in which all the forces are brought into play for some tangible purpose. The object of a Trade Union should be to avoid a conflict wherever possible, and to reserve its strength for the more important issues which have to be fought out in connection with labour. Of course, it is not always possible to avoid those minor disputes ; the Unions are not able at all times to chose their own ground, or the time ; in such cases they have to do the best they can. The most lamentable cases of disputes that could and should be avoided are those between one society and another, some of which have been very bitter and costly. In those cases employers suffer from no fault of their own, while the Unions are cutting each others' throats. There is also, at times, a tendency to exaggerate a grievance, and to exasperate an employer, by violent tirades, on the platform and in the press. If employers could but see wherein their real interest lay, they would at once communicate with the officials of the Union, and endeavour to put things right. They would find less passion, more reason, and a greater readiness to arrange terms, if they applied at once to the head-quarters of the Union. There may be exceptions, but the rule is as stated. The " New Unionists " have a special weakness of their own; they strive to extend the line of battle ; the older Unions endeavour to localize and confine it. A body with unlimited means, and having within its pale five-sixths or seven-eighths, of all the workers at the trade, might venture, if they thought fit, to cover the entire field of industry in one campaign ; but, even then, the wisdom of such a step would be doubtful. The more prudent course is to localize and limit the conflict, and to concentrate the forces on a given point. The economical and inherent weakness of Trade Unionism is that its energies and force are spent on what is at best a palliative ; it has not been able, perhaps cannot, of itself, to initiate a policy which will help to solve the labour problem, by placing production on a level with capital, or rather utilizing their own capital for the purposes of production. The fault, however, is not with the Unions ; they are bound by inexorable necessity, hand and foot.

VII. **Popular Demonstrations.**—The New Unionism has a weakness for demonstrations, bands, banners, and emblems. This is but a revival of a practice which was much more common in the second quarter of the present century than it has been since, at least until within the last two or three years. Those demonstrations often serve a useful purpose. They frequently evoke popular sympathy. At other times, however, they promote a hostile feeling, in consequence of the inconvenience, real or imaginary, which is caused by the congregation of large masses of men in the public thoroughfares. Demonstrations, such as those latterly so frequent in the metropolis, ought not to be regarded lightly. If repeated too often they lose their force. People ask—What for ? To what purpose ? What is their object ? What will or can result therefrom ? As a mere parade of force, in the shape of numbers, they may demonstrate a fact, as for example when the trades held their demonstration on the 4th of May, to signify a strong desire for an eight hour day. The Dockers had their parades to evoke public sympathy, and create enthusiasm in the ranks of those hitherto unorganized.

The miners hold their annual demonstrations, which are gala-days, for mutual congratulation and enjoyment. Useful as they may be, and are, in their way, strikes are not usually won by parades, processions, bands of music, Phrygian caps, and flags. The walls of Jericho fell to the sound of the rams'-horns, but miracles like that are not repeated in these modern days. Demonstrations, as a rule, cost money, as the Socialists found on the 1st and 4th of May, 1890 ; the trades paid their expenses quickly, but the other "demonstrators" had some difficulty in discharging the liabilities in which they were thereby involved. Whatever their value, "great demonstrations" can never become a substitute for the material forces of the Unions, represented by numbers, and a cash balance sufficient to provide for the necessities of those on strike. If at the end of the first week, the money is not forthcoming wherewith to pay the men, they become disheartened, weak, and vacillating, and they forecast failure and disaster in the end. Parades and demonstrations may infuse some life and strength into the movement, but they are hollow shams in the face of hunger, suffering, and dire distress.

VIII. **Federations.**—The New Unionists have also a weakness for federations. So strong is their faith in them that they seem to think that a federation of weak societies will supply the necessary aggregate strength. During the third and fourth decades of this century, there were similar movements in favour of gigantic federations, universal strikes, and international co-operation in labour movements. They had their day ; the dreams vanished as practical difficulties presented themselves which the leaders were powerless to remove. Groups of trades and cognate industries might be able to form a defensive federation in case of

Q.

attack; but a huge fighting federation is next to impossible. The shipping trades have recently been attempting it; to some extent they may be successful; but their real success will depend upon the attitude of the Shipping Federation, of shipowners, employers, and capitalists directly concerned in the shipping and cognate branches of industry. The less skilled in the shipping trades, represented by the Newer Unions, have also instituted a federation, but its very first move proved a failure. The miners have been more successful, but even the National Federation does not embrace the whole of the mining population. Still it is the most powerful federation in existence. The building trades, the printing trades, the textile trades, all may combine into one federation, for certain well-defined and practical purposes, but a federation of all trades is a wild dream, incapable of realization. But some men can only learn by failures; history and experience teach them no lessons, except the experience which comes from their own narrow lives, blighted schemes, and bitter failures. All handicraft labour, skilled and unskilled, has much in common; but the interests of men are diversified, not less so in the world of labour than in the professions, and in trading and commercial circles. The fusion of all trades into one gigantic association is an impossibility; and were it not so, it would be undesirable, even in the interests of labour. Its inevitable tendency would be to level down, not up; the emulation that now exists would be strangled; skill would have no pre-eminence; even character would lose its force. The Unions might co-operate, assist each other as occasions arise; but a fusion of all the elements would be destructive—they would neutralize if not annihilate each other.

IX. **Trades' Councils.**—Trades' Councils belong to the

old order of Trade Unionism. The London Trades' Council, for example, was founded in 1860; it grew out of a conference of the metropolitan trades, called into existence in 1859, in consequence of the " Builders' Strike and Lock-out." The conference was only a temporary body, brought together for a temporary purpose, but it became the nucleus of the London Trades' Council, which has existed ever since. Trades' Councils are necessarily severely limited in their sphere of action. They may pass resolutions of the most ultra character, but the bodies sending delegates may adopt or disregard them as they think fit. They have no executive authority; it is wholly delegated; it can be withdrawn at any time, if a society disagrees with the programme, proposals, or work. A vote by the council, or by the entire body of delegates summoned by it, has no binding effect, beyond the decision for the moment given; it might be endorsed, but it might also be rejected by the societies on a subsequent meeting night. A Trades' Council is a consultative body, rather than executive, but it exercises an influence in the locality in which it exists. Its greatest power consists in the focussing of the matured opinion of the trades, or of the leading men in the trades, upon general industrial questions; it helps also in maturing that opinion by discussion and public action. But it cannot step in to direct the policy of the Unions in any case, or upon any matter. If, therefore, the Socialists capture the Trades' Councils, in furtherance of their designs, they achieve little more than an empty victory. Perhaps the most important factor in the constitution of Trades' Councils is the fact that the delegates composing it represent the most active, and generally the best-informed, Trade Unionists in the district in which it is instituted. They have been most useful in many ways, during the last thirty years; and their usefulness might be greatly extended. But if they attempted to usurp executive authority their delegated power would be withdrawn, in which case it would cease to represent the trades. The jealousy with which the governing bodies of the Unions regard any interference with their distinctive authority is permanently felt in the Trades' Councils; it moulds their policy, and controls their action in every movement in which they take part.

CHAPTER X.

TRADE UNIONISM—ITS METHODS, MEANS, AND WORK :
STRIKES—CONCILIATION—CO-OPERATION—AND RESULTS.

Trade Unions not wholly responsible for methods or means employed
—Strikes—Conciliation and Arbitration—Capital and Labour in
Union—Profit sharing—Co-operation—Conclusion—New Life in
Labour Movements—Reliance upon State Aid deprecated.

TRADE UNIONS are not altogether responsible either for the
methods adopted, the means they use, or the work they
undertake. They grew out of existing conditions. They
were not able to choose even their own form of organization
and constitution, so cribbed, cabined, and confined were
they by statutory law. If, therefore, they are imperfect in
constitution, deficient in general policy, and inadequate in
their manner of dealing with social and industrial problems,
the fault does not entirely rest with the Unions. Those who
criticize them from an elevated standpoint, should remember
their origin, their history, their struggles, and their disadvantages. They do not profess to be associations for the
regeneration of the human species ; they confine themselves
to practicable questions and attainable objects, or such as
appear to be within their reach from time to time. It is
only occasionally, comparatively speaking, that a Union can
be charged with really initiating a dispute, a large proportion of them being caused by some act on the part of

employers.   The latter, however, are not always to blame for
what they do ; they also are influenced by existing conditions of trade, and other circumstances.   The relative
position of the two contending parties is much more simple
than it appears to be on the surface.   The complexity arises
from outside conditions, the outgrowth of centuries, for
which neither party is directly responsible.   Personally,
employers and employed stand thus :—The former require
labour, the latter require payment for that labour.   The
social and economical question to be solved is—how the
two parties shall best be able to make equitable bargains
and terms, so that neither shall obtain undue advantage over
the other.   Trade Unions aim at equalizing the relative
forces ; and no better method has been as yet devised for
that purpose.   A powerful Union places its members on a
par with the employers ; they are no longer eager competi-
tors, compelled to take work at any price, in order to satisfy
hunger.

I. **Strikes.**—The weapons by which Trade Unions em-
power their members to make bargains upon such equitable
terms as may be possible, and to enforce the terms when
made, are strikes.   This might be a rude way, even a brutal
way, in the estimation of the fastidious ; but what other
method have the men upon which to rely ?   Workmen do not
stand in precisely the same position as sellers of commodities,
except perhaps in the case of those who make up the materials
they purchase, and hawk and sell the articles.   But these are
no longer hired workmen ; yet their lot is sometimes quite as
hard, if not harder, than that of the hired journeyman.   The
conditions of trade and industry are such that hired labour
seems inevitable.   Certain modifications may be suggested
for mitigating this tied relationship between " capital and

labour "; but these would altogether change existing conditions. Trade Unions deal with things as they are, not as they might be. The latter involve questions of economic, social,. and moral laws. In the evolution of society, the Unions will have much to do ; they must look after the welfare of their members in the changes that may have to take place. They may also greatly assist in promoting such changes as may lead to beneficial results. But to organize a crusade to promote vast social and industrial changes would involve an abnegation of their present functions, possibly to the detriment of useful reforms, and certainly to the disadvantage of labour as now engaged and employed. Strikes may not, in themselves, be commendable; but they are defensible. Starved labour is a worse evil than strikes, which result in improved conditions for the labourer. If the latter can be obtained without strikes, so much the better for all concerned. Strikes are simply labour's weapons in the struggle for existence, upon the right use of which much depends. A wrongful use of such weapons might have, and sometimes has had, disastrous effects upon those who use them, as a defective piece of ordnance may deal out death and destruction to the defenders of a garrison, instead of havoc in the ranks of its assailants. Instances of disaster could be cited, in both cases, in abundance.

II. **Conciliation and Arbitration.**—Strikes, as a mode of settling labour disputes, ought always to be regarded as reserved power, only to be used when all other means have failed. They involve a wasteful expenditure of force at the very best. Conciliation is a first and necessary step, in all cases, for dealing with labour questions. It is essential that both parties shall agree to meet and discuss. A refusal to meet and discuss grievances and terms can scarcely be

justified in any case; in some instances such refusal is open
to severe condemnation. Nearly 90 per cent. of all labour
disputes could be averted by conciliation, under some
proper system, mutually agreed upon. Of the other 10 per
cent. 5 or 6 per cent. might be averted by arbitration, if
conciliation failed. In a few cases possibly a trial of
strength, in the first instance, would take place; could
perhaps scarcely be avoided. After some experience probably strikes might be altogether averted. The principle is
advancing in public favour, and it might be that, ere long,
some mode of conciliation and arbitration will become
general throughout the land. It is too early to predicate
what will result from the action of the Chambers of Commerce in this respect, but the efforts of the London Chamber
deserve commendation and success. The North of England
Board of Conciliation and Arbitration, the Midland Wages
Board, the Miners' Joint Committees, and similar bodies,
show that this mode of dealing with labour disputes is
practicable, and that enormous waste and suffering can
be thereby prevented. If these bodies could once agree
to deal with the question of the hours of labour, for the
several industries represented, they would be able to settle
it on a basis suitable to the exigencies of the trade in which
they are engaged. This is the rightful form in which to
deal with a subject so far-reaching in its character as the
working hours. Wages may go up and down, as under a
sliding scale; but the hours of labour cannot so fluctuate,
as a general rule. There is a need of regularity, and of
some uniformity in the various trades. All these matters
are subjects for debate and settlement by those concerned;
and in no way can they be so well dealt with as by
conciliation and arbitration.

III. **Capital and Labour in Unison.**—We have heard a great deal lately about the abolition of capitalists in the economy of industry. Reconciliation might be possible and practicable; abolition is a Utopian dream, which does not concern us in this work. There are two ways in which an adjustment is possible such as will ensure to labour its rightful dues, at least under existing conditions of general industry. But both of the systems which have been proposed, and to a certain extent have worked successfully, have been opposed by the New Unionists, namely, participation in profits, and co-operation.

(*a*) **Profit-sharing.**—This principle has not been generally adopted in any country; but in France, by the Maison Leclaire, Maison Bord, and other undertakings, and to some extent in Germany, Switzerland, and the United States, the plan has succeeded admirably. One would suppose that having a direct interest in the welfare and prosperity of the concern would be an inducement to the workmen to co-operate for the mutual advantage of all. But English workmen have not, as a rule, taken kindly to the system. In the estimation of many of them it involves too much responsibility and regulation; and those most ardently opposed to it are just the men who go in for State and municipal regulation. If they are not fit for the former, the more voluntary system, they certainly could not endure the compulsory system under legal regulation.

(*b*) **Co-operation.**—This method of production has been extensively tried in this country, and has largely succeeded. It has been worked out by working men, carried on by working men, and managed successfully. Yet, here again, those co-operative industrial undertakings have been frequently attacked, and publicly, in the Trades Union

Congress. One would have thought that any spare cash belonging to the Unions might have been usefully invested in co-operative production, as a means of helping to solve the labour problem. But not so. Men dream of co-operative production, under State regulation, centuries hence, but will not help to initiate a movement, or advance it, which might assist to mitigate the evils of the present competitive system. In one or the other of these forms labour could help to fix its own reward. But it requires some fitness, forethought, patience, even sacrifice thus to co-operate for mutual good. Perhaps the sense of unfitness causes some of them to yearn for a kind of military rule in industrial production, with State force and compulsion behind it, to enforce obedience and effect control, where self-reliance is absent or at fault.

IV. **Conclusion.**—In the foregoing pages we have endeavoured to portray the chief features of Trade Unions, and to indicate wherein the old, and what are called the "new," differ from each other. It is shown that, in all essential particulars, the constitution and aims of all *bonâ fide* Unions are practically the same; that the difference between one trade society and another consists mainly in the class and kind of "benefits" provided for, and assured to, members by the rules; and that the real difference, such as it is, which exists between the Old and the New Trade Unionism, is rather to be found in the acknowledged policy, means used, and ulterior objects sought by the new leaders, as formulated in their speeches, contributions to the press, and by resolutions passed at various meetings, than in the constitution and procedure of the Unions themselves. Even the minor differences which existed when the newer Unions were first established, have more or less disappeared, those recently formed having found by experience that, from the necessities of the case, they must proceed on the old lines.

The gain to Unionism during the last two years by the recent revival and agitations is not denied. New life has been infused into labour movements in all directions; and, above all, the mass of unskilled, or only partially skilled, workers, have been brought into line. They have been taught to understand, for the first ·time on a scale of great magnitude, that the condition of the workers can only be improved by mutual help and associative effort. Self-help and self-reliance are extended and strengthened by combination, the latter being the only method by which labour can obtain its due reward, under existing industrial conditions. But with these lessons others have been inculcated which would render nugatory the power of the Unions, namely, reliance upon State aid, State regulation, and State control. The two systems cannot co-exist; they are contradictory, and opposed. The military system applied to industry involves impossible conditions. The evils of the competitive system may at least be minimized by mutual aid, and by conciliation; they might be cured by a wise and extended system of co-operation, in which capital and labour would both obtain their fair reward.

THE END.

18, *Bury Street, W.C., January,* 1891.

MESSRS. METHUEN'S
𝔑ew 𝔅ooks and 𝔄nnouncements.
1891.

CONTENTS.

FICTION.

S. BARING GOULD.

URITH : A Story of Dartmoor. By S. BARING GOULD, Author of "Mehalah," "Arminell," &c. 3 vols. [*February.*

HANNAH LYNCH.

PRINCE OF THE GLADES. By HANNAH LYNCH. 2 vols. [*February.*

W. CLARK RUSSELL.

A MARRIAGE AT SEA. By W. CLARK RUSSELL, Author of "The Wreck of the Grosvenor," &c. 2 vols. [*February.*

W. H. POLLOCK.

FERDINAND'S CLAIM. By WALTER HERRIES POLLOCK. Post 8vo. 1s. [*February.*

R. PRYCE.

THE QUIET MRS. FLEMING. By RICHARD PRYCE. Crown 8vo. 3s. 6d. [*February.*

M. BETHAM EDWARDS.

DISARMED. By M. BETHAM EDWARDS, Author of "Kitty." Crown 8vo. 3s. 6d. [*February.*

W. E. NORRIS.

JACK'S FATHER. By W. E. NORRIS, Author of "Mademoiselle de Mersac." Crown 8vo. 3s. 6d. [*March.*

S. BARING GOULD.

TOM A' TUDLAMS. By S. BARING GOULD, Author of "Mehalah." Crown 8vo. 3s. 6d. [*May.*

LESLIE KEITH.

A LOST ILLUSION. By LESLIE KEITH, Author of "The Chilcotes," "A Hurricane in Petticoats," &c. 3 vols. Crown 8vo.

"Were it only a shade more cheerful it would be a perfect story."—*Manchester Examiner.*
"A really pathetic story full of human nature."—*Graphic.*

G. MANVILLE FENN.

A DOUBLE KNOT. By G. MANVILLE FENN, Author of "The Vicar's People," "Eli's Children," &c. 3 vols. Crown 8vo.

"A clever novel. The plot is intricate and well managed. The story abounds in strong and exciting situations."—*Speaker.*

L. T. MEADE.

THE HONOURABLE MISS : A Tale of a Country Town. By L. T. MEADE, Author of "Scamp and I," "A Girl of the People," &c. 2 vols. Crown 8vo.

"Delightfully fresh and winning."—*Scotsman.*

GENERAL LITERATURE.

S. BARING GOULD.

HISTORIC ODDITIES AND STRANGE EVENTS. Second Series. By S. BARING GOULD, Author of "Mehalah," "Old Country Life," &c. Demy 8vo. 10s. 6d. [Ready.

"Mr. Baring Gould has a keen eye for colour and effect, and the subjects he has chosen give ample scope to his descriptive and analytic faculties. The new series of 'Historic Oddities and Strange Events' is a perfectly fascinating book. Whether considered as merely popular reading or as a succession of studies in the freaks of human history, it is equally worthy of perusal, while it is marked by the artistic literary colouring and happy lightness of style."—*Scottish Leader.*

J. B. BURNE, M.A.

PARSON AND PEASANT: Chapters of their Natural History. By J. B. BURNE, M.A., Rector of Wasing. Crown 8vo. 5s. [Ready.

"'Parson and Peasant' is a book not only to be interested in, but to learn something from—a book which may prove a help to many a clergyman, and broaden the hearts and ripen the charity of laymen."—*Derby Mercury.*

W. CLARK RUSSELL.

THE LIFE OF ADMIRAL LORD COLLINGWOOD. By W. CLARK RUSSELL, Author of "The Wreck of the Grosvenor." With Illustrations by F. BRANGWYN. 8vo. [In February.

P. H. DITCHFIELD, M.A.

OLD ENGLISH SPORTS AND PASTIMES. By P. H. DITCHFIELD, M.A., Author of "Our English Villages." Illustrated. Post 8vo. [In April.

Edited by A. CLARK, M.A.

THE COLLEGES OF OXFORD: Their History and their Traditions. By Members of the University. Edited by A. CLARK, M.A., Fellow and Tutor of Lincoln College. 8vo. [In the Press.

Edited by J. WELLS, M.A.

OXFORD AND OXFORD LIFE: With Chapters on the Examinations by Members of the University. Edited by J. WELLS, M.A., Fellow and Tutor of Wadham College. Crown 8vo. [In the Press.

S. BARING GOULD.

THE TRAGEDY OF THE CÆSARS: The Emperors of the Julian and Claudian Lines. With numerous Illustrations from Busts, Gems, Cameos, &c. By S. BARING GOULD, Author of "Mehalah," &c. [In the Press.

W. G. COLLINGWOOD, M.A.

JOHN RUSKIN: His Life and Work. By W. G. COLLINGWOOD, M.A., late Scholar of University College, Oxford. Crown 8vo. [In Preparation.

H. H. HENSON, M.A.

DISSENT IN ENGLAND: A Sketch of the History and Constitution of the Principal Nonconformist Sects. By REV. H. H. HENSON, M.A., Fellow of All Souls' College, and Rector of Barking. 8vo. [In Preparation.

NEW BOOKS for BOYS and GIRLS.

W. CLARK RUSSELL.

MASTER ROCKAFELLAR'S VOYAGE. By W. CLARK RUSSELL, Author of "The Wreck of the Grosvenor," &c. Illustrated by GORDON BROWNE. Crown 8vo. 5s.

"Mr. Clark Russell's story of 'Master Rockafellar's Voyage' will be among the favourites of the Christmas books. There is a rattle and 'go' all through it, and its illustrations are charming in themselves, and very much above the average in the way in which they are produced. Mr. Clark Russell is thoroughly at home on sea and with boys, and he manages to relate and combine the marvellous in so plausible a manner that we are quite prepared to allow that Master Rockafellar's is no unfair example of every midshipman's first voyage. We can heartily recommend this pretty book to the notice of the parents and friends of sea-loving boys."—*Guardian.*

"In the frank and convincing narrative of Master Rockafellar there happens to be set a short story which should make the fortune of the book. 'La Mulette' is as fine a piece of story-telling as ever Mr. Russell has given us, and we heartily commend it to any boy who has the sense to distinguish between the author who has a story to tell, and the author who has to tell a story."—*Speaker.*

G. MANVILLE FENN.

SYD BELTON: or, The Boy who would not go to Sea. By G. MANVILLE FENN, Author of "In the King's Name," &c. Illustrated by GORDON BROWNE. Crown 8vo. 5s.

"Who among the young story-reading public will not rejoice at the sight of the old combination, so often proved admirable—a story by Manville Fenn, illustrated by Gordon Browne The story, too, is one of the good old sort, full of life and vigour, breeziness and fun. It begins well and goes on better, and from the time Syd joins his ship exciting incidents follow each other in such rapid and brilliant succession that nothing short of absolute compulsion would induce the reader to lay it down."—*Journal of Education.*

"The pick of the adventure books for this season. There is not a dull page in it. 'Syd Belton' is a capital book."—*Speaker.*

"From beginning to end the book is a vivid and even striking picture of sea-life."—*Spectator.*

Mrs. PARR.

DUMPS. By MRS. PARR, Author of "Adam and Eve," "Dorothy Fox," &c. Illustrated by W. PARKINSON. Crown 8vo. 3s. 6d.

"One of the prettiest stories which even this clever writer has given the world for a long time."—*World.* "A very sweet and touching story."—*Pall Mall Gazette.*

L. T. MEADE.

A GIRL OF THE PEOPLE. By L. T. MEADE, Author of "Scamp and I," &c. Illustrated by R. BARNES. Crown 8vo. 3s. 6d.

"An excellent story. Vivid portraiture of character, and broad and wholesome lessons about life."—*Spectator.* "One of Mrs. Meade's most fascinating books."—*Daily News.*

METHUEN'S NOVEL SERIES.

THREE SHILLINGS AND SIXPENCE.

MESSRS. METHUEN will issue from time to time a Series of copyright Novels, by well-known Authors, handsomely bound, at the above popular price. The first volumes (ready) are:

F. MABEL ROBINSON.
1. THE PLAN OF CAMPAIGN.

S. BARING GOULD, Author of " Mehalah," &c.
2. JACQUETTA.

Mrs. LEITH ADAMS (Mrs. De Courcy Laffan).
3. MY LAND OF BEULAH.

G. MANVILLE FENN.
4. ELI'S CHILDREN.

S. BARING GOULD, Author of " Mehalah," &c.
5. ARMINELL : A Social Romance.

EDNA LYALL, Author of " Donovan," &c.
6. DERRICK VAUGHAN, NOVELIST. With Portrait of Author.

F. MABEL ROBINSON.
7. DISENCHANTMENT.

M. BETHAM EDWARDS.
8. DISARMED. [*Shortly.*

W. E. NORRIS.
9. JACK'S FATHER. [*Shortly.*

S. BARING GOULD.
10. TOM A' TUDLAMS. [*Shortly.*

Other Volumes will be announced in due course.

5

English Leaders of Religion.

Edited by A. M. M. STEDMAN, M.A.

Under the above title MESSRS. METHUEN have commenced like publication of a series of short biographies, free from party bias, of the most prominent leaders of religious life and thought in this and the last century.

Each volume will contain a succinct account and estimate of the career, the influence, and the literary position of the subject of the memoir.

The following are already arranged—

CARDINAL NEWMAN.   *R. H. Hutton.*   [*Ready.*

" Few who read this book will fail to be struck by the wonderful insight it displays into the nature of the Cardinal's genius and the spirit of his life."—WILFRID WARD, in the *Tablet.*

" Full of knowledge, excellent in method, and intelligent in criticism. We regard it as wholly admirable."—*Academy.*

" An estimate, careful, deliberate, full of profound reasoning and of acute insight."—*Pall Mall Gazette.*

JOHN WESLEY.   *J. H. Overton, M.A.*
                                     [*In February.*

JOHN KEBLE.   *W. Lock, M.A.*

CHARLES SIMEON.   *H. C. G. Moule, M.A.*

BISHOP WILBERFORCE.   *G. W. Daniell, M.A.*

F. D. MAURICE.   *Colonel F. Maurice, R.E.*

THOMAS CHALMERS.   *Mrs. Oliphant.*

CARDINAL MANNING.   *A. W. Hutton, M.A.*

Other Volumes will be announced in due course.

SOCIAL QUESTIONS OF TO-DAY.

Edited by H. de B. GIBBINS, M.A.

Crown 8vo. 2s. 6d.

MESSRS. METHUEN beg to announce the publication of a series of volumes upon those topics of social, economic and industrial interest that are at the present moment foremost in the public mind. Each volume of the series will be written by an author who is an acknowledged authority upon the subject with which he deals, and who will treat his question in a thoroughly sympathetic but impartial manner, with special reference to the historic aspect of the subject and from the point of view of the Historical School of economics and social science. The Labour Question will be treated of in the volumes on Trades Unions and Co-operation: the Land Question will form the subject of another two volumes; others will treat of Socialism in England, in its various phases, and of the labour problems of the Continent also. The monograph on Commerce will be of special interest at present in view of the recent development of American commercial policy. Those on Education and on Poverty will be of similar importance in view of current discussion, and the volume on Mutual Thrift will prove a valuable survey of the various agencies for that purpose already in existence among the working classes.

The following form the earlier Volumes of the Series :—

ABOUT
Feb.   1.   **TRADES UNIONISM—NEW AND OLD.**
1891.   G. HOWELL, M.P., Author of "The Conflicts of Capital and Labour."

March. **2.   POVERTY AND PAUPERISM.**
             Rev. L. R. PHELPS, M.A., Fellow of Oriel College, Oxford.

3.   THE CO-OPERATIVE MOVEMENT OF TO-DAY.
       G. J. HOLYOAKE, Author of "The History of Co-operation."

4.   MUTUAL THRIFT.
       Rev. J. FROME WILKINSON, M.A., Author of "The Friendly Society Movement."

SOCIAL QUESTIONS OF TO-DAY *(continued)*.

UNIVERSITY EXTENSION SERIES.

Under the above title MESSRS. METHUEN have commenced the publication of a series of books on historical, literary, and economic subjects, suitable for extension students and home-reading circles. The volumes are intended to assist the lecturer and not to usurp his place. Each volume will be complete in itself, and the subjects will be treated by competent writers in a broad and philosophic spirit.

Edited by J. E. SYMES, M.A.,

Principal of University College, Nottingham.

Crown 8vo. 2s. 6d.

The following volumes are already arranged, and others will be announced shortly.

THE INDUSTRIAL HISTORY OF ENGLAND. By H. DE B. GIBBINS, M.A., late Scholar of Wadham Coll., Oxon., Cobden Prizeman. With Maps and Plans. [*Ready.*

" A compact and clear story of our industrial development. A study of his concise but luminous book cannot fail to give the reader a clear insight into the principal phenomena of our industrial history. The editor and publishers are to be congratulated on this first volume of their venture, and we shall look with expectant interest for the succeeding volumes of the series. If they maintain the same standard of excellence the series will make a permanent place for itself among the many series which appear from time to time."—*University Extension Journal.*

" A careful and lucid sketch."—*Times.*

" The writer is well-informed, and from first to last his work is profoundly interesting."—*Scots Observer.*

A HISTORY OF ENGLISH POLITICAL ECONOMY. By L. L. PRICE, M.A., Fellow of Oriel Coll., Oxon., Extension Lecturer in Political Economy. [*February.*

ENGLISH SOCIAL REFORMERS. By H. DE B. GIBBINS, M.A., late Scholar of Wadham Coll., Oxon., Cobden Prizeman.

PROBLEMS OF POVERTY : An Inquiry into the Industrial Conditions of the Poor. By J. A. HOBSON, M.A., late Scholar of Lincoln Coll., Oxon., U. E. Lecturer in Economics. [*March.*

THE FRENCH REVOLUTION. By J. E. SYMES, M.A., Principal of University Coll., Nottingham. [*In the Press.*

NAPOLEON. By E. L. S. HORSBURGH, M.A., Camb., U. E. Lecturer in History.

ENGLISH POLITICAL HISTORY. By T. J. LAWRENCE, M.A., late Fellow and Tutor of Downing Coll., Cambridge, U. E. Lecturer in History.

SHAKESPEARE. By F. II. TRENCH, M.A., Fellow of All Souls' Coll., Oxon., U. E. Lecturer in Literature.

VICTORIAN POETS. By A. SHARP. [*April.*

THE ENGLISH LANGUAGE. By G. C. MOORE-SMITH, M.A., Camb., U. E. Lecturer in Language.

AN INTRODUCTION TO PHILOSOPHY. By J. SOLOMON, M.A., Oxon., late Lecturer in Philosophy at University Coll., Nottingham.

PSYCHOLOGY. By F. S. GRANGER, M.A., Lond., Lecturer in Philosophy at University Coll., Nottingham. [*In the Press.*

ENGLISH PAINTERS. By D. S. MACCOLL, M.A., Oxon., Fellow of Univ. Coll., London, U. E. Lecturer in Art and Literature.

ENGLISH ARCHITECTURE. By ERNEST RADFORD, M.A., Camb., U. E. Lecturer in Art. With Illustrations.

THE EVOLUTION OF PLANT LIFE: Lower Forms. By G. MASSEE, Kew Gardens, U. E. Lecturer in Botany. With Illustrations. [*In the Press.*

THE CHEMISTRY OF LIFE AND HEALTH. By C. W. KIMMINS, M.A., Camb., U. E. Lecturer in Chemistry.

MESSRS. METHUEN'S NEW & RECENT BOOKS.

FICTION.

E. LYNN LINTON.

THE TRUE HISTORY OF JOSHUA DAVIDSON, Christian and Communist. By E. LYNN LINTON. Eleventh and Cheaper Edition. Post 8vo, 1s.

HISTORY AND POLITICS.

E. LYNN LINTON.

ABOUT IRELAND. By E. LYNN LINTON. *2nd Edition.* Cr. 8vo, bds., 1s.

"A brilliant and justly proportioned view of the Irish Question."—*Standard.*

T. RALEIGH, M.A.

IRISH POLITICS: An Elementary Sketch. By T. RALEIGH, M.A., Fellow of All Souls', Oxford, Author of "Elementary Politics." Fcap. 8vo, paper boards, 1s.; cloth, 1s. 6d.

"A very clever work."—MR. GLADSTONE.

"Unionist as he is, his little book has been publicly praised for its cleverness both by Mr. Gladstone and Mr. Morley. It does, in fact, raise most of the principal points of the Irish controversy, and puts them tersely, lucidly, and in such a way as to strike into the mind of the reader."—*The Speaker.*

"Salient facts and clear expositions in a few sentences packed with meaning. Every one who wishes to have the vital points of Irish politics at his finger's end should get this book by heart."—*Scotsman.*

F. MABEL ROBINSON.

IRISH HISTORY FOR ENGLISH READERS. By F. MABEL ROBINSON. *Fourth Edition.* Crown 8vo, boards, 1s.

GENERAL LITERATURE.

Edited by F. LANGBRIDGE, M.A.

BALLADS OF THE BRAVE: Poems of Chivalry, Enterprise, Courage, and Constancy, from the Earliest Times to the Present Day. Edited, with Notes, by Rev. F. LANGBRIDGE. Crown 8vo.

"A very happy conception happily carried out. These 'Ballads of the Brave' are intended to suit the real tastes of boys, and will suit the taste of the great majority. It is not an ordinary selector who could have so happily put together these characteristic samples. Other readers besides boys may learn much from them."—*Spectator.*

"The book is full of splendid things."—*World.*

Presentation Edition. Handsomely Bound, 3s. 6d. (School Edition, 2s. 6d.) Or, in Three Parts, 1s. each, for School Readers.

I. TROY TO FLODDEN. II. BOSWORTH TO WATERLOO. III. CRIMÆA TO KHARTOUM.

P. H. DITCHFIELD, M.A.

OUR ENGLISH VILLAGES: Their Story and their Antiquities. By P. H. DITCHFIELD, M.A., F.R.H.S., Rector of Barkham, Berks. Post 8vo, 2s. 6d. Illustrated.

"A pleasantly written little volume, giving much interesting information concerning villages and village life."—*Pall Mall Gazette.*

"The object of the author is not so much to describe any particular village as to give a clear idea of what village life has been in England from the earliest historical times. An extremely amusing and interesting little book, which should find a place in every parochial library."—*Guardian.*

A. M. M. STEDMAN, M.A.

OXFORD: ITS LIFE AND SCHOOLS. Ed. by A. M. M. STEDMAN, M.A., assisted by members of the University. *New Edition.* Cr. 8vo. 5s.

"Offers a full and in most respects a satisfactory description of the country through which students must travel, and affords to parents who are desirous of calculating the expenses and rewards of University education, a mass of useful information conveniently arranged and brought down to the most recent date."—*Athenæum.*

"We can honestly say of Mr. Stedman's volume that it deserves to be read by the people for whom it is intended, the parents and guardians of Oxford students, present and to come, and by such students themselves."—*Spectator.*

GENERAL LITERATURE (*continued*).

OLD COUNTRY LIFE. By S. BARING GOULD. With Sixty-seven Illustrations by W. PARKINSON, F. D. BEDFORD, and F. MASEY. Large Crown 8vo, cloth super extra, top edge gilt, 10*s.* 6*d.* *Second Edition.*

"'Old Country Life,' as healthy wholesome reading, full of breezy life and movement, full of quaint stories vigorously told, will not be excelled by any book to be published throughout the year. Sound, hearty, and English to the core."—*World.*

"Mr. Baring Gould is well known as a clever and versatile author : but he never wrote a more delightful book than the volume before us. He has described English country life with the fidelity that only comes with close acquaintance, and with an appreciation of its more attractive features not surpassed even in the pages of Washington Irving. The illustrations add very much to the charm of the book, and the artists in their drawings of old churches and manor-houses, streets, cottages, and gardens, have greatly assisted the author."
Manchester Guardian.

HISTORIC ODDITIES AND STRANGE EVENTS. By S. BARING GOULD. FIRST SERIES. Demy 8vo, 10*s.* 6*d.* *Second Edition.*

"A collection of exciting and entertaining chapters. The whole volume is delightful reading."—*Times.*

"The work, besides being agreeable to read, is valuable for purposes of reference. The entire contents are stimulating and delightful."—*Notes and Queries.*

HISTORIC ODDITIES AND STRANGE EVENTS. SECOND SERIES. By S. BARING GOULD, Author of "Mehalah," "Old Country Life," &c. Demy 8vo, 10*s.* 6*d.* [*Ready.*

"Mr. Baring Gould has a keen eye for colour and effect, and the subjects he has chosen give ample scope to his descriptive and analytic faculties. The new series of 'Historic Oddities and Strange Events,' is a perfectly fascinating book. Whether considered as merely popular reading or as a succession of studies in the freaks of human history, it is equally worthy of perusal, while it is marked by artistic literary colouring and happy lightness of style."—*Scottish Leader.*

SONGS OF THE WEST: Traditional Ballads and Songs of the West of England, with their Traditional Melodies. Collected by S. BARING GOULD, M.A., and H. FLEETWOOD SHEPPARD, M.A. Arranged for Voice and Piano. In 4 Parts (containing 25 Songs each), 3*s.* each. *Part I., Fourth Edition. Part II., Second Edition. Part III., ready. Part IV., in the Press.*

"A rich and varied collection of humour, pathos, grace, and poetic fancy."—*Saturday Review.*

YORKSHIRE ODDITIES AND STRANGE EVENTS. By S. BARING GOULD. New and Cheaper Edition. Crown 8vo, 6*s.*
[*Now ready.*

JACQUETTA, and other Stories. By S. BARING GOULD. Crown 8vo, 3*s.* 6*d.*

ARMINELL: A Social Romance. By S. BARING GOULD. New Edition. Crown 8vo, 3*s.* 6*d.*

"To say that a book is by the author of 'Mehalah' is to imply that it contains a story cast on strong lines, containing dramatic possibilities, vivid and sympathetic descriptions of Nature, and a wealth of ingenious imagery. All these expectations are justified by 'Arminell.'"
Speaker.

EDUCATIONAL WORKS.

METHUEN'S SCIENCE SERIES.

MESSRS. METHUEN propose to issue a Series of Science Manuals suitable for use in schools. They will be edited by Mr. R. Elliot Steel, M.A., F.C.S., Senior Natural Science Master in Bradford Grammar School, and will be published at a moderate price. The following are ready or in preparation—

THE WORLD OF SCIENCE. Including Chemistry, Heat, Light, Sound, Magnetism, Electricity, Botany, Zoology, Physiology, Astronomy, and Geology. By R. ELLIOT STEEL, M.A., F.C.S., Senior Natural Science Master in Bradford Grammar School. 147 Illustrations, Crown 8vo, 2s. 6d.

" Mr. Steel's Manual is admirable in many ways. The Book is well calculated to attract and retain the attention of the young."—*Saturday Review.*

" If Mr. Steel is to be placed second to any for this quality of lucidity, it is only to Huxley himself; and to be named in the same breath with this master of the craft of teaching is to be accredited with the clearness of style and simplicity of arrangement that belong to thorough mastery of a subject."—*Parents' Review.*

ELEMENTARY LIGHT with numerous Illustrations. Crown 8vo. [*February.*

,,   ELECTRICITY AND MAGNETISM.

,,   HEAT.

    Other Volumes will be announced in due course.

R. E. STEEL, M.A.
REVISED FOR NEW SESSION.

PRACTICAL INORGANIC CHEMISTRY. For the Elementary Stage of the South Kensington Examinations in Science and Art. By R. E. STEEL, M.A., Senior Natural Science Master at Bradford Grammar School. Crown 8vo, cloth, 1s. [*Now Ready.*

R. J. MORICH.

A GERMAN PRIMER. With Exercises. By R. J. MORICH, Chief Modern Language Master at Manchester Grammar School. [*In the Press.*

H. de B. GIBBINS, M.A.

COMPANION GERMAN GRAMMAR. By H. DE B. GIBBINS, M.A., Assistant Master at Nottingham High School. Crown 8vo, 1s. 6d. [*Ready.*

E. McQUEEN GRAY.

GERMAN PASSAGES for UNSEEN TRANSLATION. By E. McQUEEN GRAY. Crown 8vo, 2s. 6d. [*Ready.*

A. W. VERRALL, M.A.

SELECTIONS FROM HORACE. With Introduction, Notes, and Vocabulary. By A. W. VERRALL, M.A., Fellow and Tutor of Trinity Coll., Cambridge. Fcap. 8vo. [*In the Press.*

SELECTIONS FROM HERODOTUS. With Introduction, Notes, and Vocabulary. By A. C. LIDDELL, M.A., Assistant Master at Nottingham High School. Fcap. 8vo. [*In the Press.*

WORKS BY A. M. M. STEDMAN, M.A.

WADHAM COLLEGE, OXON.

FIRST LATIN LESSONS. *Second Edition, Enlarged.* Crown 8vo, 2s.
[*Ready.*

FIRST LATIN READER. With Notes adapted to the Shorter Latin Primer and Vocabulary. Crown 8vo, 1s. 6d. [*Ready.*

EASY LATIN PASSAGES FOR UNSEEN TRANSLATION. *Second Edition, Enlarged.* Fcap. 8vo, 1s. 6d.

EASY LATIN EXERCISES ON THE SYNTAX OF THE SHORTER AND REVISED LATIN PRIMERS. With Vocabulary. *Second Edition.* Crown 8vo, 2s. 6d. Issued with the consent of Dr. Kennedy.

NOTANDA QUAEDAM: MISCELLANEOUS LATIN EXERCISES ON COMMON RULES AND IDIOMS. With Vocabulary. Fcap. 8vo, 1s. 6d.

LATIN VOCABULARIES FOR REPETITION: arranged according to Subjects. *Third Edition.* Fcap. 8vo, 1s. 6d.

FIRST GREEK LESSONS. [*In preparation.*

EASY GREEK PASSAGES FOR UNSEEN TRANSLATION.
[*In preparation.*

EASY GREEK EXERCISES ON ELEMENTARY SYNTAX.
[*In preparation.*

GREEK VOCABULARIES FOR REPETITION: arranged according to Subjects. Fcap. 8vo, 1s. 6d.

GREEK TESTAMENT SELECTIONS. For the use of Schools. *New Edition.* With Introduction, Notes, and Vocabulary. Fcap. 8vo, 2s. 6d.

FIRST FRENCH LESSONS. [*In the Press*

EASY FRENCH PASSAGES FOR UNSEEN TRANSLATION.
Fcap. 8vo, 1s. 6d.

EASY FRENCH EXERCISES ON ELEMENTARY SYNTAX. With Vocabulary. Crown 8vo, 2s. 6d. [*Ready.*

FRENCH VOCABULARIES FOR REPETITION: arranged according to Subjects. Fcap. 8vo, 1s.

See also School Examination Series, p. 15.

SCHOOL EXAMINATION SERIES.

Edited by A. M. M. STEDMAN, M.A.

Crown 8vo. 2*s*. 6*d*. each.

In use at Eton, Harrow, Winchester, Repton, Cheltenham, Sherborne, Haileybury, Merchant Taylors, Manchester, &c.

FRENCH EXAMINATION PAPERS IN MISCELLANEOUS GRAMMAR AND IDIOMS. By A. M. M. STEDMAN, M.A. *Fifth Edition.*

A KEY, issued to Tutors and Private Students only, to be had on application to the Publishers. *Second Edition.* Cr. 8vo, 5*s*.

LATIN EXAMINATION PAPERS IN MISCELLANEOUS GRAMMAR AND IDIOMS. By A. M. M. STEDMAN, M.A. *Third Edition.* KEY (issued as above), 6*s*.

GREEK EXAMINATION PAPERS IN MISCELLANEOUS GRAMMAR AND IDIOMS. By A. M. M. STEDMAN, M.A. *Second Edition, Enlarged.* KEY (issued as above), 6*s*.

GERMAN EXAMINATION PAPERS IN MISCELLANEOUS GRAMMAR AND IDIOMS. By R. J. MORICH, Manchester Grammar School. *Second Edition.* KEY (issued as above), 5*s*.

HISTORY AND GEOGRAPHY EXAMINATION PAPERS. By C. H. SPENCE, M.A., Clifton College.

SCIENCE EXAMINATION PAPERS. By R. E. STEEL, M.A., F.C.S., Chief Natural Science Master, Bradford Grammar School. In three volumes.

> Part I.   Chemistry.
> Part II.   Physics (Sound, Light, Heat, Magnetism, Electricity).
> Part III.   Biology and Geology.   [*In preparation.*

GENERAL KNOWLEDGE EXAMINATION PAPERS. By A. M. M. STEDMAN, M.A.   [KEY. *In the Press.*

EXAMINATION PAPERS IN BOOK-KEEPING, with Preliminary Exercises. Compiled and arranged by J. T. MEDHURST, F. S. Accts. and Auditors, and Lecturer at City of London College. 3*s*.

ENGLISH LITERATURE, Questions for Examination in. Chiefly collected from College Papers set at Cambridge. With an Introduction on the Study of English. By the Rev. W. W. SKEAT, Litt.D., LL.D., Professor of Anglo-Saxon at Cambridge University. *Third Edition, Revised.*

ARITHMETIC EXAMINATION PAPERS. By C. PENDLEBURY, M.A., Senior Mathematical Master, St. Paul's School. KEY, 5*s*.

TRIGONOMETRY EXAMINATION PAPERS. By E. H. WARD, M.A., Assistant Master at St. Paul's School. KEY, 5*s*.

SCHOOL EXAMINATION SERIES

Edited by A. J. H. STIDMAN, D.A.